# The Forbidden Game

# The Forbidden Game

## A Social History of Drugs

by

## BRIAN INGLIS

CHARLES SCRIBNER'S SONS
NEW YORK

Copyright © 1975 Brian Inglis

**Library of Congress Cataloging in Publication Data**

Inglis, Brian, 1916–
  The forbidden game.

  Bibliography: p.
  Includes index.
  1. Drug abuse—Social aspects—History.  2. Drug
abuse—History.  3. Drugs.  I. Title.  [DNLM: 1. Drugs
—History.  2. Attitude to health.  QV11 I45f]
 HV5801.I55   1975b      362.2'93'09      75-12382
ISBN 0-684-14428-X

1 3 5 7 9 11 13 15 17 19 V/C 20 18 16 14 12 10 8 6 4 2

Printed in the United States of America

# Contents

| | | page |
|---|---|---|
| | INTRODUCTION | 9 |
| 1 | Drugs and Shamanism | 11 |
| 2 | Drugs and the Priesthood | 25 |
| 3 | The Impact of Drugs on Civilisation | 37 |
| 4 | The Impact of Civilisation | 49 |
| 5 | Spirits | 62 |
| 6 | The Opium Wars | 72 |
| 7 | Indian Hemp | 96 |
| 8 | The Poet's Eye | 110 |
| 9 | Science | 116 |
| 10 | Prohibition | 132 |
| 11 | The International Anti-drug Campaign | 154 |
| 12 | Heroin and Cannabis | 178 |
| 13 | The Collapse of Control | 200 |
| 14 | Psychopharmacology | 210 |
| | POSTSCRIPT | 225 |
| | ACKNOWLEDGEMENTS | 231 |
| | SOURCES | 233 |
| | BIBLIOGRAPHY | 234 |
| | INDEX | 245 |

# The Forbidden Game

# Introduction

WE TAKE DRUGS FOR TWO MAIN REASONS; EITHER TO RESTORE
ourselves to the condition we regard as normal — to cure infections, and to take away pain; or to release us from normality —
to enable us to feel more lively, or more relaxed; to alter our
mood, or our perceptions. It is with this second category (of drug
use, not of drugs; the drugs themselves may be the same) that I
am concerned. For some reason, there is no generally accepted
colloquial description. 'Narcotic' is quite familiar, but it has
acquired a pejorative tinge, and in any case it should properly be
used only about a drug used to induce drowsiness or stupor.
For a while 'dope' did service, but by the time Tom Lehrer was
singing about the old dope peddler spreading joy wherever he
went, it had begun to slip out of favour, and is now more commonly used to describe what is taken by athletes to improve their form,
or given to racehorses to upset the odds. I have stuck simply to the
term 'drugs'.

I have used words like 'addiction' in their colloquial rather than
their more specialised clinical sense; and I have tried to avoid the
jargon of the pharmacologists, except when quoting it. Their
term for the mood-altering drugs, 'psychotropic', has established
itself; but they have yet to agree on how best to describe a drug
used to alter perception. The term most often employed, 'hallu-
cinogen', is both ugly and misleading, as the experiences are not
necessarily hallucinatory; but the commonest alternative, 'psycho-
tomimetic', is even uglier and more misleading, as the experiences
do not often resemble psychosis. 'Phantastica', which Louis Lewin

tried to popularise, has not caught on; nor, mercifully, have 'psychotogenic' or 'psycholitic'; and Humphrey Osmond's 'psychedelic' has shifted its meaning, in popular usage. I have preferred 'vision-inducing'.

There is another category of drugs which I had intended to include; aphrodisiacs. I found, though, that virtually all the drugs known to man, not to mention all sorts of foodstuffs and drinks which are not ordinarily regarded as drugs, have had the reputation at one time or another of stimulating sexual appetite, or improving sexual performance. As the same drugs, at other times, have often had the reputation of diminishing desire, and spoiling performance, it is doubtful whether the category of aphrodisiac can be accepted, except subjectively.

I have also dealt only in passing with the economic consequences of drug use. For centuries, a vast acreage has been given over to growing the plants which provide the raw material of drugs. Huge sums have been spent on processing, distributing and retailing the finished products, and on providing the accessories, from public houses to hubble-bubbles. States have extracted immense revenues from drug duties and used them to pay for everything from social services to guided missiles. Obviously the influence of drugs on the world's economy has been incalculable; but to deal adequately with this aspect of the subject would require another, and a very different, book.

The reasons for some other omissions will be found in the section on sources. But there is also one inclusion, which I find sometimes causes surprise. Alcohol is clearly a drug; *the* drug, of our civilisation and many before. But it has also long been consumed, often primarily, as a beverage. I have dealt with attitudes to drink, and legislation designed to control drinking, only when they have been inspired by fears of its effects when used as a drug.

# 1
# *Drugs and Shamanism*

WHY DID MAN FIRST TAKE TO DRUGS? IT IS UNLIKELY THAT
we will ever know for certain; archaeological discoveries — the
seeds of drug plants found in pots; cave drawings of the plants
themselves — indicate that the practice must be many thousands
of years old, and the information is too scanty to justify anything
more than speculation. Our main source of evidence about early
drug practices comes from explorers, missionaries, traders and
colonial administrators, and more recently from anthropological
field workers, who have described what they have seen in primitive
communities. Unluckily, what they saw was often so alien to the
preconceptions which they brought with them from civilisation
that they rarely described it with detachment. Still, certain patterns
emerge, with a reasonable consistency.

## From the New World

The most revealing accounts of drug use by savages, as they were
long described by men accounting themselves civilised, are in the
chronicles of the followers of Columbus, reporting what they saw
and heard in the Caribbean islands, and later in North and South
America. They found a great variety of plant drugs in use there:
cohoba, coca, peyotl, certain species of mushroom, datura
(jimsonweed), ololiuqui (morning glory), caapi, and others —
tobacco being the commonest. None of these plants was known in
Europe at the time; nor was any drug in use there for the purpose
for which they were most widely taken in the New World, to
generate energy. The only drug then in common use in Europe

was alcohol; and wine or beer were ordinarily taken mainly for refreshment. The American Indians, the chroniclers reported, chewed tobacco or coca leaves as a substitute for refreshment — to give themselves a psychological 'lift', as if into a mild form of trance. This, they claimed, enabled them to work long hours, or travel long distances, or fight protracted battles, without the need for food, drink, or sleep.

Drugs were also taken in America as alcohol was in Europe, for intoxication — but again, with a difference. As Girolamo Benzoni reported in one of the early published accounts of life there, an Indian would settle down to fill himself up with tobacco smoke until to outward appearances he was hopelessly drunk. But he was putting himself out of his mind with a purpose; for 'on returning to his senses, he told a thousand stories of his having been at the council of the gods, and other high visions'; and such stories were taken very seriously by the tribe.

Although the same drug might be taken both for everyday working purposes and for intoxication, it would as a rule be used as an intoxicant only by — or with the supervision of — a medicine man, qualified by character and training to interpret what was seen or heard. The visions, the Indians believed, were glimpses of a world on a different plane of reality, but just as real; inhabited by spirits who had access to useful sources of knowledge. In particular, they would reveal what was in store for the tribe, or individual members of it. The process was described by the chronicler Gonzalvo Fernando d'Oviedo y Valdez. The Indians of Hispaniola, he wrote,

> had secret means of putting themselves in touch with spirits whenever they wished to predict the future. This is how they set about the matter. When a chief called one of those priests of the desert, this man came with two of his disciples, one of whom bore a vase filled with some mysterious drink, and the other a little silver bell. When he arrived, the priest sat himself down between the two disciples on a small round seat in presence of the chief and some of his suite. He drank the liquor which had been brought, and then began his conjurations, calling aloud on the spirits; and then, highly agitated and furious, he was shaken by the most violent movements . . . He then seemed

to be plunged into a kind of ecstasy and to be suffering curious pains. During all this time one of the disciples rang the little bell. When the priest had calmed down, and while he lay senseless on the ground, the chief, or some other, asked what they desired to know, and the spirit replied through the mouth of the inspired man in a manner perfectly exact.

The Spanish chroniclers did not doubt the accuracy of the information collected. They were quite prepared to believe that the drugs induced visions, and that in them, the future could be foretold. But the whole process — the convulsions, the strange voices — was reminiscent of what they knew, and feared, as diabolic possession. Such visions, they were aware, might come from God; but it was unthinkable that God should have provided such a valuable service for the heathen. The only possible explanation was that, as the Dominican Diego Duran put it, 'the devil must be speaking to them in that drunken state'. As it was not considered safe to investigate the devil's handiwork, for fear of falling into his clutches — or, later, the Inquisition's — the opportunity to investigate drug-induced divination was not grasped.

### Travellers' tales

Ironically, the emergence of a more sceptical attitude also discouraged inquiry; for a reason hinted at by Nicolas Monardes in his *Joyful News out of the New Found World*, which contained the first attempt at a survey of the American plant drugs. Monardes did not dispute that the devil was involved. Having knowledge of herbal lore, the devil must have revealed it to the Indians, 'that they might see the visions he had prepared for them, and so deceive them'. But Monardes doubted the authenticity of the information transmitted by the medicine men. It was simply their attempt to make sense of their incoherent visions, he felt — and had often to be deliberately left obscure, so that whatever happened the medicine men could claim to have predicted it. As a member of the Church, in other words, he took divination seriously; as a man of science he was reluctant to do so.

During the seventeenth and eighteenth centuries, though reports continued to filter back to Europe from time to time of remarkable divinatory feats by medicine men under the influence of drugs, they attracted attention only as curiosities. A typical example was the reaction to the account which Count Filip von Strahlenberg, a Swedish army officer who had spent years as a prisoner of war in Siberia, gave of the Koryak tribesmen, in which he described how they used the red-capped amanita muscaria mushroom — the 'fly agaric' — as an intoxicant. Only the better-off families, Strahlenberg explained, could afford to buy them, and store them for the winter. Whenever they had a feast, they would pour water over them, boil them, and enjoy the visions. 'The poorer sort', he went on,

> who cannot afford to lay in a store of these mushrooms, post themselves on these occasions round the huts of the rich, and watch the opportunity of the guests coming down to make water; and then hold a wooden bowl to receive the urine, which they drink off greedily, as having still some virtue of the mushroom in it, and by this way, they also get drunk.

A story like this helped to give 'travellers' tales' their derisory reputation. It slipped easily into the repertory of the ranconteur — and of the satirist; Oliver Goldsmith used it to lend point to some remarks on the degeneracy of the English nobility. And even when later visitors to Siberia — voluntary or involuntary — were to confirm that it was true, they were interested less in the purposes for which the drug was taken, than by the fact that it could retain its intoxicating properties even when recycled through urine four or five times; and that reindeer, too, were susceptible — a discovery which the Koryaks had been able to exploit. Gavril Sarychev, who spent from 1785 to 1793 in the region, found that the Chuckchi herdsman kept a sealskin container for his urine; whenever he wanted to round up his reindeer, 'he only has to set this container on the ground and call out 'Girach, Girach!', and they promptly come running toward him from afar'.

Only rarely did commentators note that the intoxication which the fly agaric induced was of a very different kind from that which followed the consumption of alcohol; or that it was used by the Siberian shamans for the same purpose as the American medicine men used tobacco or peyotl. But an account by another exile, Stephan Kraseninnikov, of his enforced residence in Kamchatkaland showed the similarities. A man under the influence of the fly agaric, he wrote in 1755, could be recognised by

> the shaking of the extremities, which will follow after an hour or less, after which the persons thus intoxicated have hallucinations, as in a fever; they are subject to various visions, terrifying or felicitous, depending on differences in temperament; owing to which some jump, some dance, others cry and suffer great terrors, while some might deem a small crack to be as wide as a door, and a tub of water as deep as the sea. But this applies only to those who over-indulge, while those who use a small quantity experience a feeling of extraordinary lightness, joy, courage and a state of energetic well-being.

### Anthropology

Travellers' tales merge imperceptibly into anthropology; but one of the landmarks on that road was *Travels in Peru*, by the respected Swiss naturalist J. J. von Tschudi. He had read accounts by Pizarro's followers, describing how the Indians could perform prodigious feats of endurance by chewing coca leaves; and he was able to verify them when he arrived in the 1830s, finding that the porters he employed could go for five days and nights with no food and very little sleep. Coca was also used by the medicine men; but datura was preferred, being more potent — as Tschudi reported, after watching its effects on an Indian who took it.

> Shortly after having swallowed the beverage, he fell into a heavy stupor. He sat with his eyes vacantly fixed on the ground, his mouth, convulsively closed, and his nostrils dilated. In the course of about a quarter of an hour his eyes began to roll, foam issued from his half-opened lips, and his whole body was agitated by frightful convulsions. These violent symptoms having subsided, a profound sleep of several hours succeeded. In the evening, when I saw him again, he was relating to a circle of attentive listeners the particulars of his vision, during which he alleged he had held communication with the spirits of his forefathers.

Accounts of this kind, from investigators whose trustworthiness was not in question, began to be increasingly common — particularly from South America, where new tribes, and new drugs, were continually being discovered. In his geographical survey of Ecuador, published in 1868, Manuel Villavicenzio described the effects of ayahuasca — also known as caapi, or yagé

> In a few moments it begins to produce the most rare phenomena. Its action appears to excite the nervous system; all the senses liven up and all faculties awaken; they feel vertigo and spinning in the head, then a sensation of being lifted into the air and beginning an aerial journey; the possessed begins in the first moments to see the most delicious apparitions, in conformity with his ideas and knowledge. The savages say that they see gorgeous lakes, forests covered with fruit, the prettiest birds who communicate to them the nicest and the most favourable things they want to hear, and other beautiful things relating to their savage life. When the instant passes they begin to see terrible horrors about to devour them, their first flight ceases and they descend to earth to combat the terrors who communicate to them all adversities and misfortunes awaiting them.

By 1871, when Edward Tylor published his *Primitive Culture* — the first serious attempt at a comparative survey of tribal life and lore — a mass of such information had become available, and it was remarkably consistent. Almost all communities, in every part of the world, had their medicine men, witch doctors, or shamans, selected mainly on account of their ability to communicate with the spirits. To visit the spirit world, the medicine man had to be able to enter a state of trance; and this was frequently attained with the help of drugs. In this state he behaved as if he were drunk, or in a kind of fit; but he would be able to recall his visions when he recovered. Or he might appear to be possessed, describing what he was seeing (or hearing) in a voice not his own. Either way, his function was to bring back information of use to his tribe: the answers to such questions as what the enemy tribes were planning; where more game might be found; how to detect a witch; and what treatment to give a sick member of the tribe.

The evidence presented Tylor with an embarrassing problem. His great ambition was to divest anthropology of its 'travellers' tales' label, and secure its recognition as an academic discipline (as eventually he was to do; he became the holder of the first Chair of Anthropology at Oxford). He was aware that the scientific Establishment of the time rejected the validity of divination, and he agreed, describing it as a 'monstrous farrago'. But they also refused to admit the existence of the trance state, and possession. Reviewing the evidence, Tylor found it impossible to accept that the state of 'ecstasy', as it was then commonly called, in which a man is transported out of his right mind, was always spurious. But to accept it, let alone to admit its importance to primitive man, might lead to the anthropologist being classified with the mesmerists, hypnotists and spiritualists, all at the time busy trying to batter down orthodoxy's defences; and this would have been fatal to his academic prospects. So Tylor skirted round the subject, with such discreet phrases as 'North American Indians held intoxication by tobacco to be supernatural ecstasy, and the dreams of men in this state to be inspired'. In doing so, he set the fashion followed by Sir James Frazer in *The Golden Bough*, and by most orthodox anthropologists to this day.

Reports from explorers, naturalists and anthropologists, however, continued to pour in, revealing the great respect in which the drug-induced trance state was held by primitive tribes. In Guiana in the 1870s, for example, Everard Im Thurn discovered that before a youth was initiated into his tribe he had to move away from it for a period of fasting, and at the same time accustom himself to drink 'fearfully large draughts' of tobacco juice mixed with water. Then, 'maddened by the draughts of nicotine, by the terrors of his long solitary wanderings, and fearfully excited by his own ravings, he is able to work himself at will into those most frantic passions of excitement during which he is supposed to hold converse with the spirits, and to control them'. If he learned to control them, he could become a medicine man, second only in importance to the chief of the tribe, and sometimes even more influential. Was it really possible that these and other primitive tribes, throughout history, throughout the world, had been taken in by a total imposture?

At last, in the 1890s, experiments with hypnosis finally convinced the scientific establishment that the trance state existed; and the way was opened for a fresh look at the phenomenon. But the investigators arrived as blinkered as before; because orthodoxy, in accepting the trance state, classified it as a form of mental disorder. In retrospect, this is understandable; medicine men under the influence of drugs tended to behave in ways which, in any civilised country, would have led to their being certified insane. Russian anthropologists, in particular, investigating shamanism — a term loosely applied to the whole medicine man/witch doctor/ shaman complex — lent confirmation by attributing it to the fearful sub-Arctic living conditions, and dismissing the visions which the shamans claimed to see under the influence of the fly agaric as no more meaningful than the pink elephants seen by an alcoholic with delirium tremens.*

The 'Arctic mania' was a preposterous theory, in view of the fact that shamanism in one form or another existed wherever primitive tribes were found. But research of a kind which might have led to a more plausible explanation was hampered not only by continuing scientific scepticism, but by the undisguised hostility of missionaries — hoping to stamp out what they felt were pagan drug cults; and of colonial administrators, anxious to demonstrate that they, rather than the shaman, witch doctor or medicine man, were in command. In the early years of the century, therefore, when it would still have been possible to investigate drug-induced trances in tribes untainted by much contact with civilisation, little serious research was done, except by a few interested individuals, and they were often frustrated. Frank Melland, who in the early years of the century was a shrewd observer of African customs in Rhodesia, described in a book about his experiences how he had the good fortune to hear about some secret native dances. One was named after the drug taken by the dancers, which gave them extraordinary endurance; those who took it, he was told, could travel a hundred miles in the course of a night. In the other the participants, after

* The anthropologists did, however, fully confirm the old travellers' tale. According to Vladimir Jochelson, writing in 1905, reindeer no longer even needed to be summoned with the call *Girach! Girach!*

Frequently the reindeer come running to camp from a far off pasture to taste of snow saturated with urine, having a keen sense of hearing and of smell, but their sight is rather poor. A man stopping to urinate in the open attracts reindeer from afar, which, following the sense of smell, will run to the urine, hardly discerning the man, and paying no attention to him. The position of a man standing up in the open while urinating is rather critical when he becomes the object of attention from reindeer coming down on him from all sides at full speed.

taking the drug, were hypnotised by the witch doctor so that they too could enter the spirit world. But he was unable to verify the information, because the Africans feared that if the colonial government came to know the dances were held, they would be banned; and Melland, as a magistrate, would be required to enforce the prohibition.

### The possessed

It was only when young anthropologists began to undertake intensive field work, which involved staying long enough with a tribe to win its trust and to understand its customs, that drug-induced divination began to be taken a little more seriously. One of these field workers was destined to be influential: Edward Evans-Pritchard, subsequently Professor of Social Anthropology at Oxford University. When he went out to the Sudan in the 1920s to study the Azande, he watched the witch doctors at work; and from his observations, he drew a revealing picture of the process, and the part drugs played in it.

A predecessor there, Monsignor Lagae, had described how the witch doctor's object was to reach a state where the drug he had taken 'glows (*brille*) through his body, and through it he begins to see witchcraft clearly'. This, Evans-Pritchard found, was an accurate description. The 'medicine', as they thought of it — not so much the drug itself, when one was used, but its effect — 'goes to their stomachs, and dancing shakes it up and sends it all over their bodies, where it becomes an active agent, enabling them to prophesy'. The prophecies were not necessarily verbalised; the witch doctor 'does not only divine with his lips, but with his whole body. He dances the questions that are put to him.' Evans-Pritchard's houseboy, who himself qualified as a witch doctor, described the process. While he was dancing, he had to await the verdict of the drugs. 'When the medicines take hold of him, a man begins to dance with reference to someone. He dances in vain, and goes in the soul of the medicine and arrives at another man. He sees him and his heart cools about that man. The witch doctor says to himself: that man does not bewitch people.' But eventually 'his heart shakes about him' and he knows that the man in front of him is a witch. Even if the witch should be from his own family, 'the medicine will stand alert within him', compelling him to reveal the truth.

By the time Evans-Pritchard's work on the Azande appeared, in 1937, there was more willingness to concede that shamanism might not be simply a form of hysteria. Though Freud's theories still met with resistance, his basic premise of an unconscious mind had come to be accepted; and he had surmised that from the unconscious, man could have access to information which was not available to him through his five senses — a proposition that Jung accepted and expanded. If so, was it not possible that what the diviner was trying to explain, when he claimed that the medicine 'stood alert within him', was that in some way it liberated instinct, which answered the required questions without the intervention of consciousness? In primitive communities, after all, instinct may well be a surer guide, on many issues, than imperfect reasoning ability. 'There seems no reason to doubt', M. J. Field concluded from her long experience working in Ghana, 'that the utterances of a possessed person, concentrating on a narrowed field, may exceed in wisdom those he can achieve when exposed to all the distractions of normal consciousness.' However odd such a method of getting information might appear to the materialist, Field found that it worked — 'by their fruits ye shall know them, and the fruits of most spirit possession in Ghana are wholesome and sustaining'. Michael Gelfand came to a similar conclusion from his experience in Rhodesia. Irrational though their technique might seem, it could be very effective; the practitioner might be no scientist — he wrote in his *Witch Doctor* — 'but he practices his art with superb skill'.

In any case, the fact was that most primitive communities used divination as a guide in their everyday affairs; and anthropologists began to realise that to ignore or depreciate its influence was like an atheist refusing to study the effect of Christianity on history on the ground that he did not believe in God. And gradually, a hypothesis has evolved to account for divination, and to explain its social role.

Like other forms of animal life, man originally had instinct as his guide, supplemented by the five senses. But with the development of consciousness, reasoning power, and memory, the capacity to consult instinct was gradually lost, except when it broke through as the 'sixth sense', or intuition. For primitive man, the loss would have been serious, had it not been for the fact that certain individuals retained the ability to dissociate — to throw off consciousness, and to liberate instinct.

Dissociation took various forms. The diviner might dance out the required answers, as Evans-Pritchard had observed; he might become possessed, as if taken over by a disembodied personality; or he might have visions in which the spirits would show him or tell him what he wanted to learn. How the information was secured, though, did not much matter, so long as it appeared to be relevant and useful. But as man came to rely more on memory and reasoning power he found it more difficult to enter the required trance state; and it was at this point that drugs came to be used, to induce it — man being guided, perhaps, by instinct to the required plant drugs, just as animals are guided to the right plants to make up for vitamin deficiencies.*

In his *Shamanism*, published in 1951, Professor Mircea Eliade interpreted this development as being a sign of decadence. Narcotics — as he called them, with obvious distaste, lumping tobacco, alcohol and the fly agaric together — were a recent innovation, 'only a vulgar substitute for pure trance', and 'an imitation of the state which the shaman is no longer capable of attaining otherwise'. Recently, however, this verdict has been challenged, notably by R. G. Wasson in his *Soma*, and by some of the contributors to the first full scale academic symposium on plant drugs, held at the University of California in 1970 — the proceedings of which were subsequently edited by Professor Peter T. Furst and published as *Flesh of the Gods*. Drugs are indeed a substitute for the ability to enter the trance state voluntarily, but that is not necessarily a symptom of decadence; if man can find such substitutes for faculties which he has lost in his evolution, that may be held to be to his credit. And there is no evidence that the trance state induced by drugs is necessarily any different from the state attained by other means.

* Compare 'Palinurus' — Cyril Connolly — in *The Unquiet Grave:*

The mystery of drugs: how did savages all over the world, in every climate, discover in frozen tundras or remote jungles the one plant, indistinguishable from so many others of the same species, which could, by a most elaborate process, bring them fantasies, intoxication, and freedom from care? How unless by help from the plants themselves?

*Horizons beyond*

One question remains unanswered. Until very recently, to take divination seriously enough even to consider the possibility that extra-sensory perception might be involved, as a product of the drug-induced trance state, was to court ridicule. But orthodox science has been shifting its stance, moving towards guarded acceptance of the proposition that some phenomena, formerly regarded as supernatural, may acquire scientific respectability. Certainly the former prejudice against research studies in this field is disappearing.

The historical evidence for links between taking certain drugs and the ability to practise divination would fill a book. Constantly, men have believed that they have been on the verge of proving it — like Joseph Kopek, a Polish general exiled to Siberia in the 1790s, whose experiments with the fly agaric not merely made him believe he was a diviner, but enabled him to correct the mistakes of the local shaman ('I warned him to improve in those matters; and I noticed that he took those warnings almost as the voice of revelation'). Could anybody now deny, Kopek went on,

> that in spite of our vast knowledge of natural phenomena, there still exist almost countless phenomena about which we can only guess? Can one put a limit to nature at a point that delimits the possibilities of enquiries and discoveries of human research? Innumerable effects of recently discovered magnetic forces, effects that cannot be detected by physical means nor pinpointed with any degree of precision to some specification on the human body, seem to reconcile in some measure the controversy concerning this mushroom. It is possible that in the sleep brought by the influence of this mushroom, a man is able to see at least some of his real past and, if not the future, at least his present relations.

In the letters and memoirs of travellers, missionaries and colonial administrators over the past century and a half there are countless stories, some of them well attested, of witch doctors accurately describing what was happening in distant places, or correctly forecasting future events. But they were all, by their nature, 'anecdotal'; and it was always possible to pick holes in an anecdote — as, for example, in the case of an episode recounted at the turn of the century by the respected South African merchant David Leslie, who had decided out of curiosity to test a local diviner. Leslie had eight native hunters out working for him, searching for elephant; could the diviner tell him how they were faring? The diviner made eight fires, and threw roots into them; then, he took a drug, and fell into a convulsive trance. When he came round, he raked out the fires one by one, describing as he did so what was happening to each hunter; how some had been fortunate; others had done badly; and two had been killed. The account, Leslie claimed, had proved to be true in every particular. But could the diviner not have cheated? Dudley Kidd argued in *The Essential Kafir*, published in 1902, that he could have combined local knowledge with intelligent guesswork. Leslie, though he might be convinced that this explanation was inadequate, had no way of proving that the diviner really had been using second sight.

Tales of the kind that Leslie told have continued to be heard from many parts of the world, particularly from those regions of America where peyotl can be found. Dr Rafael Bayon, working in Colombia at the beginning of the century, became convinced that with its help the local shaman could see and hear distant events on behalf of a patient, 'consistent with exact observations of things of which the patient neither has, nor could have, the least previous knowledge'. Twenty years later the French missionaries assured the pharmacologist Andre Rouhier that shamans who were asked a question only needed to take peyotl, 'and they obtain a solution to the problem before them in an auditory form — a person appearing to them and telling them what they want to know; or visually — as if, for example, they were to see the landscape, the persons or the plants which would serve them to the end desired'. Recently, Carlos Castaneda has described Don Juan's paranormal faculties in his books; and in *Flesh of the Gods*, Douglas Sharon — an anthropological field worker — has given a convincing account of the powers of the Peruvian shaman Eduardo Calderon Palomino.

When Palomino realised that he had a vocation to be a *curandero*, a healer/diviner, he began to practise with the help of tobacco, which gave him 'very rapid sight, mind and imagination'. (It was

for this purpose, he surmised, that people had originally taken
snuff; the *curanderos* found it helped to clear their minds and
speed their thoughts.) But when he wanted to induce visions, he
took the potent San Pedro cactus. He described the effects to
Sharon:

> . . . first, a slight dizziness that one hardly notices. And then a
> great vision, a clearing of all the faculties of the individual. It
> produces a slight numbness in the body and afterwards a tran-
> quillity. And then comes a detachment, a type of visual force
> in the individual, inclusive of all the senses; seeing, hearing,
> smelling, touching, etc. — all the senses, including the sixth
> sense, the telepathic sense of transmitting oneself across time
> and matter.

The cactus drug, Palomino thought, developed the power of
perception, enabling a man to 'distinguish powers or problems of
disturbances at a great distance, so as to deal with them'.

This evidence — and there is a great deal more of it — suggests that drug-induced divination as practised in primitive communities deserves more serious attention than it has received.
If it can be demonstrated that drugs are capable of liberating the
clairvoyant faculty in certain individuals, so that with the help of
their training as shamans they can use it for the benefit of the
tribe, there will have to be a radical reappraisal both of shamanism
and of the drugs associated with it. R. G. Wasson has even suggested that they may have had an evolutionary role, by giving
primitive man a glimpse 'of horizons beyond any that he knew
in his harsh struggle for survival'.

# 2

# *Drugs and the Priesthood*

THE CHANGE OF ATTITUDE TO DRUGS, BY WHICH THEY CAME TO BE
regarded as a threat rather than as an asset to society, was connected with the decline of shamanism and the emergence in its
place of organised religions and their priesthoods; an evolution
which the earlier anthropologists took to be a sign of progress,
towards less irrational forms of belief, but which can now be
interpreted rather differently.

### Shaman to priest

As man's reasoning power developed, and his capacity to consult instinct declined, fewer men could be found who had the
ability, with or without a drug, to slip into the trance state; and it
became progressively more difficult to interpret the pronounce-
ments of those who could. More powerful doses of whatever drug
was in use could not have helped, as they would have promoted
simple intoxication, without benefit of revealing visions. The
medicine no longer 'stood alert' within the shaman, leading him
inexorably to the answer he was seeking, uncovering the identity
of witch or thief. He began to need aids, as if to pick up and
amplify instinct's weak transmissions. Just as there are some water
diviners who search for underground sources unaided, while others
need to use a forked hazel twig or a pendulum, so there were (and
still are) some shamans who needed no aids, while others had to
employ devices — horns, say, which they could hold, and which
seemed to dictate their movements. And in the next stage, they
began to seek their visions in smoke, or in bowls of liquid —

much as a present-day fortune teller consults a crystal ball; or to throw bones, and observe the pattern they formed as they fell; or to examine the entrails of animals.

So long as these techniques were employed as a means to induce a trance — so long as the smoke or the entrails were simply a way of rousing the unconscious mind to take over — drugs still had their part to play in making the process easier. But the time was to come when divination by such means became standardised. The pattern in which the bones fell, the state of the entrails, were consciously 'read', as were omens; a bird flying past from one direction meant one forecast; from another direction, a different forecast. In time, divination was reduced to rote — to routine. Dissociation was then no longer needed; and drugs became superfluous.

At the same time, the development of patterns of belief — religions — made dissociation an untrustworthy and unnerving experience, because the material pouring out of the unconscious might be at variance with approved doctrine. A safer way was to employ ritual; the regular repetition of words and actions, designed to break down consciousness without inducing a full trance. Ritual required more self-control on the shaman's part, in order that he should be able to reproduce the formula exactly, time after time. Dissociation was no help; and drugs were a positive handicap. As a result shamans began to be chosen on other grounds than their ability to induce trances; and it was at this point that, in effect, they became priests.

The priest, as the American anthropologist A. L. Kroeber defined him half a century ago,

is an official recognised by the community. He has duties and powers. He may inherit, be elected, or succeed by virtue of lineage subject to confirmation. But he steps into a specific office which existed before him and continues after his death. His power is the result of his induction into the office, and the knowledge and authority that go with it. He thus contrasts sharply with the shaman — logically at least. The shaman makes his position. Any person possessed of the necessary mediumistic faculty, or able to convince a part of the community of his ability to operate supernaturally, is thereby a shaman. His influence is essentially personal.

The demarcation line, as Kroeber emphasised, cannot always be clearly drawn; in early civilisations, shamanism and religion often co-existed, particularly where potent plant drugs were available — peyotl, datura, the fly agaric. The most striking example emerges from the verses of the *Rig Veda* — the testimonies of the shaman/priesthood which was one outcome of the Aryan influx into India, three thousand years ago

> We have drunk soma, have become immortal
> Gone to the light have we, the gods discovered
> What can hostility do against us?

These hymns to a plant deity, as Wasson pointed out in his *Soma*, were composed over a period of centuries, by men who lived far remote from each other, but shared the same experiences from it;

> ... In the hierarchy of Vedic gods certain others took precedence over Soma: but since Soma was a tangible, visible thing, its inebriating juice to be ingested by the human organism in the course of the ritual, a god come down and manifesting himself to the Aryans, Soma played a singular role in the Vedic pantheon. The poets never tire of stressing Soma's sensuous appeal ... The priests, after imbibing the juice, seem to have known, for the nonce, the ecstasy of existence in the World of the Immortals. The divine element was not just a symbol of spiritual truth as in the Christian communion: Soma was a miraculous drink that spoke for itself.

It remains uncertain from which plant Soma was extracted. (Wasson's contention that it must have been the fly agaric makes more sense than most early theories, which even proffered such unlikely candidates as rhubarb); and the testimonials cannot be regarded as a wholly reliable source of information about its qualities — a similar collection of eulogies of beer or tobacco could be collated from English sources which would be hardly less idolatrous. Nevertheless the impression left of Soma's transcendental

qualities is significant, because it reveals that the drug —
whatever it may have been — was being taken for a different end.
The purpose was no longer basically functional — to secure access
to useful information. Rather, it was to lift the mind to a higher
plane of perception. The suggestion has even been made that the
shaman priests did not take the drug to try to achieve artificially
the exalted state of mind that mystics achieved through yoga. The
mystics, through yoga, may have been trying to recapture the
exalted states of mind which formerly had required the assistance
of Soma for their attainment.

In many other parts of the world, plant drugs which had
originally been used to facilitate access to the spirits came to be
regarded, and later worshipped, as spirits, or deities, in their own
right. In Peru, Tschudi reported, 'it was believed that any business
undertaken without the benediction of coca leaves could not pros-
per, and to the shrub itself, worship was rendered'. Chewed coca
was thrown on veins of ore in the Peruvian mines, in the belief
they would be softened, and easier to work. A few years later the
French traveller H. A. Weddell, exploring Bolivia, found that
married men going on a journey would throw a dollop of chewed
coca leaf on to a rock, in the belief that if it did not still adhere
to the rock when they returned, it would be proof that in their
absence their wives had not adhered to their marital vows.
Many innocents, Weddell feared, must have suffered a *bastonnade*,
as a result. In the 1920s Alexander Goldenweiser described how
the Chuckchi tribesmen in Siberia took the fly agaric in the expectation that the mushrooms would appear to them in the guise
of mushroom men, who would 'lead the dreamer through the
world and show him real and imaginary things'. Later, Wasson
observed the same process in Mexico, where the mushrooms had
begun to take command:

They speak through the *curandero* or shaman. He is as though
not present. The mushrooms answer the questions put to them
about the sick patient, about the future, about the stolen money
or the missing donkey ... similarly the eater of the fly agaric
comes under the command of the mushrooms, and they are
personified as amanita girls or amanita men, the size of the
fly agaric,

## The fruit of the vine

Drugs, therefore, remained an essential part of shamanism, where it survived. But wherever religions established themselves in its place, and in particular where the religion was monotheistic, the need for them disappeared, because the kind of divination they inspired was regarded as a threat. Rulers did not care for untamed sources of information, which might turn out to be subversive; and priests, brooding over their entrails, looked with envy on shamans, drawing their information directly from the spirit world — 'the priest realises clearly where the danger lies', as Michelet observed in his study of sorcery; 'an enemy, a menacing rival, is to be feared in this High-Priestess of Nature he pretends to despise'. Divination in such circumstances became regarded as the devil's doing — unless the diviner's probity or position was such that this interpretation was unthinkable, or perhaps unmentionable. It was equated with witchcraft, and the death penalty imposed for anybody who practised it — except when, as in the case of the witch of Endor, it happened to be the State, in the person of King Saul, who needed the prognostication. And drugs which had been used to induce the trance state were naturally suspect.

There was one drug available, however, which in this respect was relatively safe: wine. Whereas other drugs appeared to give access to information transmitted from a different world, what wine released — though it was often revealing: *in vino veritas* — was mundane. It induced visions only when taken in excess, over a protracted period; and they were not of any divinatory value to a shaman, or anybody else. As an intoxicant, in fact, alcohol's function was — in the phrase that has been so often echoed — to 'take away understanding'. It removed a man from the cares of the world, without precipitating him into another. Although his behaviour when in this condition might be anti-social and dangerous to himself and his companions, it presented no real threat to the authority of Church or State.

Wine, though, was taken chiefly as a beverage. It was decidedly safer to drink, in many regions, than water — as well as tasting agreeable. The Old Testament writings demonstrate that wine was never, in that era, looked on with suspicion. Drunkenness was condemned as a sin, but wine was no more held responsible for it than meat was held responsible for the sin of gluttony. So far from wine being suspect, it was usually coupled with bread as God's great gift to man. An abundant grape harvest signified divine pleasure; a superabundant harvest was taken to herald the coming of the Messiah. Temperance reformers were later to point to the existence of tribes or sects who renounced wine; but this was not because of disapproval of its intoxicating properties, but because they objected to the cultivation of the grapes. Nomads tended to despise those who settled down to the sedentary life of the farmer or town dweller; the Rechabite injunction 'ye shall drink no wine' was accompanied by 'neither shall ye build house, nor sow seed'. And where ascetic sects emerged, their worry was that wine-bibbing was a form of self-indulgence. John the Baptist would have objected as strenuously to the consumption of agreeably flavoured non-alcoholic drinks.

Wine had two effects, however, which eventually aroused debate on whether it ought to be — in effect — reclassified as a drug. One was the possible consequences for society of intoxication, when it unfitted men to do their jobs. It was up to the individual to regulate his own drinking, Plato's Athenian argued in the *Laws*; but the State had a right and a duty to protect citizens from the effects of that drinking, should it put them at risk:

> ... if the practice is treated as mere play, and free licence is to be given to any man to drink whenever he pleases, in what company he pleases, and when engaged on any undertaking he pleases, I could no longer vote for allowing any indulgence in the wine-cup to such a city, or such a man. I would even go further than the practice of Crete and Lacedaemon and propose an addition to the Carthaginian law which prohibits the very taste of this liquor to all soldiers in the field, and enforces water-drinking throughout the duration of a campaign. I would absolutely prohibit its taste in civic life to slaves of both sexes, to magistrates throughout the year of their office, and equally absolutely to captains of vessels and jurymen when on duty, and likewise to any member of an important council when about to attend its meetings. Further I would prohibit its use during the day absolutely, except under the orders of a trainer or physician, and at night also to any person of either sex contem-

plating the procreation of children, to pass over the many other cases in which wine is not to be drunk by rational men with a sound law.

The Greeks were concerned only about how to prevent drinking from becoming a security risk. Some early Christian sects, however, began to take the argument a stage further, and suggest that there was a more serious hazard: that it would imperil men's souls. Gnostics, Manicheans and others argued that as wine was notoriously an aphrodisiac, and the occasion of sin, to drink it must be sinful, and wine itself must be inherently evil. Against them were ranged those fathers of the Church on whom Greek thought still exercised a decisive influence, and who contended that 'it is not what entereth in that defileth a man' — as Clement of Alexandria put it in the second century A.D. — 'but that which goes out of his mouth'; a view echoed by St. Chrysostom, two centuries later:

> ... the simple ones among our brethren, when they see any person disgracing themselves from drunkenness, instead of reproving such, blame the fruit given them by God, and say, 'Let there be no wine'. We should say then in answer to such, 'let there be no drunkenness; for wine is the work of God, but drunkenness is the work of the devil'. Wine makes not drunkenness, but intemperance produces it. Do not accuse that which is the workmanship of God, but accuse the madness of a fellow mortal.

## Hashish

The knowledge that Jesus had been a wine drinker — and had even promised the disciples at the last supper that he would enjoy wine with them in Paradise — did not prevent the leaders of early Christian sects from arguing that wine was the occasion of sin, because they could claim that as Jesus was without sin, wine had no power over him. But to the ordinary believer, the argument sounded specious; and when Mahomet decided to instruct his followers to forgo wine, one of the reasons — it has been suggested — was that this would help to distinguish them from the wine-loving Christians.

As this was the first attempt of its kind to prohibit the consumption of a popular drug, it would be interesting to know more about how the ban worked. Given a zealous priesthood, it would have been relatively easy to enforce, because the location of the vineyards would be known. They could easily have been destroyed; and wine is too bulky to be easily smugg'.d in any quantity on camel caravans. The evidence, however, h: s yet to be sifted, to find what were the prohibition's effects. Ironically we know more — thanks to the work of Franz Rosenthal — about one of the side-effects of Mahomet's law: the controversy which followed in the Moslem world whether hashish, the drug made from the hemp plant, ought also to come under the ban, though it had not been formally indicted in the Koran. In *The Herb*, published in 1971, Rosenthal presented an illuminating sample of the opinions of philosophers and priests, public health officials and poets, on the issue of whether and how the consumption of hashish should be restricted, or stopped altogether: a foretaste of many a similar campaign to come.

To judge from a brief account in Herodotus of the way the Scythians threw hemp on heated stones and 'carried away by the fumes, shout aloud', the hemp plant must long have been known to have intoxicating qualities; and Moslem sects, such as the Sufis, continued to take it in traditional shamanist ways. By Mahomet's time, though, it seems to have been utilised chiefly as a medicine for, among other disorders, dandruff, diarrhoea, earache, gonorrhea and worms. But then — perhaps because of the ban on wine — hemp came again to be eaten, or drunk in some form of infusion in the Moslem world. There are difficulties, Rosenthal warned, in the way of any assessment of its precise effects on people, because 'hashish', the term ordinarily used, not merely covered a variety of different hemp preparations, but also took in opium and henbane, and was loosely used about herbs in general. Hemp, Rosenthal surmised, must gradually have come to be identified with hashish because it was regarded as *the* herb; 'the most representative and, probably, the most widely used of the hallucinatory drugs employed by medieval Muslims'. And when the authorities realised it was being increasingly adopted as a substitute for wine, they began to cast around for excuses to stop it. The Koran, they argued, banned wine because it could be an intoxicant; hashish was being taken as an intoxicant; therefore hashish should be banned. The upper classes tended to agree — particularly employers: hashish-eating was mainly a working class habit. It was bad for the working man's health, they explained; damaging his complexion, giving him halitosis, and eventually leading him to immorality, insanity, and mental exhaustion (much the same arguments, in fact, as were later to be used in England against masturbation).

The supporters of hashish argued that it had not been banned in the Koran precisely because it did *not* intoxicate — not, at least, in the same way as wine. Wine caused quarrelsomeness; hashish induced 'languid placidity' — as even its critics appear to have conceded; in the attacks on the drug, Rosenthal could find no mention of any really violent actions against others under its influence. In some people, it created a pleasant stupor; in others, it excited the imagination; that was all. It could not be condemned as anti-social. The law should therefore not meddle with it. As a jurist put it ingeniously in a verse:

Hashish intoxication contains a hidden secret
Too subtle for minds to explain
They have declared it forbidden without any justification
  on the basis of reason and tradition
Declaring forbidden what is not forbidden is forbidden

As hashish was admitted to be less intoxicating than such alternatives as opium and henbane — and even nutmeg, which enjoyed a considerable reputation as a narcotic — any attempt to suppress it, its supporters added, might only lead its purchasers to more dangerous drugs.

These arguments did not impress the authorities, who determined to try to curb the consumption of hashish. But how? Should it be banned outright; or should it be permitted for specific purposes, with penalties for misuse? Periodically, outright prohibition was attempted; but enforcement proved impracticable. The hemp plant grew wild; and even if it had not, it would have been impossible to stop cultivation, as it was valuable for other purposes — for making fibre, as well as medicine. It was quite easy to transport, or if necessary to smuggle, to those who wanted it; and because it was cheap there was a ready demand even from the poorest classes — 'I am satisfied', as a poet put it:

> ... with a morsel of porridge
> And a round pill of hashish,
> Why should I reproach time from which individual
> Destiny proceeds, by complaining about lack of means?

The pattern which emerges from Rosenthal's research is significant, because it has recurred again and again up to the present day. Drugs come under attack because they make Church and State uneasy, for fear that they will render people, particularly the young, less amenable to discipline. As the authorities do not care to admit that this is their real reason for wanting to stop drug-taking, they claim they are only concerned with their subjects' health, morals, and welfare. They then find that prohibition simply does not work. The anti-hashish campaigners, according to Rosenthal, were forced to admit that they were 'fighting a losing battle with the reality of the social environment', and eventually they sank into 'complete resignation'. It was the first in a long line of such losing battles in authority's protracted war to control drugs.

*Witch's brew*

There are other gaps in the history of drugs in this era which will have to await research like Rosenthal's to fill in. Some are unlikely ever to be filled. We will probably never know for certain what the constituents were of Homer's nepenthe; or what drug was used in the shamanist Eleusinian cult in ancient Greece, in which the initiate was given a potion designed to induce delectable visions, after which he could never be the same again. In general, the information about drugs and their social effects in classical times, and in the Middle Ages, is too scanty and unreliable to serve as the basis for anything more than enjoyable speculation. And although there is plenty of evidence about the attempts to control drunkenness — Solon established the death penalty for magistrates who were found under the influence and numerous regulations were made to prohibit slaves, or minors, or women from drinking — there is very little evidence how such laws worked in practice.

Apart from wine, there does not seem to have been any drug in common enough use in Europe to disturb the authorities' peace of mind. Drugs crop up chiefly in connection with witchcraft. Professor Michael Harner has recently argued that they were of central importance to witchcraft in Europe, but that this has been obscured by the fact that so much of the source material, most of it in Latin, has never been studied by anybody with an interest in this aspect of the subject. From the later evidence of witchcraft trials, it is clear that witches employed such plants as henbane and deadly nightshade — sometimes making them into unguents, and smearing them on parts of their bodies — as a way of liberating themselves. to undertake their Sabbat rides. It is also clear that, like shamans, they believed that while they were under the influence of these drugs they really could fly through the air. One seventeenth-century witch, more fortunate than many in that she had a shrewd priest dealing with her, boasted she could prove it;

rubbing ointment on herself to the accompaniment of magic incantations, she lay her head back and immediately fell asleep. With the labor of the devil she dreamed of Mistress Venus and other superstitions so vividly that, crying out with a shout and striking her hands about, she jarred the bowl in which she was sitting and, falling down from the stool, seriously injured herself about the head. As she lay there awakened, the priest cried out to her that she had not moved; 'for heaven's sake, where are you? You were not with Diana and as will be attested by these present, you never left this bowl'. Thus, by this act and by thoughtful exhortations he drew out this belief from her abominable soul.

Harner cites a number of similar examples, suggesting that witchcraft was not, as some historians have suggested, a symptom of mass hysteria, having no existence in its own right, but a debased form of shamanism, which the hostility of the Church had prevented from coming out into the open.

The prevailing belief in diabolic possession, however, meant that the drugs a witch used were not regarded as responsible for her conduct; and there is no indication that drugs were otherwise employed, except as medicines. Consequently, they were not an issue. Drunkenness continued to be condemned, and legislated against — but as a social nuisance rather than as a sin. So when Columbus's men returned with their descriptions of the purposes for which drugs were used in the New World, they were too unfamiliar to be feared as a threat to faith or morals in Europe. They could be welcomed, in fact, for the medicinal properties they were believed to possess.

# 3

# The Impact of Drugs on Civilisation

*Tobacco: herba panacea*

THERE WAS SOME DISPUTE AT THE TIME — AMONG SCHOLARS, THERE still is — over who deserved the praise or execration for introducing tobacco into Europe. The Spanish colonists soon took to it, in spite of official disapproval. Bartholomew de las Casas found some of them on the island of Hispaniola who had been reported for smoking; when remonstrated with for indulging in so vicious a habit, they had replied it was 'not in their power to stop'. And sailors brought the habit home. But it gained its initial popularity in Europe as a medicine. Its value in treating fevers and other disorders led Jean Nicot, French Ambassador at the Portuguese Court, to take tobacco plants to France, when he returned there in 1561, as a present for Catherine de Medici; and by the time Nicholas Monardes published his *Joyful News out of the New Found World*, a few years later, it had begun to be regarded as the great cure-all: *herba panacea*, valuable whether taken into the lungs, or into the digestive system — or applied externally, to wounds; effective alike against headaches, carbuncles, chilblains, worms, or venereal disease.

This was not illogical, in the prevailing climate of orthodox medical opinion, based on the assumption that health depended on a correct balance of the humours: blood, bile, and phlegm. A medicine which could 'cleanse the superfluous humors of the brain' could be expected to remove whatever symptoms that superfluity had brought on, mental or physical; and also to preserve health — those who took it, according to the mathematician Thomas Hariot, who was with Raleigh's expedition to Virginia in 1585, were 'not subject to many grievous diseases with which we in England are sometimes afflicted'.

It was for this reason, presumably, that Raleigh brought tobacco plants back from Virginia to plant on his Irish estate; his friend Edmund Spenser, who used to stay there, listed 'divine tobacco' in *The Faery Queen* as one of the herbs Belphoebe gathered to staunch the flow of blood from Timais's wound. But Raleigh began to enjoy tobacco in its own right, smoking it in a pipe as the Indians did in Virginia. Friends and acquaintances, introduced to smoking, caught the habit; and soon, it became the fashion.

Tobacco caught on not because it induced a trance state, and visions. Young Englishmen of the time would have been terrified if it had. They took to the drug simply because it was fashionable and — as soon as they got over the initial reaction of giddiness or nausea — enjoyable. It provided a mild 'lift', when that was desired; or it assisted relaxation. But it had one unwelcome consequence. It created a craving so powerful that by the 1890s, the writer of an English herbal was complaining that some men could not restrain themselves from having a smoke, 'no, not in the middle of their dinner'.

Smoking happened to become fashionable in England at a time when Puritanism was also establishing itself, based on an ethic closer to that of John the Baptist than of Jesus. The Puritan was not then in a position to deny tobacco's medicinal virtues, but it did not escape him that the people who smoked it were rarely concerned for their health. It was consequently possible to argue that because tobacco 'drinking' (as it was then often described, in the sense of 'drinking it all in') was not confined to specific doses at certain times of day, it could actually be harmful — like other drugs whose dosage was inadequately regulated: particularly to the young. Here, the Puritan found allies in the nobility and gentry who, even if they themselves liked to smoke, were apt to be indignant when their sons insisted on following the fashion. Ben Jonson portrayed the type — the clown Sogliardo in *Every Man out of his Humour*, 'so enamoured of the name of a gentleman that he will have it, though he buys it. He comes up every term to learn to take tobacco'. The parents suffered — 'the patrimony of many noble young gentlemen', Edmund Gardner, author of the *Trial of Tobacco*, observed, had 'vanished clear away with this smoky vapour'.

It was this aspect of the dangers of tobacco that 'Philaretes' emphasised in his *Work for Chimney Sweepers*, which appeared in 1602, denouncing smoking as a 'pestiferous vice'. Still fresh in the memory, he recalled, were reports

> that divers young Gentlemen, by the daily use of this tobacco, have brought themselves to fluxes and dysentries, and of late at Bath a scholar of some good account and worshipful calling was supposed to have perished by this practice, for his humours being sharpened and made thin by the frequent use of tobacco, after that they had once taken a course downward, they ran in such violence, that by no art or physician's skill could they be stayed, till the man most miserably ended his life, being then in the very prime and vigour of his age.

Philaretes explained how this had happened. Tobacco, he asserted, worked by evaporating man's 'unctuous and radical moistures' — as was demonstrated in the fact that it was employed to cure gonorrhea by drying up the discharge. But this process, if too long continued, could only end by drying up 'spermatical humidity', too, rendering him incapable of propagation. Experience also showed that tobacco left men in a state of depression, 'mopishness and sottishness', which in the long run must damage memory, imagination and understanding. Nor was it any use the defenders of tobacco arguing that the Indians took it without such ill-effects; the Indians had accustomed themselves to taking it from childhood.

## Tobacco: counterblast

*Work for Chimney Sweepers* was the first of scores of similar pamphlets which were to appear later on the same theme, denouncing the use of tobacco — and later of other drugs — for non-medical purposes. Whatever the drug, the writer was likely to claim that it was physically and mentally destructive, if not in its immediate effects, then in the long term; that it put the youth of the country particularly at risk — as some scarifying illustration from Bath (or Baden, or Ballston Spa, N.Y.) would demonstrate; and that it had a sinister past record. As the composer of the proto-typical broadside, Philaretes could be cited as deserving of some small niche in the history of drugs. But his offering was to be over-shadowed by the more famous *Counterblast to Tobacco* which came out two years later, in 1604 — its anonymous author's identity not being concealed for long: James I, newly ascended to the British throne.

In certain respects, the *Counterblast* was ahead of its time. James did not waste time trying to explode tobacco's reputation as a cure-all by citing examples of its failures; he contented himself with exposing the contradictions in the claims made on its behalf.

It cures the gout in the feet and (which is miraculous) in that very instant when the smoke thereof — light — flies up into the head, the virtue thereof — as heavy — runs down to the little toe. It helps all sorts of agues. It makes a man sober that was drunk. It refreshes a weary man, and yet makes a man hungry. Being taken on going to bed, it makes one sleep soundly; and yet being taken when a man is sleepy and drowsy, it will, as they say, awake his brain, and quicken his under-standing. As for the curing of the Pox, it serves for that use only among the poxy Indian slaves. Here in England it is refined, and will not deign to cure here any other than cleanly and gentlemanly diseases. Omnipotent power of tobacco!

James also emphasised tobacco's most commonly encountered pernicious effect: 'many in this kingdom have had such a continual use of taking this unsavoury smoke, they are not now able to resist the same, no more than an old drunkard can abide to be long sober'. But he spoiled his case by clearly hinting at one of the reasons for his dislike of tobacco: his hatred of Raleigh. Nor could he resist the temptation to set out his arguments against tobacco in the form of literary conceits. Tobacco, he sought to prove, was 'the lively image and pattern of hell', because it had in it all the vices for which man might expect hell to await him:

to wit; first, it was a smoke; so are the vanities of this world.

Secondly, it delighteth them who take it; so do the pleasures of the world delight the men of the world. Thirdly, it maketh men drunken, and light in the head; so do the vanities of the world, men are drunken therewith. Fourthly, he that taketh tobacco saith he cannot leave it, it doth bewitch him; even so, the pleasures of the world make men loath to leave them, they are for the most part so enchanted with them; and further, besides all this, it is like hell in the very substance of it, for it is a stinking loathsome thing; and so is hell.

It was a little too pat, confirming that James was less the shrewd observer of the effects of the drug that he appeared to be, than the diligent collector of all the possible rationalisations which could be mustered against it.

That autumn, James informed the High Treasurer of England that all importers of tobacco would have to pay, in addition to the customs duty of 2d a pound that Elizabeth had imposed, the sum of 6/8d; an increase of 4,000 per cent. It was the first attempt of its kind to get rid of a drug by indirect prohibition — by imposing a tax so heavy that only the very rich would be able to afford to buy it. And this discrimination was deliberate. When tobacco had been discovered, the preamble recalled, it had been taken 'by the better sort', only as physic. But it had recently, 'through evil custom and the toleration thereof, been taken in excess by a number of riotous and disorderly persons of mean and base condition who, contrary to the usages of which persons of good calling and quality make, spend most of their time in idle vanity, to the evil example and corrupting of others'. They also spent too much of their wages, which they ought to be spending on their families, 'not caring at what price they buy'; so that people's health was being impaired, making them unfit for work, and consuming their resources, and also the country's, because 'a great part of the treasure of our land is spent and exhausted by this drug alone'. James, in other words, had been moved to action less because of the drug's effect on his subjects' health, than because it might make them less loyal and hard-working. Men who took time off to smoke could be expected to expend much of that time in talk; and the talk might turn to gunpowder, treason and plot . . .

To judge by the *Counterblast*, James would have preferred to ban tobacco outright; but that could possibly have been dangerous, with so many pipe-smokers among the Court circle; and it would certainly have been difficult, with tobacco in such demand as a medicine. So the intention — the preamble continued — was simply to provide a restraint on consumption, in order to reduce the amount being imported, while leaving 'sufficient store to serve for the necessary use of those who are of the better sort, and have and will use the same with moderation to preserve their health'. But the new duty, James soon found, had precisely the opposite effect to that which he had intended. The people who used tobacco to cure ailments, finding it so expensive, were forced back on older herbal remedies which cost little or nothing. Those who had begun to smoke for pleasure, however, and become addicted could not bear to do without their pipefuls. And although with so heavy a duty to be paid, merchants did indeed, as James had hoped, find it less profitable to import tobacco, this only meant that they found it more profitable to smuggle it. In the decade that followed the introduction of the duty, tobacco consumption continued to increase, not least among the poor. 'There is not so base a groom' — the pamphleteer Barnabe Rich complained in 1614 —

> that comes into the alehouse to call for his pot, but he must have his pipe of tobacco, for it is a commodity that is now as saleable in every tavern, inn, and ale house, as either wine, ale or beer, and in apothecaries' shops, grocers' shops, chandlers' shops, they are (almost) never without company, that from morning to night are still taking of tobacco; what a number are there besides, that keep houses, or open shops, which have no other trade to live by but the selling of tobacco.

### Tobacco: fund-raiser

In ordinary circumstances James, with his sublime intellectual arrogance, would have been likely to try stiffer measures to check smuggling. But that would have meant increased expenditure, which he was in no position to undertake. He was chronically desperate for funds; and the signs that tobacco smoking was on the increase had suggested a way to secure them. In 1608 he had ordered a reduction in the duty to a shilling a pound, selling the right to collect it to one of his favourites, Philip Herbert, Earl of

Montgomery. Tobacco imports began to rise so rapidly that James found he had sold himself short; in 1615 he revoked the deal (paying Montgomery compensation) so that he could sell the right to collect the duty for a sum more closely approximating to what it would be worth to the patent holder — £16,000 a year, by 1620.

For the remainder of James's reign solvency was the essential consideration. By farming out the duty, he in effect ensured that it would be kept as high as it could go without causing the importer to switch to smuggling. But the importers were not the only problem. Distributors and retailers, it was found, were stretching their stocks by adulterating the tobacco with ground up stalks and leaves of other plants, and disguising the thinness of the flavour by adding small quantities of spirits, and spices, to delude the customer — unlike Jonson's Abel Drugger:

> He lets me have good tobacco, and he does not
> Sophisticate it with sack, lees, or oil
> Nor washes it in muscadel and grains
> Nor buries it in gravel, underground
> Wrapped up in greasy leather, or piss'd clouts.

'Sophistication' was frowned on by the authorities because it lost them revenue. When half of what was sold was no longer pure tobacco, this meant, in effect, that duty was being paid only on one out of two pipefuls smoked. The practice became so notorious that James had to intervene to authorise the inspection of stocks held by retailers. As a result, before the end of his reign he found himself setting himself up as guardian of the purity of the drug which twenty years before he had tried to suppress. And the irony only began there. The British colonists in Virginia, who for some years had almost despaired of being able to survive, experimented in 1611 with growing tobacco. The flavour happened to appeal to the British smoker. It was very much in James's financial interest that this taste should be encouraged because, as the House of Commons was told in 1620, the amount of sterling leaving the country in bullion to pay for tobacco had reached six figures. Such vast (for that period) sums were better channelled into British colonies — helping them to become self-supporting, and eventually to contribute to the Treasury — than shipped to swell the treasure chests of Portugal and Spain.

Without wishing it, therefore — to the end of his life, James continued to recall 'the dislike which we have always had of the use of tobacco in general', and to share the uneasiness of the Virginia Company about allowing the colony's economy to rely on a 'deceivable weed', the fashion for which 'must soon vanish into smoke' — the British Government had embarked upon a course of economic imperialism, based on two assumptions. One was that as colonies were revenue-raising enterprises — or at least, it was hoped, financially self-supporting — they must be allowed, and if necessary encouraged, to produce any commodity which could be sold profitably, even if it were not regarded as desirable in itself. The other was that if the commodity were *not* regarded as desirable in itself, its manufacture and sale could always be excused by pointing out that people were going to buy it anyway, so they might as well buy a British product. By this means, quality would be ensured; and the profits would benefit the British taxpayer.

### Tobacco: banned

Hypocritical though James's attitude to tobacco became, at least his policies were flexible enough to be administratively feasible. In other parts of the Old World, the reaction of rulers to the introduction of tobacco was generally the same, but they often preferred to take what must have appeared to be the simplest course; outright prohibition of the drug, with severe penalties for anybody caught selling or taking it.

Visiting Constantinople in 1611, George Sandys was told that on the orders of the Sultan Amurath a man caught smoking had been paraded through the streets mounted facing backwards on an ass, with a pipe drawn through the cartilage of his nose. In Iran, the Sultan's brother Shah Abbas imposed similar penalties; Sir Thomas Herbert, arriving there with a British delegation in 1628, found that Abbas had sentenced two merchants who had been caught importing tobacco to have their noses and ears cut off; and their consignment, forty camel loads, was burned — its 'black vapour gave the whole city infernal incense for two whole days and nights together'. Both rulers, when such punishments proved insufficient to check smuggling, introduced the death penalty. Jean Tavernier, visiting Iran in the 1670s, was told that some rich merchants found smoking in an inn had been punished, by Abbas's heir, as befitted the nature of their crime, by having molten lead poured down their throats. In India, the Great Mogul Jehangir Khan decreed that anybody found smoking should have his lips slit. When ambassadors from the Duke of Holstein arrived in Moscow in 1634, they saw eight men and a woman publicly knouted for selling tobacco, and the death penalty was decreed that year for habitual offenders.

The fashion of tobacco-smoking for some reason took longer to spread through Europe; but by the middle of the seventeenth century several states had laws against it. In the Canton of Berne, where the laws were related to the Ten Commandments, tobacco smoking was put in the same category as adultery, punishable by fines, the pillory, and imprisonment. And when this failed, the Canton set up a special Tobacco Court, modelled on the Inquisition, with payments for informers and harsh penalties for those who were convicted.

These laws and penalties, admittedly, were not based exclusively on the objection to tobacco as a drug. The Tsar Michael claimed also to be concerned about fire hazards; there were objections to the fumes and the spitting which accompanied smoking; and there was the fear that where men smoked together, they might be conspiring together. But whatever the motive, and however savage the penalties, the result was everywhere the same; prohibition was an utter failure. Sandys noted that in spite of the warning given by the sight of the convicted smoker paraded round Constantinople, people continued to smoke clandestinely. Tavernier found men and women in Persia 'so addicted to tobacco that to take their tobacco from them, is to take away their lives'.

Everywhere, eventually, the ban had to be lifted, and tobacco allowed in. Its consumption was in future to be restricted only by a variety of Government expedients to make money out of it by the levying of customs or excise duties — or by a state monopoly of the kind Richelieu introduced in France and which lasts to this day; and by local by-laws, directed not against tobacco as a drug, but against its unwelcome social side-effects.

*Tobacco: tamed*

How did it come about that tobacco, from being the drug most commonly used to induce visions in the New World, should have soon been domesticated in Europe; so that, as the flow of tributes from essayists and poets reveal, it was welcomed as a mild mental stimulant, stirring ideas, and as a mild tranquilliser, soothing away nervous tensions? The tobacco smoked in Europe may not have been as strong as that used by the Indians, and it was probably not taken in such powerful doses; but that is not sufficient to account for the difference. The most likely explanation is that the European mind had been carried too far from its moorings in instinct for tobacco to be capable of producing the trance state; and there was no shamanist tradition which could have been taken up to exploit tobacco in the way the medicine man was accustomed to do.

When tobacco smokers were seen to be physically no worse off for their indulgence — their semen did not dry up, and many of them lived on into old age — suspicions died; and during the Great Plague, tobacco attained respectability even among those who, like Samuel Pepys, had feared it as a dangerous drug. In the spring of 1665 he saw how a cat could be killed by 'the oil of tobacco'; but a month later the sight of doors marked with a red cross and the inscription 'Lord Have Mercy Upon Us' prompted him to resort to it: 'I was forced to buy some roll-tobacco to smell and to chew, which took away the apprehension.' And with a growing sense of Britain's maritime destiny, the tobacco trade attained full respectability, coming to be regarded not simply as a commercial, but as a national, asset. When an increase in the tobacco duty was mooted in 1685, a critic of the project was quick to point out that in addition to bringing in so much revenue, and providing the colonists with the wherewithal to buy vast quantities of English manufactures, 'the tobacco trade employed nearly two hundred ships, the breeding ground of many mariners'.

In America, too, tobacco-smoking among the colonists followed the pattern newly established in Europe. Even the Indians began to use it more for ritual and symbolic purposes — the 'pipe of peace'. In some States where tobacco was not grown attempts were made to curb consumption: Massachusetts banned smoking in company (even among consenting adults) in 1632, and three years later tried to stop its sale by retailers. But such regulations proved unenforceable, and tobacco developed into an industry second only in importance to alcoholic liquor. The effects on the health of the community cannot now be estimated; but some idea of the social and economic significance of the development was provided by Joseph C. Robert in *The Story of Tobacco in America*, published in 1949. Tobacco not merely saved the Virginia settlement; it

> created the pattern of the Southern plantation; encouraged the introduction of Negro slavery, then softened the institution; begot an immortal group of colonial leaders; strained the bonds between mother country and Chesapeake colonies; burdened the diplomacy of the post-Revolutionary period; promoted the Louisiana purchase; and, after the Civil War, helped to create the New South ... Dispute and violence are milestones along this tobacco road; Culpeper's Rebellion marked the seventeenth century, the Black Patch war the twentieth. Colonial Virginians used tobacco as money; in the confusion following the Second World War the American cigarette was currency 'from Paris to Peking'.

*Tea: coffee*

Tobacco was the only drug from the Americas which caught on in the Old World; but in the middle of the seventeenth century two other drugs which had not been known before in Europe began to appear from the East: tea — which Pepys recorded as a novelty in 1661 — and coffee. Both were originally introduced, as tobacco had been, for medicinal purposes — the apothecary telling Mrs Pepys it was 'good for her cold and defluxions'. Both, like tobacco, aroused authority's suspicion when it was found they were being taken for pleasure.

Coffee came from the Middle East, where its appearance had so alarmed the authorities in Mecca and Cairo that they had tried to prohibit its sale, with regulations that all stocks found should be burned, and all people found drinking it punished. As with Indian hemp, earlier, the accusation was that coffee was an intoxicant — a reputation which Sir Anthony Shirley, one of three brothers with a reputation as travellers in far-away lands, confirmed after he had tasted it in Aleppo in 1598. So when it was introduced into Europe, a number of rulers reacted to it as their forbears had reacted a century before to tobacco, decreeing fines, imprisonment and corporal punishment for those involved in its distribution or consumption. But the tendency was to regard it as a danger chiefly to the lower orders; the aristocracy reserved the right to drink coffee. Inevitably such qualified prohibition proved unworkable; and rulers soon switched to the method King James had pioneered, taxing it instead.

Tea did not attract the same hostility because, except in Britain, it continued for two centuries to be sold by druggists, and bought by the public, chiefly as a remedy for internal disorders (it was to surprise the town of Angoulême when Balzac's Mme Bargeton gave a tea party, as tea was still sold there in chemists' shops for indigestion — for which purpose the curé of Yonville was to recommend it to Madame Bovary). In Britain, where it became popular as a pick-me-up, it provoked some virulent attacks from satirists and from politicians; Henry Savile told Mr Secretary Coventry in 1678 that it was a base, unworthy and filthy substitute for wine. But by then it was too late. One of Charles II's first acts at his restoration had been to impose a duty on tea; and it had proved to be one of his most profitable fiscal expedients. When the traveller and philanthropist Jonas Hanway tried to launch a campaign against it a century later, he had against him not only Dr Johnson — 'a hardened and shameless tea drinker' as he described himself, 'who with tea amuses the evening, with tea solaces the midnight, and with tea welcomes the morning' — but also almost the entire population of Britain, poor and rich alike, who by this time were consuming it in such quantities that it had become one of the State's chief sources of revenue.

# 4

# *The Impact of Civilisation*

THE FACT THAT SO SMALL A NUMBER OF PLANT DRUGS WERE KNOWN in the Old World, compared to the new, has naturally led to speculation: why? The reason, the American anthropologist Professor Weston La Barre has suggested, is simple; that shamanism had survived in the Americas, and it was 'so to speak, culturally programmed for an interest in hallucinogens and other psychotropic drugs'. And not only for an interest in them: the medicine man, by training as well as by instinct, knew how to exploit drugs. The Europeans, taught as they were to regard divination as the work of the devil, were culturally programmed to regard vision-inducing plant drugs as his instrument. In Europe, this was not a problem; though witches might use them, they were not ordinarily encountered in everyday life, and few people would have thought of experimenting with them. But the drugs found in use in the New World appeared to be a direct threat to Church and State — not then differentiated; and the tendency, wherever shamanist drug-practices were found, was to try to suppress them.

## Coca

Drugs came under attack even when they were widely used for secular purposes, as medicines, or to increase endurance — as in the case of coca, in Peru. The Inca religion had retained an element of shamanism, and coca was one of the drugs used by the diviner-priests to help themselves into a trance; or, where that art had been lost, the diviner burned the leaves so that he could 'see' coming events in the curling smoke. Infusions of coca were taken at festivals; corpses were buried with coca, to help them over the Inca equivalent of the Styx; there was a 'Coca Mama' — the equivalent of the Corn Mother of other cults; and coca was included in sacrifices, on the principle that whatever was most valued should be given up to the gods. Appalled at these manifestations of idolatry, missionaries and priests were soon denouncing coca. It was formally condemned at the first Ecclesiastical Council held in Lima in 1551, and again in 1567 as connected with the work of idolatry and sorcery, 'strengthening the wicked in their delusions, and asserted by every competent judge to possess no true virtues; but, on the contrary, to cause the deaths of innumerable Indians, while it ruins the health of the few who survive.'

The civil authorities had their own reasons for mistrusting coca. Anything so closely linked with Inca tradition was likely to become identified with it, in the minds of those who cherished the hope of overthrowing Spanish rule. There was also a more practical reason for suppressing the use of the drug. It was taken by workers throughout the day, pouched in the cheek, and replenished when necessary. The need for replenishment did not suit employers, who felt it was an unnecessary expense. By a simple device, they had ensured that labour in Peru would be both readily available and cheap; a tax had been imposed on every Indian of working age, which meant that the male population had to find work, in order to be able to pay it. The tax was nicely judged to leave the worker with only nominal wages — a penny a day — and his keep. As part of his keep, however, he expected a ration of coca. Why, employers naturally asked themselves, should they have to provide him not only with food and water but with a luxury — worse, a drug condemned by the Church?

Prohibition was demanded, and in ordinary circumstances, could have been expected to follow. But those Spaniards who had established themselves as the owners of the coca plantations on the slopes of the Andes had quickly made their fortunes. From 1548 to 1551, the Spanish chronicler Cieza de Leon recalled, 'there was not a root, nor anything gathered from a tree, except spice, which was in such estimation', and they grew rich on the proceeds. They were not inclined to let the source of their wealth be wrested from them; and their profits gave them the means to campaign in Lima and in Madrid to save their business from extinction. Prohibition, they claimed, would be impracticable. The coca plantations might be ploughed up, but this would not stop the plant from being grown illicitly. And what evidence was there that coca was bad for the Indians? On the contrary, not merely did it help them to work long hours; it provided them with the necessary stimulus to do the work — coca being the only currency available to them.

These were arguments which could be expected to make some impression on the Government, in its capacity as an employer. More surprisingly, they also made an impression on the Church. A Spanish priest, Blas Valera, who worked in Peru in the early years of the seventeenth century — and who thought highly of coca, particularly as a medicine — described how the change of heart came about. Some people, he recalled, had been hostile, 'moved only by the fact that in former times the heathen offered coca to their idols, as some wizards and diviners still do'. Because of this, they had argued that coca should be suppressed. If the Incas had offered coca and nothing else in their sacrifices, this might have been reasonable. But they had also sacrificed cattle; was beef therefore to be banned? On reflection, it had been decided that it would be best not to ban coca, but instead, to instruct the natives how to avail themselves of God's gifts in a Christian fashion. This resolution, Valera noted, had not been without its benefits to the Church; 'the income of the bishop, canons and other priests of the Catholic Church of Cuzco is derived from the tithe on the coca leaf'.

So the Indians, though they were punished if they were caught using coca in religious observances, were allowed to take it while working, in order that they might be able to put in still longer hours. The consequences were to be summarised four centuries later by John Hemming, in *The Conquest of the Incas*:

Coca plantations lay at the edge of humid forests, thousands of feet below the natural habitat of the Andean Indians. This did not deter Spanish planters and merchants who made huge profits from the coca trade. They forced highland natives to leave their *encomiendas* and work in the hot plantations. The change of climate was devastating to Indians with lungs enlarged by evolution to breathe thin air. Antonio de Zúñiga wrote to the King: 'Every year among the natives who go to this plant a great number of Your Majesty's vassals perish.' There were also ugly diseases in the plantations. A tiny mosquito-like dipterous insect that lives between 2,500 and 9,500 feet in the Andean foothills carries the destructive 'verruga' or wart disease, in which victims die of eruptive nodules and severe anemia. Coca workers also caught the dreaded 'mal de los Andes' or *uta*, which destroys the nose, lips and throat and causes a painful death. Bartolomé de Vega described the native hospital of Cuzco 'where there are normally two hundred Indians with their noses eaten away by the cancer'. Those who escaped the diseases returned to their mountain villages debilitated from the heat and undernourishment; they were easily recognisable, pale, weak and listless. Contemporary authorities estimated that between a third and half of the annual quota of coca-workers died as a result of their five-month service.

Decrees from Lima, and even from King Philip in Madrid, tried to regulate working hours and conditions. The frequency with which they had to be repeated — one Viceroy, Francisco de Toledo, issued over twenty ordinances designed to protect the Indians — suggests that they were not obeyed; not, at least, until wastage reduced the supply of labour to the point when the employers in their own self-interest had to begin to treat their workers with more consideration, or risk having too few of them to harvest the coca crop.

This pattern was to be repeated in colonised territories. Missionaries disliked shamanism and the drugs associated with it because they were pagan; the colonial authorities, because they might be a focus for unrest, and for law-breaking. But where a plant drug could be exploited commercially, farmers, entrepreneurs and traders would find reasons for permitting, and encouraging, its consumption. They would use their influence to persuade the colonial authorities that it was essential to the colony's economy; and — particularly if they could extract revenue out of the drug — the colonial authorities would usually allow themselves to be persuaded.

### Peyotl

Where commercial considerations were unimportant, either because the drug was taken exclusively in shamanist rites, or because it could not be cultivated, the Church was more likely to have its way: as it did with the peyotl cactus. As late as the middle of the seventeenth century, when Francisco Hernandez published his pioneering work on the flora and fauna of Mexico, he was still careful to intimate his disapproval of the way certain of the plants he described were used. By eating peyotl, he noted, the Indians 'can foresee and predict anything; for instance, whether enemies are going to attack them the following day? Whether they will continue in favourable circumstances? Who has stolen household goods? And other things of this sort.' Far from being impressed, when Hernandez described what peyotl looked like he observed that it 'scarcely issues forth, as if it did not wish to harm those who discover it and eat it'. Similarly with *ololiuqui* — the 'morning glory'; when the priests wished to commune with their gods, and to receive messages from them, they ate it to induce a delirium, in which 'a thousand visions and satanic hallucinations appeared to them'. A catechism used in Mexico in that period reveals the priests' attitude. 'Art thou a soothsayer?' each convert would be asked.

Dost thou foretell events by reading signs, or interpreting dreams, or by water, making circles and figures on the surface? Dost thou suck the blood of others, or dost thou wander about at night, calling upon the demon to help thee? Hast thou drunk peyotl, or hast thou given it to others to drink, in order to find out secrets or to discover where stolen or lost articles were?

In 1620, peyotl was formally denounced:

We, the Inquisitors against heretical perversity and apostasy, by virtue of apostolic authority declare, inasmuch as the herb or root called peyotl has been introduced into these provinces for the purposes of detecting thefts, of divining other happenings, and of foretelling future events, it is an act of superstition, to be condemned as opposed to the purity and integrity of our holy Catholic faith. The fantasies suggest intervention of the devil, the real authority of this vice.

The civil authorities shared the Inquisition's views. They, too —

according to the chronicler Fr Joseph de Acosta — were impressed by the evidence that under the influence of peyotl shamans were able 'to report mutinies, battles, revolts and death occurring 200 or 300 leagues distant, on the very day they took place, or the day after'. That divination could provide such a rapid communication service was an excellent reason for banning consumption of the drug. With characteristic cunning, however, the devil had provided alternatives; as well as ololiuqui, there were tobacco, datura and certain types of mushroom. All that Church and State could do was ban the drug cult ceremonies; and when the risk of holding them openly became too great, the cults continued underground.

### Alcohol: Siberia

Suppression was not the only weapon with which colonists could attack indigenous drug cults. They brought their own substitute drug with them: alcohol. Along with beer and wine, they introduced spirits: brandy, whiskey, gin and rum. Traders found it convenient to use them to lubricate negotiations, buying and selling; and then, as merchandise in their own right.

The results were often depressing. When the Russians began the conquest of Siberia at the end of the sixteenth century, they determined to put down shamanism; and to that end they banned the consumption of the fly agaric — a futile gesture; the naturalist Nikolai Sljunin observed in 1900 that the law was 'completely ignored'. The introduction of vodka by traders proved a more effective weapon. Vodka was cheap — and readily available, unlike mushrooms, all the year round. But not merely did it fail to provide the shaman with visions; it actually blocked them — coming to be regarded, according to Sljunin, as an antidote to the mushroom's effects. The evidence, in fact, suggests that it was not drugs which made Siberian shamanism decadent, as Mircea Eliadé claimed; it was one particular drug, alcohol, which destroyed the shaman's ability to induce a trance, and tempted him to fake it, and delude the company with conjuring tricks.

### Alcohol: Tahiti

Traditionally, the saddest story of the effects of alcohol concerns Tahiti. When the island was discovered in the 1760s, the crews who had been there returned with glowing accounts of a paradise, where the people lived free from worldly cares, doing little work because most of their wants were provided for by nature; enjoying sexual relations uninhibitedly because they were untroubled by the taboos or the guilt which Christianity had attached to them; and in general appearing to lead a wonderfully contented existence. Their only mild intoxicant came from a root which, when ground up, could be made into the drink kava; and was taken only on ceremonial occasions. Though Captain Cook's crew were told that it could make men drunk, they never saw this happen. When first offered alcoholic drinks, their Tahitian guests took them in all innocence, became drunk, and — after experiencing hangovers — took care not to get drunk again, 'shunning a repetition of it', Joseph Banks observed in his account of the visit, 'instead of greedily desiring it as most Indians are said to do'. It was as if the islanders, close to nature as they were, had no need of artificial intoxication; they lived in the happy state which Europeans tried in vain to reach with the help of alcohol.

Before long, however, as more ships began to call, some Tahitians began to develop a taste for alcohol; particularly members of the ruling families, who were recipients of much of the hospitality. The missionaries, who by this time were establishing themselves, abetted the process. On arrival, they had determined to compel the Tahitians to cover their nakedness, and to cease their uninhibited sexual play. They were also anxious to put an end to Tahitian religious rites — among them, the ceremonial drinking of kava — because they were pagan. To implement these reforms, however, they had to win the Paramount Chief's support. The heir, Pomare II, intimated that he was willing to back the missionaries, so long as they did not interfere with his personal pleasures. Arriving in 1802 on his voyage round the world John Turnbull found the royal family demoralised by excess, and Pomare an alcoholic and a public menace. Under the influence of drink, Turnbull feared, he would not scruple to kill anybody who annoyed him.

What possible benefit — Diderot had asked — could Christians with their hypocrisy, guilt and ambition, bring to the South Sea islanders? They would arrive, he warned, 'with crucifix in one hand and dagger in the other, to cut your throats or force you to accept their customs and opinions'. Gin bottle in the other, would have been nearer the mark; but Diderot's warning — 'one day under their rule you will be almost as unhappy as they are' — was soon shown to be justified. Tahitians lost their childlike innocence, which made even their pilfering endearing; they had to wear 'Mother Hubbards'; they had to work; they were no longer happy; and they drank. When William Ellis arrived on Tahiti as a missionary in 1817, he found Turnbull's fears had been justified. Under Pomare, intemperance prevailed 'to an awful and unprecedented degree'. On impulse, men would get together to erect a still, and then over a period of days consume its product, 'sinking into a state of indescribable wretchedness, and often practising the most ferocious barbarities'. While the liquor lasted they were more like demons than human beings; and after it was finished,

> sometimes in a deserted still-house might be seen fragments of the rude boiler, and the other appendages of the still, scattered in confusion on the ground; and among them, the dead and mangled bodies of those who had been murdered with axes or billets of wood in the quarrels that had terminated their debauch.

As soon as they had established their authority, the missionaries tried to stop the islanders from drinking spirits; but with so many ships coming in, the task was hopeless. Among the arrivals was the *Beagle*, in 1835. When Darwin offered the Tahitian guides a drink they 'put their fingers before their mouths and uttered the word "missionary"' — but they did not refuse. 'The natives having nothing at all to do', Gauguin reported half a century later, 'think of one thing only: drinking.'

Was alcohol the cause of the destruction of Tahiti's island paradise, or were there more insidious reasons? Other Pacific islands were given much the same introduction to colonialism and Christianity; not all of them were so marked by it. Pondering this on his tour of the Pacific, early in the 1890s, Robert Louis Stevenson came to the conclusion that it was unwise to put the blame for what had happened there either on gin or on 'Tartuffe insisting on unhygienic clothes'. No single cause, he felt, was responsible for decay, where it was to be found. What was decisive was the amount of dislocation involved in the islanders' way of life: 'where there have been fewest changes, important or unimportant, salutary or hurtful, there the race survives. Where there have been most, important or unimportant, salutary or hurtful, there it perishes.'

J. W. Anderson, who had travelled around among the Pacific islands in the 1870s, was of the same opinion. He cited the stability of Fiji as an example. There, he found, yangona (as kava was known) was still taken in an elaborate ritual. First, young men and women with good teeth were employed to chew the root, until it was of the right consistency to be put in a bowl of water and its juices squeezed out. The resulting liquid appeared 'greenish-grey and muddy-looking'; it tasted to him like 'a mixture of rhubarb, magnesia and soapsuds'; and it left those who drank it rather unsteady on their feet. So the missionaries wanted to ban the ceremony — as did some employers, who disapproved of the time it wasted; islanders would drop whatever they were doing to attend. But it had not been banned; rightly, Anderson felt. The chewing process might appear to be disgusting (and to spread unmentionable diseases); the kava itself might be debilitating, to anybody who took it to excess. But in moderation it did no harm. The islanders, in fact, regarded it as a purifier of the blood. And even those who took so much of it that they became intoxicated displayed 'neither unseemly behaviour nor incoherency of speech', but rather showed 'an inclination to remain mute in a mood of happy dreaminess'. In the circumstances, Anderson hoped, kava drinking would continue, 'for the chances are that by and by, its substitute will be "*yangona papalangi*" that is, white man's grog; and we are too well aware what havoc the fire water plays among savages who once take a liking to it'.

*Alcohol: America*

As Anderson's reference showed, alcohol had become notorious for its effects on primitive communities; particularly in North America, where distilled liquors had been unknown before the arrival of the colonists from Europe. As in the Pacific, it was the traders who introduced the American Indians to 'fire water'; and the Indians, unaccustomed to intoxication (tobacco was ordinarily used for that purpose by the shaman, but not by members of the tribe, except under his guidance) developed a craving for it.

Towards the end of the seventeenth century missionaries were beginning to report the dire consequences, 'Lewdness, adulteries, incest, and several other crimes which decency keeps me from naming' — Father Chrestien Le Clerq wrote of a tribe on the Gulf of St. Lawrence — 'are the usual disorders which are committed through the trade in brandy, of which some traders make use in order to abuse the Indian women, who yield themselves readily during their drunkenness to all kinds of indecency.' The places where the Indians drank brandy, another missionary wrote in 1705, were 'an image of hell. Fire flies in all directions, blows with hatchets and knives make the blood flow on all sides. They commit a thousand abominations — the mother with her sons, the father with his daughters, and brothers with their sisters. They roll about on the cinders and coals, and in blood.'

It was stories such as these to which Anderson (and Banks, a century earlier) were referring; the assumption then being that alcohol had been the really destructive influence. But this view has recently been challenged by Craig MacAndrew and Robert Edgerton in their *Drunken Comportment: a social explanation*, published in 1969. They were able to show that the American Indians, like the Tahitians, when they first tried spirits were attracted by the novelty of the experience — 'a merry-go of the brain', as one of them described it — but for a while were not adversely affected. So long as their experience was 'untutored by expectations to the contrary' — MacAndrew and Edgerton claimed — 'the result was neither the development of an all-consuming craving nor an epic of drunken mayhem and debauchery'. That epic only came when their way of life had been destroyed by the settlers, and their culture debased — another instance of the destructive power of change which Stevenson had observed.

But there was more to it, MacAndrew and Edgerton decided, than simple change. The consumption of spirits brought out a trait which had already existed in their tribal societies: cruelty. The Red Indians had been notoriously cruel to captured foes, practising tortures on them of the most savage but sophisticated kind. They now learned from the white traders that a man should not be held responsible for what he did under the influence of drink. Alcohol therefore provided them both with the stimulus and the excuse to repeat the kind of behaviour they had formerly indulged in, with tradition's sanction, when they captured a member of an enemy tribe.

It was not the drug, therefore, that was responsible for the way people behaved under its influence. The drug was simply the release mechanism, the behaviour being largely conditioned by expectations. Where the expectations from an established drug were of gentle intoxication, as with kava, it was in the colonists' self-interest to encourage it, and discourage the sale of spirits; and where this became settled policy, as on Fiji, the results appeared satisfactory — as Basil Thomson, who spent many years in Fiji around the turn of the century, recalled in his memoirs. Although the missionaries had continued to wage their campaign against yangona with 'a fiery zeal', the civil authorities had contented themselves with regulations chiefly designed to try to restrict its use to precisely the ceremonial occasions that the missionaries most deplored. As a magistrate, Thomson had to enforce this policy; and he came to the conclusion it was justified, because the vice of kava drinking 'if it is a vice at all, cannot reasonably be condemned for bringing in its train any of these social evils that are due to alcohol'.

But colonial authorities were sometimes less far-sighted; and they could not, as a rule, stop the introduction of alcohol. Nor was it easy for them to prevent the erosion of traditional cultures and beliefs. Shamanism had been based on certain assumptions which Christianity and, later, the even more powerful force of rationalism challenged. Inexorably, the shaman's authority was eroded. He might still get his visions from tobacco, or other drugs. But they were of little comfort to the tribe if they predicted, correctly, that it was futile to oppose the superior power wielded by the white man — and disastrous when they incorrectly roused expectations, as occasionally they did, that the white man was going to be destroyed by a whirlwind, or some other form of divine retribution. When Sitting Bull smoked, and gave a hundred pieces of his flesh, before dancing the Sun Dance, his aim was to receive a vision; and he had one, which revealed that white soldiers were coming, and that the Sioux would slaughter them. The Sioux duly did, when Custer and his force appeared. But the vision had not revealed what was to follow: the massacre of the Indians at

Wounded Knee, which banished their last hope of successful resistance.

In such circumstances, vision-inducing drugs were a hazard; and shamanist observances came to rely more upon ritual — or on alcohol. Where alcohol was involved, they often came to resemble saturnalia, of the kind Ruth Underhill described in her study of the religion of the Papago Indians. At the annual rain-making ceremony the shaman was still employed, but only as a subordinate. The most important role was that of the brewer, who made the fermented liquor from cactus fruit; the shaman being required simply to protect the brew from harmful influences. If he failed, he rather than the brewer would suffer for it. The principle which had attached itself to the ceremony was that 'the saturation of the body with liquor typifies and produces the saturation of the earth with rain'; the aim was to get everybody concerned 'full', without any expectation of visions, let alone of clairvoyance. Neophytes, admittedly, were encouraged to 'dream' songs which could be added to the tribal repertoire: but to judge by the samples Underhill obtained suitability was not equated with any great originality of insight.

> Come and sing!
> Come and sing!
> Sing for the evening!
> The sun stands there.
> Sing for it!
> For the liquor delightfully sing!

And in the traditional songs and speeches, the emphasis was on the pleasures of inebriation for its own sake. To each recipient of the brew, the cup-bearer would say

> Drink, friend! Get beautifully drunk
> Hither bring the wind and the clouds.

Nor did the use of the term 'beautifully' mean that the Papagos were under any illusions as to the effects of the liquor — as one of the songs sung during the progress of the ceremony indicated:

On the morning of the second day
They come hastening from all directions
They grow drunk, they stagger, they grow very drunk
They crawl around in their vomit

Much dizziness,
Much dizziness
Within me is swelling
And more and more
Every which way I am falling

# 5

# *Spirits*

---

## *Gin*

IT WAS NOT, THEN, ALCOHOL AS SUCH WHICH WAS THE DESTRUCTIVE influence, but the fact that a potent variety — spirits — was introduced to communities suffering from social dislocation after the loss of their old stability. And Britain, in the early seventeenth century, was taught the same lesson by gin.

Until 'Geneva', as it was originally known, began to become popular, distilled liquors had not been drunk in Europe on any substantial scale — except among the rich, who enjoyed their brandy. But in the seventeenth century Geneva drinking spread to Holland, and among those who acquired a taste for it was William of Orange. Chronically in need of funds to finance his campaigns against the French, he had become aware of the value of drugs as a source of revenue; part of the price he demanded for consenting to oust James II was that he should be awarded the revenue from the tobacco duties; and when he and Mary ascended the throne, one of his first actions was to break the London Distillers' Guild monopoly, and allow anybody to manufacture spirits on payment of a duty. The conflict with France, checking the import of brandies, provided a further inducement to British distillers; and production began rapidly to increase.

That spirits could have the attributes of a drug was remarked upon by the economist Charles D'Avenant in 1695. Brandy-drinking, he wrote, was becoming a growing vice among the common people (he was presumably using brandy as a synonym for spirits, as few of the common people could have afforded cognac), 'and may in time prevail as much as opium with the Turks, to which many attribute the scarcity of people in the East' — opium having won the reputation of diminishing sexual appetite, and eventually of weakening sexual performance. So far as Government and Parliament were concerned, though, the new taste for spirits was a godsend. 'It pays rent for our land, employs our people', Daniel Defoe noted in his *Review* in 1713; distilling had become 'one of the most essential things to support the landed interest' (which happened to be supporting him, at the time; he was working as an undercover agent for the Government). It should consequently, he urged, be 'specially preserved, and tenderly used'.

Distilling was tenderly used — more tenderly even than brewing. Gin cost around 18p a gallon to manufacture, so it could be sold at a price which would enable anybody who wished to get drunk to do so for less than it would cost to get drunk on beer.It began to replace beer as the tipple of the poor, at least in London; and the results alarmed the London magistrates. A committee they appointed to investigate reported in 1726 that gin was sold in one house in ten in some London parishes (one house in five, in one parish); that as a result of its availability and cheapness, the poor were giving themselves over to vice and debauchery; and that even in the workhouses, where the sodden creatures ended their days, gin was smuggled in. The inmates were prepared to suffer any punishment 'rather than live without it, though they cannot avoid seeing its fatal effects by the death of those among them who had drunk most freely of it'.

The fate of the poor in workhouses was of little concern to Members of Parliament. What was disturbing to them about the report was the suggestion that soldiers and, worse, servants were being daily suborned by gin; it was scarcely possible for them to go anywhere 'without being drawn in either by those who sell it or by their acquaintances, whom they meet with in the street, who generally begin by inviting them to a dram'. M.P.s, though, shared a landed interest. Distilling from grain pushed up their income. The Prime Minister, Robert Walpole, did not want to lose his majority; nor did he care to sacrifice the revenue from the duty paid by the distillers. Even when increasingly horrifying reports drove him in 1729 to put a curb on the sale of gin, the outcry from the farmers, coupled with the fact that enforcement proved impossible, soon led to its being withdrawn.

The London magistrates — responsible for the city's health, as well as for law and order — began again to warn that the situation was deteriorating; and in a further report in 1736 they presented a picture of the degeneration of the poor too ugly to be ignored. Spirits were clearly responsible. The workers were being encouraged to drink the whole week 'upon score', and 'too often without minding how fast the score runs against them, whereby at the week's end they find themselves without any surplusage to carry home to their families, which must of course starve, or be thrown on the parish'. Their wretched wives were also becoming gin drinkers 'to a degree hardly possible to be conceived. Unhappy mothers habituate themselves to these distilled liquors, whose children are born weak and sickly, and often look shrivel'd and old as though they had numbered many years. Others again daily give it to their children.'

### Gin: prohibition

The worry was not that gin made men and women drunk. Drunkenness, as distinct from what people might do when they were in that condition, was not in this period regarded as a heinous offence: 'an honest drunken fellow', Defoe had noted in 1702, 'is a character in man's praise'. If the Londoner had got roaring drunk on gin the way the Irish and the Scots were reputed to get drunk on whiskey — because they liked to get drunk on whiskey, from time to time — he would have caused the magistrates little concern. But he was using gin as a quick, cheap way of escape — not as an intoxicant, but as a narcotic. This was, in fact, the prototype of future drug scares, presenting many of the features which were to become so familiar; among them, the first reported parliamentary debate on the issue of prohibition.

Appalled by the evidence, Sir John Jekyll proposed in the Commons that a duty of 20 shillings a gallon should be put on spirits sold by retail. The motion was opposed by Sir William Pulteney. This was not, Pulteney emphasised, because he had anything to say in favour of the consumption of spirits, which had become excessive and mischievous, sapping the people's health and morals. His criticism was that the measure amounted to prohibition.

Prohibition, Pulteney explained, was doubly unjust; in principle, because it struck at spirits, rather than at their misuse (nobody had argued that spirits consumed in moderation did harm, so to stop them being sold for consumption in moderation was 'carrying the remedy much farther than the disease'); and in practice, because it was the Government itself which had encouraged men to sink capital in distilleries and in shops — 'it is a dangerous, it is, Sir, a terrible thing to reduce many thousands of families at once to a state of despair'. But the essential objection to prohibition was that it did not work — as the earlier experience of the Walpole government had shown. The spirits which had previously been available were simply replaced by an illicit liquor 'which, I believe in derision of the Act, they called "Parliament Brandy" '. If legal channels dried up, spirits would inevitably begin to flow in through other, illegal channels.

Parliamentary debates were not at the time legally reported, and only the outline of the prohibitionists' reply to Pulteney survives; but it indicates why they were not prepared to listen to his warning. He had concluded by saying that in so far as the measure did not amount to total prohibition — spirits could still be bought by the hogshead — this too was unjust, because it would allow the rich to buy and drink as much as they liked, when they liked, while stopping the poor from buying a glass of gin over the counter. This, Jekyll's supporters made clear, was precisely their aim. As one of them put it, the justification for the Bill was that it would keep spirits out of the reach of 'persons of inferior rank', who were 'the only sort of people apt to make a custom of getting drunk with such liquor'. Nor was it possible to cater for those who would, if allowed to drink, drink in moderation. Where spirits were available in the shops, 'few would keep themselves within any bounds, because a small quantity deprived them of their reason, and the companions they usually met with at such places encouraged them to drink to excess'. The only concession the supporters of the measure were prepared to make was that spirits should still be available when prescribed by a physician, in cases of illness. Otherwise, if the law was found to amount in practice to prohibition so far as the poor were concerned, so much the better.

Against Walpole's advice — he was mainly concerned with the loss of revenue, but he agreed with Pulteney that prohibition would not work — the measure was passed. The consequences were to be described by Walpole's biographer, Coxe. The people, he recalled, reacted

> in the usual mode of riot and violence. Numerous desperadoes availed themselves of the popular discontents, and continued the clandestine sale of gin in defiance of every restriction. The demand of penalties, which the offenders were unable to pay, filled the prisons, and removing every restraint, plunged them into courses more audaciously criminal. It was found that a duty and penalty so severe as to amount to an implied prohibition, were as little calculated to benefit the public morality, as the public revenue.

The Act failed partly because the Government's enforcement officers, the excisemen, were universally hated. When they were active, they were in danger of their lives; but frequently they were inactive, because they preferred to come to terms with the lawbreakers. Where demand was strong enough, as Walpole had warned after his earlier experience, the smuggler could afford 'to blind the officer with a large bribe', especially as he knew that once a bribe had been accepted, the officer 'is, and must be, his slave for ever'.

The means which were adopted to enforce the Act also had unfortunate consequences. To catch those who manufactured, sold, or purchased illicit spirits, a reward of £5 had been offered for information leading to a conviction. The preliminary results were gratifying: over four thousand such convictions were secured, and payments made for them, in the first two years. By that time, though, it was becoming apparent that an unascertainable but substantial proportion of the convictions had been obtained by perjury, to get the £5 which, to an unskilled labourer, represented almost three months' wages. And many other people who had been detected consuming drink purchased illicitly had paid the standard blackmail fee of £10 to avoid prosecution.

*Gin: licensing*

After Walpole's fall, his successors decided to repeal the Act. As

Lord Bathurst* explained to the House of Lords in 1743, perjuries had become so common and flagrant, 'that the people thought all informations malicious; or at least, thinking themselves oppressed by the law, they looked upon every man that promoted its execution, as their enemy'. Intimidation and violence — some informers had been murdered in the streets — had made it impossible to bring offenders to court, 'so that the law, however just might be the intention with which it was enacted, or however seasonable the methods prescribed by it, has been now for some years totally disused'.

Experience, therefore, had shown that it was impossible to prevent the retailing of spirits. 'What then' — Bathurst asked the House —

> are we to do? Does not common sense point out the most proper method, which is to allow their being publicly retailed but to lay such a duty upon the distillery and upon licenses as without amounting to a prohibition will make them come so dear to the consumer that the poor will not be able to launch out into an excessive use of them?

The expedient was not new; James I had resorted to it with tobacco, when prohibition failed. And the motive on this occasion appeared to Opposition peers to be the same: the Treasury's need for more revenue, to pay for Britain's contribution to the war on the Continent. This was deplorable, Lord Chesterfield thought. If spirit-drinking were a vice, it ought to be punished as such.

> Would you lay a tax upon a breach of the Ten Commandments? Would not such a tax be wicked and scandalous because it would imply an indulgence to those who would pay the tax? No reasonable man would suppose you intend to discourage, much less prohibit, this vice, by giving every man that pleases an indulgence to break out himself, or to promote it in others upon condition of his paying a small tax annually.

Lord Hervey was equally scathing. All that was wrong with the

* As reported from memory by Samuel Johnson, then working for the *Gentleman's Magazine*.

law, he insisted, was that it had not been enforced. Now, instead, they were to have a duty whose proceeds were being mortgaged to pay for the war. In other words, they were establishing the worst sort of drunkenness to pay for an expense which in his opinion was both unnecessary and ridiculous, 'like a tradesman mortgaging the prostitution of his wife or daughter, for the sake of raising money to supply his luxury or extravagance'. And he went on to inveigh against drunkenness, 'of all vices the most abominable'.

Drunkenness happened not to be one of Hervey's vices; drink gave him gall-bladder trouble. But when Lord Sandwich, who entertained his Hell Fire Club friends to drunken orgies at which the Black Mass was celebrated, told the House that his regard for the morals of the people compelled him to oppose the Bill, Bathurst could not resist remarking that he hoped that all public houses were not going to be regarded as chapels of the devil, simply because a man might eat or drink too much in them. 'According to this way of reasoning, I am afraid, many of your lordships' own houses would come under the same denomination, and you yourselves would not be quite free from the character of being devils.'

Patiently, Bathurst explained that though the Government hoped to make money from the duty, the measure must at the same time reduce spirit-drinking, because spirits would cost more. To those critics who wondered whether, if the price rose, the measure could be enforced, he replied that this time the Government would have allies; if, as had been surmised, 50,000 publicans took out licences to sell spirits, 'there will likewise be 50,000 informers against unlawful traders'. In any case, as spirits would now be legally available, the public would no longer side with the sellers of illicit liquor.

So it was eventually to prove. For a while the distillers, fearing for their profits, managed to secure a modification of the Act; but by 1751 the consequences were so manifestly shocking — reflected in Henry's Fielding's *Reasons for the Late Increase in Robbers*, and Hogarth's 'Gin Lane' — that the Act's original provisions were reimposed. The dire warnings of Chesterfield and Hervey were quickly shown to have been unjustified. The consumption of spirits in Britain, which had been estimated at eight million gallons in 1743, fell to two million in the 1760s and to around one million in the 1780s. Only one of Chesterfield's forecasts proved correct;

that if Governments once began to enjoy the considerable revenue which would accrue to them from the duty, they would never let it go. They never did.

## Gin: scapegoat

Gin-drinking had spread 'with the rapidity and the violence of an epidemic', the historian Lecky was to write: 'small as is the place which this fact occupies in English history, it was probably, if we consider all the consequences that have flowed from it, the most momentous in the eighteenth century — incomparably more so than any event in the purely political or military annals of the country.' And in a celebrated passage, he went on to describe the degradation that gin had wrought, with the retailers 'accustomed to hang out painted boards announcing to their customers they could be made drunk for a penny, dead drunk for twopence, and have straw for nothing; cellars strewn with straw were accordingly provided into which those who had become insensible were dragged, and where they remained until they had sufficiently recovered to renew their orgies'.

Contemporary accounts suggest that Lecky did not exaggerate. Speaker after speaker in the 1743 debate, regardless of his politics, showed how appalling the effects of drinking spirits had become, producing 'not only momentary fury', Lord Lonsdale claimed, 'but incurable debility and lingering diseases; they not only fill our streets with madmen, and prisons with criminals, but our hospitals with cripples'. The statistical evidence points the same way. The birth rate in London fell, in the early part of the century; so did the expectation of life among young children. Nearly ten thousand children under the age of five were dying annually, the Commons were told in 1751, because of the effects of 'the grand destroyer' on their parents. 'Inquire from the several hospitals in this city', Corbyn Morris wrote the same year, 'whether any increase of patients, and of what sort, are daily brought under their care? They will all declare, increasing multitudes of dropsical consumptive people arising from the effects of spirituous liquors.'

Yet those spirituous liquors were not really to blame for what had happened in England — any more than for what was to happen on Tahiti. It was the way that gin had been virtually thrust down Londoners' throats which had been responsible;

coupled with the condition of London's poor at the time. Gin drinking was not merely, as Dorothy George described it in her *London Life in the Eighteenth Century*, 'essentially a disease of poverty'; it was a disease of the ugly kind of poverty portrayed by Fielding, Morris and many another writer. The picture that emerges is of a squalor and degradation far worse even than in the London of the Great Plague; and it was from this that the London poor were seeking escape.

Even so, had spirits come gradually into use Londoners might have learned to come to terms with them, as the Dutch had. But not only were they a novelty in Britain; their sale was relentlessly pushed by the distillers (whose trade, Hervey complained, became the most profitable of any in the kingdom — 'except that of being broker to a Prime Minister'). And the distillers themselves had been given every encouragement by the Government, hungry for more revenue — and by the landowner M.P.s, hoping for higher rents.

It was the way gin was introduced, coupled with the environment, that made its effects destructive. When Bishop Berkeley boasted that Britain was the freest country in Europe, the Bishop of Gloucester wrote to him to say there was indeed freedom of a kind — for unbounded licentiousness: 'there is not only no safety living in this town' he wrote from London, 'but scarcely in the country now, robbery and murder are grown so frequent . . . Those accursed spirituous liquors which, to the shame of our government, are so easily to be had, and in such quantities drunk, have changed the very nature of our people.' The crimes which so disturbed the Bishop, though, were not as a rule committed in drink — or even for drink, in the sense of a man robbing to pay for it, though that must have been common enough. The worst crimes were committed by those who worked for the illicit distiller and the smuggler, because the demand for his illicit goods was sufficient to enable him to pay them well enough not merely to work for him, but if necessary to commit crimes of violence, even murder, for him. Nor was it simply the London gin-drinkers who had provided the demand. Long before they had begun to worry the magistrates, the British ruling class had shown that they were determined to continue to buy their claret and their cognac, regardless of whether the Government wanted to exclude them, as when Britain was at war with France. And at other times, when they were admitted legally on payment of duty, the M.P.s who voted for the tax had no compunction in buying their own supplies more cheaply, knowing they must have been smuggled in.

The lesson the gin plague taught, in fact, was not so much that prohibition was futile, as that it was futile unless the Government enjoyed public confidence and support. Where it was known that the members of the ruling class — Walpole himself being notoriously one of them — did not feel that prohibition should apply to them, the law fell into contempt. Efforts to enforce it, therefore, tended simply to inflame the public; often even those citizens who were not spirit drinkers, and would have liked to see consumption stopped, but were more deeply concerned about the corruption that attempts to stop it involved. That was why, as Bathurst had realised, prohibition had been unworkable. It was impossible to find anybody willing to undertake 'a task at once odious and endless, or to punish offences which every day multiplied, and on which the whole body of the common people — a body very formidable when united — was universally engaged'.

# 6

# *The Opium Wars*

THE GIN PLAGUE OF LONDON HAD SHOWN HOW A GOVERNMENT, and a governing class, could encourage the spread of drug-taking in its own financial interest, with destructive consequences; but at least it had been possible for them to reverse the policy when those consequences became apparent. A plant drug which grew in Britain's new colonial territory in India was to prove even more profitable; and as the bulk of it was sold away from British territory, there was no need to worry what the consequences might be.

Opium had long been manufactured from the sap of the poppies grown in the Middle East and in India; and traveller after traveller in those regions had reported that unlike in Europe, where it was employed mainly as a sedative, it was taken as a stimulant, particularly when Dutch courage was required. 'There is no Turk who would not buy opium with his last penny', the French naturalist Belon noted in the sixteenth century, 'because they think that they become more daring, and have less fear of the dangers of war.' In India, John Fryer observed in the 1670s, wrestlers took it to help them to perform feats ordinarily beyond their strength, and warriors, 'to run up on any enterprise with a raging resolution to die or be victorious'.

Had the British arrived in India as colonists, they would probably have felt bound to try to suppress opium consumption as a danger to law and order — and to health; it could create a powerful craving, as Robert Clive, who became addicted to it, was to find. But apart from the risk of addiction, opium represented no threat to the East India Company, so long as it remained primarily a mercantile body. The Moguls possessed a monopoly of opium production in Bengal, and they were disposed to restrict consumption, as far as possible, to themselves and their circle. They were willing, though, to sell it to the Company; and the Company's ships began to take it to the East Indies and to China.

## Warren Hastings

Opium had long been used in China medicinally; and in the seventeenth century people had begun to burn small quantities of it in the flame of a candle, to inhale the fumes — the idea presumably deriving from seeing tobacco smoked. Disturbed by reports of the spread of the new fad, the Emperor decreed in 1729 that opium must no longer be imported, except under licence. But by this time it had won too many adherents. The flow continued in defiance of the ban, just as with tobacco in those countries which had tried to enforce prohibition a century before.

Most of the opium was brought in from the Middle East by the Portuguese, through Macao; but when the East India Company inherited the Mogul empire after Clive's victory at Plassey, they also inherited the Mogul's opium monopoly, and the prospect of selling more of it in China, with her estimated 300,000,000 population, was attractive. There was a snag, however: foreigners were permitted to trade with China only through Canton. The Company enjoyed a monopoly of British trade there — including opium brought in under licence. Its rights might be forfeited if it were caught smuggling. The Company therefore began to sell its opium in India to the owners of merchant ships who were prepared to smuggle it into China; and these 'country ships', as they came to be called, took it to Macao.

For a while, the operations were on a very small scale; but when Warren Hastings took over the management of the Company in 1772, becoming Governor-General of British India, he soon grasped the tremendous potential of the traffic and set about expanding it for the benefit of the Company's finances. Hastings had no illusions about what he was doing. He described opium as a 'pernicious' commodity, 'which the wisdom of the Government should carefully restrain from internal consumption' — that is, from consumption in British India. Foreign commerce was

a different matter. When war with the Dutch temporarily closed
the opium market in their colonies in the East Indies, Hastings
switched a consignment to Canton, in a privateer armed at the
expense of the Company. The venture was not a success. Black-
mailed by the Canton merchants' guild with the threat of dis-
closure, the Company's Canton agents had to sell the opium
to them for a derisory price. But the 'country ships' continued to
provide a safe and increasingly lucrative method of distribution.

Shortly before the end of the century another imperial edict
against opium was promulgated; and it was to be followed by
many more, pleading, warning, threatening. Far from paying any
attention, the 'country ships' began to extend their activities;
'some ill-disposed individuals', the Emperor was informed in 1807,
had even begun to carry the opium they brought over the mountain passes into the interior. Soon, it reached Pekin. In 1813 he
discovered to his horror that members of his bodyguard, and some
of the court eunuchs, had become enslaved by the habit. Stiffer
penalties were decreed, flogging and the wearing of the *cangue* —
a kind of portable pillory; but without success. The lower classes,
it was found, were taking to the habit; 'vagabonds clandestinely
purchase and eat it' a further edict complained in 1815, 'and
eventually become sunk into the most stupid and besotted state,
so as to cut down the powers of nature and destroy life.'

The situation was unprecedented. Doubtless the French
Government had been very willing, a century earlier, that French
wine and brandy should continue to be smuggled into Britain,
the proceeds going to help the French wine industry, and at the
same time depriving the British Government of needed revenue.
But the French Government had not itself acted as a principal;
whereas the Government of British India — as the Company had
virtually become — were by this time purchasing the entire poppy
harvest in their territories, with the deliberate intention of processing the opium and sending the bulk of it to China. To avoid
jeopardising their legal commercial undertakings — in particular,
the tea trade, which had reached massive proportions — they
still had to pretend that they were not engaged in smuggling. Nor,
technically, were they, as the 'country ships' did not sail under
the Company's flag. But they were licensed by the Company — no
ship could take opium out of India without such a licence. Their

operations, too, were financed by the Company, whose Canton agents received the price for the opium from the Chinese merchants who purchased it. The Company's money was also laid out, where necessary, in bribes. When a new Governor from Pekin arrested some of the Cantonese who were involved in the traffic, and compelled them under torture to confess, the Company's Canton agents warned that sales might be subject to some delay; but they made it clear that this would be only until a new bribery scale had been agreed with the 'officers and police people employed to prevent the sales', to compensate them for the additional risk they had run.

If criticised for this involvement in drug smuggling, the Company's line was that it was up to the Chinese, if they wanted, to enforce their own laws; and in this the Company was doing its best to help by restricting production, and keeping up the price, so that most people would not be able to afford it. 'Were it possible to prevent the use of the drug altogether', the Governor-General virtuously claimed in 1817, 'except strictly for the purpose of medicine, we would gladly do it in compassion to mankind'. The Company's directors in London expressed their approval, but added that restriction of the supply was a policy which would be acceptable only so long as it meant higher profits; otherwise, 'the expediency of proportionately increasing the annual provision will naturally engage your attention'.

Very soon, the Indian Government's attention was duly engaged. Attracted by the rising price of opium, Princes in the Indian Native States were beginning to encourage production; and in quantity and quality 'Malwa', as it was known, began to rival the Company's opium from Bengal. The Company hastily abandoned its policy of restricting consumption, reduced its prices, and in 1827 resorted to what was described as a policy of 'voluntary persuasion' of the Princes to sell their opium only through the Company, in Calcutta or Bombay. The voluntary persuasion took the form of telling the Princes that they had to make a choice between keeping the friendship, or incurring the enmity, of the British Government. Past experience had shown that an Indian ruler who incurred the enmity of the British Government was liable to lose his throne, and sometimes his life. Friendship, on the other hand, meant a subsidy to compensate for the loss of revenue from opium. It was not long before the great bulk of the Malwa opium produced in the Native States was under the Company's control.

### The Napier incident

At the Canton end the Company had also had a setback; but it, too, had turned out in the end to be an advantage. By 1820 the system of bribery had become so well-established that the 'country ships' were actually sailing up the Canton estuary to Whampoa, the port of Canton, confident that officials would look the other way when the consignments were unloaded. Once again, however, a new Governor, determined to carry out Pekin's instructions — or at least appear to be carrying them out — arrested a number of the Chinese involved. He also ordered that all ships coming up the Canton river must be searched; any ship found carrying any opium would have not merely the opium, but its entire cargo confiscated, and would thereafter be banned from the China trade.

The smugglers departed — but only as far as Lintin island, at the mouth of the estuary. There, they set up what was in all but name, a British base. The opium clippers were fast and well-armed, more than a match for Chinese junks which were sent to intercept them. They brought their cargoes to Lintin, packed in chests-of-drawers, containing about 140 lbs of opium made up into balls about the size of a small grapefruit; discharged the chests in depot ships; and returned to India for more. From Lintin, the opium was either taken by country ships farther along the coast, or transferred locally to 'fast crabs', or 'scrambling dragons' — the names by which the Chinese authorities denounced them, in a proclamation in 1826 — shallow-beamed boats manned by thirty or forty oarsmen, designed so that they could skim over bars and shallows, and along remote creeks. The penalty for being caught was death; but this actually helped the traffic, because the smugglers had no hesitation in fighting it out if, owing to some breakdown in the bribery chain, they were intercepted. Lintin was ideally suited to 'fast crab' activities. It also saved port dues for the larger ships; and it was free from Chinese interference. During the 1820s, as a result, the amount of Indian opium imported into China quadrupled.

There was no question, as yet, of the Company's trying to justify the opium traffic on any other ground than *caveat emptor*. The taking of opium for pleasure was still regarded as a destructive vice — and not just in India; Stamford Raffles denounced it as a malign influence on the people of Java, 'degrading their character and enervating their energies'. De Quincey's *Confessions*, too, when they were published in 1821, alerted public opinion at home to the agonies of addiction. So when the House of Commons Committee was set up to investigate the affairs of the East India Company in 1830, the Company's line was that it must be allowed to retain its opium monopoly, because only in that way could production be restricted, and consumption kept down by 'making the price as high as possible'. It would have required little research by the Committee to find that so far from trying to keep the price up and consumption down, the Company was selling four times as much opium to the Chinese at a considerably lower price than it had ten years before; but the Company had another argument in reserve, which was to prove decisive. The value of the opium sold in China amounted to well over two million pounds — getting on for half the amount then annually devoted to paying for the Crown and the Civil Service in Britain. If the Government of India was deprived of the revenue from opium, it would have to be raised from other sources, and the British taxpayer might have to be called upon. It would not be desirable, the Committee recommended, 'to abandon so important a source of revenue as the opium trade, the duty upon opium being one which falls principally on the foreign consumer'. The Government gratefully accepted the recommendation; and although the Company was stripped of its other privileges, the opium monopoly was retained.

This meant, in effect, that the British Government was now directly responsible for the opium traffic, through the Government of India, 'the Company' being hardly distinguishable from the Indian civil service. Even the pretence that production was being kept down to keep prices high and consumption low was abandoned. The Company's agents were instructed to put pressure on the Bengal peasants to sow more poppies; as the agents were paid on a commission basis, they needed no inducement, using various forms of blackmail to bring recalcitrant peasants into line.

Largely due to the pioneer efforts of Jardine Matheson's 'opium clippers', too, new areas were opened up to the smuggling traffic along the Chinese coast to the north of Canton. Language was a difficulty; William Jardine shrewdly solved it by employing a missionary, Charles Gutzlaff, as interpreter. 'We look up to the ever-blessed Redeemer, to whom China with all its millions is given', Gutzlaff wrote; 'in the faithfulness of His promise we anticipate the glorious day of a general conversion, and are willing to do our utmost to promote the good work'; the good work being the introduction of the Chinese to the bibles, tracts, and ointments, which he distributed wherever his duties as interpreter, in the haggling over opium prices — which brought much satisfaction and profit to Jardine Matheson — permitted.

Some members of the Whig Government, though, were uneasy about the traffic. It did not pass unnoticed abroad that the Government which, in 1833, had paraded its devotion to the cause of humanity by abolishing the slave trade, had now taken over the role of principal in the most massive smuggling operation the world had ever known, designed to keep the Chinese people supplied with a notoriously dangerous drug, consumption of which was generally restricted, and in some places prohibited, on British territory. The remedy, Lord Palmerston decided, was to persuade the Chinese Government to end the Canton monopoly, and to open up other ports to foreign trade — which would be accompanied, the expectation was, by the legalisation of opium. In 1834 he despatched Lord Napier to China, to negotiate the deal.

A naval officer turned sheep farmer, Napier knew nothing of China or the Chinese, and succeeded only in irritating the Canton authorities. Recriminations followed; and the viceroy put a ban on trade of any kind by British ships. Napier's reply was a show of force: two British frigates managed to fight their way up the river to Canton. The Chinese blocked their way back, with stakes and fireships. Napier realised he was trapped. Harassed, and suffering from fever, he had to accept the offer of a Chinese boat for his return journey from Canton down to the sea. It deposited him at Macao where, a few days later, he died.

*The prohibition debate*

Up to this point, information about the effects of the opium on the Chinese had been scanty; and it was never to be wholly reliable. But in 1832 two American missionaries founded the *Chinese Repository*, a monthly magazine which, amongst other things, provided translations of Chinese documents ranging from imperial decrees to fly-posters; and the evidence pointed to growing alarm about the drug. The army, in particular, had succumbed. Of a thousand soldiers sent as reinforcements to help put down a rising in the province of Canton, the commanding officer had had to reject two hundred as unfit for service; and opium was blamed when the rebels defeated the imperial force. The son of the Governor of Canton, it also transpired, had been smuggling it through to his friends in Pekin in the equivalent of the diplomatic bag. Chinese historians have suggested that this attraction opium smoking had for the sons of men of wealth and position may have been decisive, in what was to follow: for the Emperor himself — Tao-Kwang, who had succeeded to the throne in 1820 — was a victim; his three eldest sons all died of opium addiction.

The difficulty which confronted the Emperor was how to suppress the opium traffic, now that it had obtained such a hold. The story of the opium in the diplomatic bag had come out only because it turned out to be of such poor quality that the merchant concerned was to be proceeded against, just as if it were legal merchandise; and how deeply both merchants and civil authorities were involved was revealed again in 1834. The *Repository* reported that the new Governor of Canton (the old one having been sacked for his failure to suppress the traffic), angry at finding that he had been overcharged for his opium supply, had attempted to arrest the suppliers, only to find they had already absconded. When the authorities did take action against smugglers — the *Repository* explained — it was not to stop smuggling, but to ensure that it was kept in existing channels: 'it would seem that the smuggling trade is becoming a monopoly of the Government.'

The fact, too, that so many respectable citizens — or their sons — were opium smokers encouraged extortion and blackmail. Since the beginning of the century, the American merchant Charles W. King — one of the very few merchants of any nationality in Canton who had refused to have anything to do with the traffic — complained in a letter to the British Superintendent of Trade:

the British merchants, led on by the East India Company, have been driving a trade in violation of the highest laws and the best interests of the Chinese empire. This cause has been pushed so far as to derange its currency, to corrupt its officers, and ruin multitudes of its people. The traffic has become associated, in the politics of the country, with the axe and the dungeon; in the breasts of men in private life, with the wreck of property, virtue, honour and happiness. All ranks, from the Emperor on the throne to the people of the humblest hamlets, have felt its sting. To the fact of its descent to the lowest classes of society, we are frequent witnesses; and the Court gazettes are evidence that it has marked out victims for disgrace and ruin even among the imperial kindred.

Law-abiding citizens were not necessarily safe as Gutzlaff was to lament, when he came to write the life of the Emperor. The great bane of China, Gutzlaff — of all people — argued, had been the introduction of opium by foreigners. The rewards offered to informers in the attempt to suppress it made them 'both numerous and unscrupulous; whoever had a grudge against his neighbour, denounced him as a transgressor of the laws against the drug'; and the excuse 'searching for the drug', had been used by officials to commit thefts, and other outrages. Thousands of innocent people, Gutzlaff lamented, had been the victims.

The failure of the prohibition policy, and the disastrous consequences arising out of the effort to enforce it, had attracted the attention of some of the teachers at an academy which had been founded in 1820 in Canton. Perhaps because it had not settled into the traditional academic grooves, the possibility of legalising opium imports, subject to a duty, had been discussed; and among those influenced by the arguments in favour of that course was Hsü Nai-chi, who had later become an imperial official in the province of Kwantung, and seen for himself the effects of the failure of prohibition. In May 1836 he addressed a memorial to the Emperor, putting the case for admitting opium legally, on payment of duty.

Hsü did not dispute that 'so vile a practice', and the evils arising out of it, should if possible be stopped. His argument was that prohibition not merely had failed to stop the evils, but had created many more; and the severer the interdicts against it became, 'the more widely do the evils arising therefrom spread'. When it had first been found that prohibition was not working, flogging and the *cangue* had been introduced; then, exile, imprisonment, and even death. Yet 'the smokers of the drug have increased in number, and the practice has spread almost through the whole empire'. Supporters of the prohibition policy had been forced back on the argument that it was not the regulations, but how they were carried out, that was the trouble; 'it is said, the daily increase is owing to the negligence of officers in enforcing the interdicts!' But this negligence, Hsü insisted, was the fault of the interdicts. The more severe they became, the greater the incentive to criminals to employ violence, or corruption, or both.

In its general approach, the memorial was remarkably similar in its line of argument to Bathurst's in the House of Lords nearly a century before. But Hsü's analysis went a little deeper in its recognition of why the severity of a penal code, so far from helping in the effort to suppress a drug, must make it easier for the importer. As he was not himself at risk, the penalties did not matter to him. At worst, all that he had to worry about was having to pay out more in bribes. But even that could be, in the end, to his advantage. The higher the payment offered, the easier it became to find officials who would succumb.

The Emperor was sufficiently impressed by Hsü's memorandum to refer it, in June, to the Governor of Canton, Teng T'ing-chen, who had taken office earlier that year. Teng had already been converted to the legalisation policy: his recommendations followed the line Hsü had laid down. But other advisers expressed horror at the proposal — in much the same terms as Hervey and Chesterfield had used about the Spirits Licensing Bill. 'When have not prostitution, gambling, treason, robbery, and suchlike infractions of the laws afforded occasion for extortionate underlings and worthless vagrants to benefit themselves, and by falsehood and bribery to amass wealth?', Chu T'sun, Sub-Chancellor of the Grand Secretariat, asked. 'But none, surely, would contend that the law, because in such instances rendered ineffectual, should therefore be abrogated!' The consequences of such a step would be disastrous:

The laws that forbid the people to do wrong may be likened

to the dykes which prevent the overflowing of water. If any one, then, urging that the dykes are very old, and therefore useless, should have them thrown down, what words could express the consequences of the impetuous rush and all-destroying overflow!

The damage, Chu feared, might already have been done, simply by the knowledge that there was a move in favour of legalisation: 'the instant effect has been, that crafty thieves and villains have on all sides begun to raise their heads and open their eyes, gazing about and pointing the finger, under the notion that when once these prohibitions are repealed, thenceforth, and forever, they may regard themselves as free from every restraint'.

Another memorialist added a recommendation which may well have been decisive. The opium sellers, he pointed out, were actually living in Canton: even Jardine himself. Why? Why not arrest *them*, for breaking the imperial law? Why not send all their ships back, and allow no resumption of trade of any kind until all opium smuggling activities had ceased? 'If commands be issued of this plain and energetic character, in language strong, and in sense becoming, though their nature be the most abject — that of a dog, or a sheep — yet, having a care for their own lives, they will not fail to seek the gain, and to flee the danger.'

This was the policy that the Emperor elected to follow. For having raised the hopes of the opium smokers that the drug might be legalised, Hsü Nai-chi was removed from his post. An official who had sent in detailed plans showing how prohibition could be enforced, Lin Tse-hsu, was despatched early in 1839 to Canton as Imperial Commissioner, charged with the suppression of the opium traffic.

### The first Opium War

The story of Lin's commissionership, which provoked the first Opium War, has often been told; in recent years by, among others, Maurice Collis, in *Foreign Mud*; Arthur Waley, in *The Opium War through Chinese Eyes*; and Hsin-Pao Chang in *Commissioner Lin and the Opium War*. It represents the classic example of the limitations of honesty, integrity and assiduity in carrying out a campaign to suppress the traffic in a drug. Yet Lin felt he was well-placed to achieve his aim. He had a half-Nelson on the British merchants, because he knew they could not afford to risk the loss of the tea trade, through Canton; and he determined to exploit the hold this gave him. The British merchants, he announced after his arrival, must surrender all their opium stocks. When, thinking to placate him, they offered to surrender a thousand chests, he took the opportunity to show that he knew exactly how much more opium they had, and to inform them that until they handed it over, all trade with British vessels, and all movement of British shipping up and down the Canton river, would cease.

At this point the Chief Superintendent of Trade, Captain Charles Elliot, managed to get up to Canton. As Chief Superintendent, he was a kind of unofficial British Consul in China; and he had written time after time to Palmerston to warn him that if the opium traffic was allowed to develop unchecked, a crisis must develop. It now had; and, though he had no official powers, he decided there was no help for it but to hand over all the opium: more than 20,000 chests. Lin put an end to the blockade, took delivery of the opium, and personally supervised its destruction. It was mixed with salt and lime, dissolved in water, and flushed away into the sea.

Lin had achieved his first objective; but it availed him nothing. Elliot ordered all British subjects and all British ships out of the Canton river, so that they could no longer be held virtually as hostages — the American merchants, most of whom had been involved in the opium traffic, staying in Canton to act as agents for the British, so that the tea trade would not be disrupted. The opium arriving from India was simply switched to points along the coast, as an Imperial Censor, Pu Chi-t'ung, had warned would happen, in a memorial to the Emperor. And Lin found himself unable to check the smuggling. After the destruction of the opium, he intended to have a purge of the customs officials; but too many of them, he found, were implicated in the traffic. Even where he managed to stir them to action, this only — as he explained to the Emperor in the spring of 1840 — led to the smugglers adopting more ingenious ruses to circumvent them. Sometimes opium would be hidden in the rear apartments of houses, where the women lived, their presence embarrassing the searchers. Sometimes it was buried in forests, or in the precincts of temples. It had even been put into chests disguised as coffins, and laid to rest, until required, in tombs.

And Lin was finding it hard to get informers, because they were no use to him unless they knew the traffic — in which case they would work for the smugglers, who could afford to pay them more.

What was being demonstrated, for the first time on such a large scale, was the impracticability of prohibition as a way to suppress the traffic in a drug, particularly in a drug as addictive as opium. Addicts, who felt they had to have it, would pay whatever the smugglers charged. If supplies dwindled owing to more effective customs work, the price rose, allowing a bigger margin of profit out of which to bribe the customs officials into connivance. And as smuggling was so extensive, many thousands of people, from the rowers of the fast crabs to the opium smokers, had a common interest in breaking the law, and protecting others who broke it. Where respectable citizens or officials were involved, there were opportunities for extortion and for blackmail; and the higher the legal penalties for opium offences, the greater the risk that those involved would commit acts of violence and even murder, rather than allow themselves to be caught.

All this, Lin was to learn in the months which elapsed between the departure of the British from Canton, and the arrival of the expeditionary force which Elliot had asked for, to punish the Commissioner for his presumption. Elliot had not altered his views about opium. 'No man entertains a deeper detestation of the disgrace and sin of this forced traffic', he wrote to Palmerston, in November 1839 'than the humble individual who signs this despatch. I see little to choose between it and piracy.' But British property had been extorted by compulsion, and destroyed; that, he felt, was 'the most shameless violence which one nation has ever yet dared to perpetrate against another'. While awaiting Palmerston's instructions, he used the small naval force he had at his disposal to protect the British merchant fleet, which lay at anchor off Hong Kong, and to inflict some punishment on presumptuous Chinese naval junks.

The British force arrived in June 1840; including what Lin described as 'cartwheel ships, that can put the axles in motion by means of fire, and can move rather fast'. Still more important, the new steamships could move in a flat calm, or directly up wind. They did not, however, waste any time trying to move up the river to Canton. They went north, to put more direct pressure on

Pekin. Lin, who had been basking in the Imperial favour, was abruptly removed from his post, and sent into exile. His mistake — as the Censor, Pu, had realised — lay in imagining that the threat of closure of the legitimate British trade would suffice to bring the opium traffic to an end. It mattered little to the British merchants that instead of picking up their tea at Canton, they had to leave the Americans to collect it there, and receive it from them at Hong Kong. What was vital was that the flow of their imports of opium should continue; and Lin had been unable to stop it.

It was not seriously impeded even by the hostilities which followed, as militarily the resistance was insignificant. By some judicious diplomatic manoeuvres and some injudicious attempts at deception, the Chinese managed to avoid capitulation until the summer of 1842, when they were finally compelled to accept the British terms. By then, the opium traffic was back to normal.

## The treaty of Nanking

The war had not, admittedly, been fought exclusively to legitimise the opium traffic. Palmerston could claim that he was mainly concerned with compelling the Chinese to accept free trade. But opium happened to be by far the most profitable commodity involved. 'Had there been an alternative', Commissioner Lin's biographer Hsin-pao Chang commented, ' — say, molasses, or rice — the conflict might have been called the Molasses War, or the Rice War'. But there was no alternative. Not merely was opium the only British import for which there was any substantial demand in China: the demand had grown enormously. In the late 1820s the Company exported an average of less than 10,000 chests annually to China; that figure had increased, in the year before Lin was appointed, to 40,000. Palmerston was fully aware of the situation; Jardine, who had returned to England just before Lin arrived at Canton, had been called in to brief him, 'I have to instruct you' — Palmerston accordingly informed Captain Elliot — 'to make some arrangement with the Chinese Government for the admission of opium to China as an article of lawful commerce.'

Palmerston knew, though, that it would be unwise to make this instruction public. The Chinese plenipotentiaries, he went on, must not be given the idea that it was 'the intention of H.M. Government to use any compulsion'. Had H.M. Government been seen to be forcing the Chinese to legalise opium, its enemies abroad and at home would have been handed a serviceable weapon; and its shaky majority, which had narrowly survived a debate on its China policy in the Commons in 1840, would have been again imperilled. The line to take to the Chinese, Palmertson suggested, was that they should offer to legalise opium in their own interest. They should be reminded that they could not stop it coming in, for even if the supply of opium from India could be checked, 'plenty of it would be produced in other countries, and would thence be sent to China'; and they should allow themselves to be gently persuaded to profit out of necessity by taxing it.

When Elliot was sacked in 1841, similar instructions were given to his successor, Sir George Pottinger. The British Government, the Chinese plenipotentiaries were to be told, did not insist; but it must be impressed on the Chinese how very much in their own interest the legalisation of opium would be. Pottinger duly presented Palmerston's view, only to be met with a blank refusal even to discuss the possibility of legalisation. Opium, they told him, was an evil, growing daily worse. They could not, even if they wanted to, countenance the proposal, as the Emperor would repudiate them. Pottinger's instructions left him no room to manoeuvre; and the change of Government in Britain in 1841 promised to make his task still more difficult — the Tories in Opposition having come out strongly against the opium traffic in a debate in the Commons the year before.

In the event, though, the Tories' principles underwent a rapid change when they crossed the floor of the House. They did not care to put any further pressure on the Chinese to admit opium; Pottinger was told he could accept the continuance of the ban. But he was instructed to warn the Chinese that, so far as British shipping was concerned, they 'need not trouble themselves whether our vessels bring opium or not'. In other words, British ships suspected of smuggling must not be searched. As the Chinese would presumably ask the British Government, in these circumstances, not to allow British ships to be used for smuggling, Pottinger was told he should instruct their owners to conform — leaving the traffic to 'Chinese fast boats and other craft', as before. And it was this system — 'mutual connivance', as Pottinger's successor Sir John Davis tetchily described it — that came into operation after the peace settlement.

## The Arrow War

Mutual connivance was an unsatisfactory basis for peace. It survived only because in the immediate post-war period, the Chinese were in no mood to risk a resumption of hostilities. In 1850 the new Emperor, Hsien-feng, issued a fresh edict against opium smoking, giving offenders a brief period of grace in which to break the habit, after which anybody caught would be beheaded, and his family sent into slavery. But a few months later the Taiping — the 'long-haired ones' — rose in rebellion; and although they were opposed to the use of drugs of any kind — tobacco smoking, even, was punishable by death — their victories benefited the opium traffic. The leaders of the Taiping were too preoccupied with the struggle against the imperial troops; and at the same time, it became difficult for the Emperor to enforce prohibition, even in those regions which still nominally adhered to his cause.

The traffic, too, was greatly facilitated by the fact that under the terms of the Treaty of Nanking the British had taken Hong Kong. Pottinger had assured the Chinese plenipotentiaries that the exportation of opium from Hong Kong to China would be forbidden; and it was. But the ban was never enforced. There was nothing to prevent opium from being smuggled out to the mainland. As soon as the smugglers realised that the Canton authorities, rather than risk precipitating another war, were not searching British vessels, they began to register the smuggling craft as British, and sail them openly up the Canton estuary, with the Union Jack as their flag of convenience.

Opium also poured into Northern China through Shanghai which, as the northernmost of the ports opened to foreigners by the Pottinger treaty, served a hitherto largely inaccessible region. In the ten years following the treaty, the opium traffic to China doubled. This roused British hopes that the Emperor, realising his ban had failed and needing funds to mount more effective operations against the Taiping, might be converted to the policy of legalisation, as some of his courtiers desired. But he remained determined to stamp out opium smuggling. To this end, he had sent Yeh

Ming-Chen, a disciple and friend of Commissioner Lin's, to Canton
to resume Lin's policies. Caution, and the need to deal with the
Taiping, meant that there was no immediate confrontation of the
kind Lin had precipitated; but Yeh cleverly fanned the anti-British
feeling which had arisen since the war among the Cantonese.
There were ugly incidents, and the British merchants began to
realise that they and their commerce were in growing danger.

An excuse would be needed, though, for a new campaign. Yeh
provided it in the autumn of 1856, when Mandarins arrested the
crew of the lorcha *Arrow*, lying off Canton. Lorchas were a hybrid
species, with a Western-style hull and eastern-style sails; they had
been found convenient for smuggling, and the *Arrow* was one of
many which, though Chinese-owned, had been registered as
British for that purpose in Hong Kong. For form's sake, the master
was British; but the crew were Chinese, some of them being
criminals known to the Chinese authorities. So far as the British
authorities were concerned, this made no difference. Criminals or
not, they were under the protection of the British flag. (The discovery that the *Arrow*'s registration had expired, so that it was no
longer a British vessel, caused only momentary embarrassment; it
could legally have re-registered, the explanation was, the next time it
arrived in Hong Kong.) When Yeh refused to apologise, the navy
was called in, and proceeded to shell his official residence in Canton.

The Tory Opposition were outraged. The *Arrow* affair, they
complained, was a shoddy excuse for the war which Palmerston
now clearly proposed to wage; and in an impassioned debate in
the Commons, they did what they had failed to do in 1840, winning
the Radicals to their side and defeating the Government in a vote.
It was just the opportunity Palmerston had needed. He held a
general election, taking care to ensure it was fought on the issue of
the insult to the British Crown. 'An insolent barbarian wielding
authority at Canton,' he told the electors of Tiverton, 'has violated
the British flag, broken the engagement of treaties, offered rewards
for the heads of British subjects in that part of China, and planned
their destruction by murder, assassinations and poisons.' The
electorate, their patriotic passions aroused, enthusiastically voted
him and his supporters back into office.

The Emperor managed to delay the final capitulation, as his
predecessor had, by some judicious stalling, and some injudicious

deception. Lord Elgin, leading the British expeditionary force, had to occupy Pekin and burn down the Emperor's Summer Palace, to convince him that when terms were accepted, even under duress, they must be kept. And one of the terms imposed, on this occasion, was that in future imports of opium would be legally permitted, on payment of a duty. As before, it was possible to maintain that this was not what the war had been fought about — a view which suited Elgin, who personally thought the flimsy *Arrow* pretext scandalous, and was so digusted with what he saw of the effects of opium in China that he declined to treat it as a significant item on the negotiation agenda. It had, in fact, by this time become part of a much wider set of objectives: shared by the French, who had commercial designs on China, and had joined in the fighting, and the Americans, who had helped in spite of their neutrality. The common aim was to compel the Chinese to conform to the ways of the West in diplomacy and in trade. Nevertheless opium was still, for the British, the main consideration. The returns of the years between the wars had shown no great improvement in legal exports to China; the East India Company and the opium merchants, not British manufacturers, had been the chief beneficiaries of the opening of Shanghai to foreigners. How much importance the British delegation attached to opium was demonstrated when they persuaded the American plenipotentiary, William B. Reed, who had been formally instructed to accept the right of the Chinese to maintain prohibition, to repudiate his brief.

As expected, legalisation produced a rapid increase in the demand, which the manufacturers in India were ready to meet. From fewer than 60,000 chests in 1859–60, the figure rose almost to 90,000 ten years later, and to over 105,000 in 1879–80. And as it was no longer possible to hope that opium could be kept out, the Chinese had a powerful incentive to cultivate poppies, from which to manufacture their own. There had been occasional reports since the early 1830s of illicit poppy cultivation, but not on a scale sufficient to cause the Imperial government much alarm. Now, farmers who grew poppies could feel they were performing a patriotic duty, helping to reduce the drain of currency out of the country. For a while, though, the home product did not pose any threat to imports. In the Treaty negotiations the Chinese plenipotentiaries, anxious to demonstrate that there had been no change of view — that the drug was still objectionable on moral grounds — had argued for a high import duty, to reduce consumption. The British, determined to keep the price of their product competitive, demanded the right to decide what rate of duty should be levied, and reduced by half the rate the Chinese had proposed, so that when the cost of smuggling operations was taken into account, the new selling price need not be substantially higher than the old. As the Indian product was considered greatly superior, there need be no immediate fear of any abatement of demand.

For form's sake, the Government's argument was that the Chinese had voluntarily abandoned prohibition; but few who were in a position to know their attitude were deceived. 'Nothing that has been gained was received from the free will of the Chinese', Sir Thomas Wade, one of the British negotiators, was to write ten years later; 'the concessions made to us have been from the first to the last extorted against the conscience of the nation — in defiance, that is to say, of the moral convictions of its educated men.' And Wade was in no doubt that the consequences for the Chinese had been terrible. In all the cases in his experience, opium had led to 'the steady descent, moral and physical, of the smoker'.

### Opium: bane or benefit?

Up to this point, the assumption that opium was injurious to the health and morals of the Chinese had hardly been questioned. The most commonly cited authority on the subject was the missionary W. H. Medhurst, who had gone out in 1816, and whose book *China* was published in 1840. By his reckoning, the amount of opium smuggled in at that time was enough to demoralise nearly three million people

> When the habit is once formed, it becomes inveterate; discontinuance is more and more difficult, until at length, the sudden deprivation of the accustomed indulgence produces certain death. In proportion as the wretched victim comes under the power of the infatuating drug, so is his ability to resist temptation less strong; and debilitated in body as well as mind, he is unable to earn his usual pittance, and not infrequently sinks under the cravings of an appetite which he is unable to gratify.

Thus they may be seen, hanging their heads by the doors of the opium shops, which the hard-hearted keepers, having fleeced them of their all, will not permit them to enter; and shut out from their own dwellings, either by angry relatives or ruthless creditors, they die in the streets unpitied and despised.

The opium habit, Medhurst estimated, reduced life expectation by about ten years, destroyed health while life lasted, and at the same time ruined countless families because of the drain on the smoker's resources.

In the 1840 Commons debate, a few voices had been raised in opium's defence, but the contention had been simply that its evils had been greatly exaggerated, and that its effects were no worse than those of over-indulgence in ardent spirits, all too familiar in the West. Between the opium wars, however, there were occasional intimations that opium need not have dire effects. The comments from Chinese sources remained implacably hostile, and so did the bulk of the reports from missionaries; but Dr Benjamin Hobson, who had worked for years as a doctor among the poor in Canton, was one of those who realised that there was not necessarily any inevitability about the process of degeneration, even for addicts. 'I have found' he wrote,

the habitual use of opium even compatible with longevity . . . though its tendency is to undermine the constitution, and only support the system by a false and dangerous stimulus, yet, if it can be taken regularly and of good quality, it does not abridge the duration of life to the extent that might reasonably be expected that it should do.

The opium merchants took their cue. The ending of prohibition after the second Opium War relieved them of their worries in China; but they still had to watch public opinion in Britain. The Palmerston era was ending; the Conservatives had always been hostile to his China policy; and the anti-opium campaign, led by Lord Shaftesbury, was gaining influential non-party support. It was time, the merchants realised, to present their wares in a more positively favourable light; and on November 28th, 1867, Jardine Matheson put them in a letter to the Governor of Hong Kong.

The ugly picture formerly drawn of the effects of opium on the Chinese, they claimed, had been forgotten; 'since 1860 it has been rendered abundantly clear that the use of opium is not a curse, but a comfort and a benefit to the hard-working Chinese'.

Had it been only Jardine Matheson who took this line, it could safely have been ignored. And when similar views were expressed by British consuls in the Treaty Ports in China, and transmitted to the Foreign Office, it was possible to suspect that they might be more concerned with British trade than with British moral prestige. But the cause was eventually supported by men who had no direct interest in opium, and who were unlikely to have been deluded or suborned; including Sir George Birdwood, a former Professor of *Materia Medica* in Bombay. Opium smoking, he told the readers of *The Times* in a letter published on December 26th, 1881, was 'almost as harmless an indulgence as twiddling the thumbs, and other silly-looking methods of concentrating the jaded mind'. The following year a book by William Bretherton, a retired Hong Kong solicitor, cited a number of testimonials to opium from men of standing on the island; and in 1892, an even more impressive array of its supporters was paraded by G. H. M. Batten, a former Indian civil servant, in a paper read in London to the Society of Arts.

The opportunity to solve the mystery came in 1893, when the pressure of public opinion in England, and a motion in the House of Commons, pushed the Government into setting up a Royal Commission to investigate the subject. Their verdict was that opium in general was used in moderation, and led 'to no evident ill-effects'. One member of the Commission, admittedly, dissented in a scathing minority report; and later, Joseph Rowntree was able to produce quite a damning critique of the report itself — showing, for example, that although forty-nine out of the fifty-two missionaries from China who had given evidence had condemned opium, the report had quoted only the opinions of two of the three who had been less critical. Nevertheless the minutes of evidence showed that as well as merchants and colonial civil servants, many doctors and some missionaries believed that the opium habit was on balance harmless, and could even be regarded as socially desirable.

How was it possible that two such mutually contradictory sets of evidence could each be supported by so much knowledgeable and trustworthy testimony? There was one obvious clue. Most of the witnesses who condemned opium had worked in China. In India, where the Commission had held most of its sittings, most witnesses were in opium's favour. Could it not be — some of them had suggested — that the explanation was simple; the Chinese smoked opium, whereas the Indians ate it, or drank it?

But evidence from other colonies failed to support this proposition. In the Malay peninsula, the colonial authorities agreed, the reverse was the case; 'Opium eating in all its forms', the Auditor-General of the Straits Settlements claimed, 'when once established as a habit, produces an invariable bodily and mental condition which imperatively calls for a constant, if graduated, increase of the drug. Now, this is not the case with opium smoking.' And evidence from the same region upset another hypothesis; that the Chinese might be in some way hereditarily susceptible to addiction. In the Straits Settlements, Major McCullum informed the Commission, only the 'indolent Malays' suffered ill-effects from the drug. For the Chinese it was 'a harmless, even a beneficial stimulant'.

Reading between the lines it is clear that the Royal Commission, baffled, came to assume that the explanation must be looked for in the circumstances in which opium addiction was observed. The 'anti-opiumists', as they were described, must have seen the effects of the abuse of opium; they must have seen, or heard about, only the addicts, and been thereby misled into thinking that addiction was inevitable. Again and again, in the reports from China, the emphasis was on the inescapable nature of the perdition awaiting the opium smoker. As the Rev. A. Elwin, a missionary in China for over twenty years, put it, there was no such thing as a moderate smoker; 'the dose is always, I believe, increased by degrees'. But there were scores of witnesses in India to demonstrate this was nonsense — including missionaries; Dr H. Martyn Clark testified that he knew of no 'hardier, thriftier or more careful people' than the peasants of the Punjab, where he had worked; yet most of them regularly took opium, a habit which 'seems to interfere neither with their longevity nor with their health'. The most reasonable explanation, therefore, was that the missionary, an alien in China, had been dealing with the cast-offs, the derelicts;

whereas in India, he was familiar with all levels of the community.

Although there was a measure of truth in this, it would not account for the whole range of different reactions to opium described over the course of the century, in different regions — or in the same region, in different periods. When opium had been introduced into Assam, along with cheap labour for the new tea plantations, an official had protested in 1839 that in the course of a few years the opium plague had 'depopulated this beautiful country, turned it into a land of wild beasts'; and in the process, it had 'degenerated the Assamese from a fine race of people to the most abject, crafty and demoralised race in India'. Yet fifty years later, though the consumption of opium there was higher per head than in any other part of India, it was giving no trouble. 'They take their opium', Commissioner Driberg reported, 'just as a good Englishman would take his "peg".'

Again, R. L. Stevenson's surmise — that it was the rapidity of the social changes which was disruptive, leading as it did to the abuse of drink or drugs — seems the most likely explanation. Opium had come suddenly into Assam, along with an influx of cheap labour, disrupting the community's old way of life. It did the same in Burma, the only British colony where it gave serious trouble. And it was a menace in China, in those regions which the smugglers could reach to 'push' the Indian produce. But in India itself, it posed no problem, being used mainly not as a narcotic, but, like coca in Peru, as a way of 'enabling the taker to undergo severe and continuous physical exercise' — Dr Francis Anstie noted in his treatise on drugs in the 1860s — 'without the assistance of ordinary food'. It was for this purpose, Dr W. Myers told the Royal Commission, that the chair-bearers, couriers and coolies of Formosa took opium. He had been forced to alter his 'preconceived prejudices with reference to the universally baneful effects of the drug', when he found that they used it every day, as a matter of course, rarely needing to increase the amount.

Significantly, where the Chinese were allowed to smoke opium, outside their own country's jurisdiction, they did nothing to disturb the authorities. The opium smoker learned to discriminate, choosing his own brand, and savouring it with the relish of a connoisseur. In a book describing his experiences as an attaché in Pekin, published in 1900, A. B. Freeman Mitford — the future

Lord Redesdale — could seriously claim that to deprive the Chinaman of his Indian opium, and to condemn him to the 'miserable substitute' grown in China, 'would be like forbidding the importation of champagne and Chateau Lafitte into England, and driving our epicures and invalids to the necessity of falling back on cheap and nasty stimulants'.

Mitford, though, had lived in a region where the inhabitants had come to terms with opium. He had never seen, as missionaries had seen, the destruction and misery that the drug could cause before it was domesticated. In any case, the British Government could not claim that it had only been trying to keep the Chinese supplied with an agreeable pastime, because it had not made that its excuse. Throughout the century, its aim had been to make the maximum profit from the drug, regardless of its effect on the Chinese. For a brief period at the beginning production had been restricted, but this was to increase profits; the pretence that it was to keep down consumption was abandoned the moment profits began to fall. Two campaigns — three, if Napier's is included — had been undertaken mainly to compel the Chinese to take the drug, preferably legally. The reasons given, that they were designed to punish the Chinese for seizing British property, and for insulting the British flag, were transparently spurious; the property was a smuggled drug, in the first instance, and the flag was flown by a drug smuggler in the second. It was the most protractedly sordid episode in British Imperial history; and it was also an intimation that where revenue was involved, a government could be just as grasping, and just as unscrupulous, as any entrepreneur. Governments have since often thundered out denunciations of the men who manufacture and sell opium and heroin. It was a Government which taught them how.

# 7

# *Indian Hemp*

*Hemp drugs; the legends*

THE LONG STRUGGLE TO END THE OPIUM TRAFFIC FROM INDIA TO China had one curious and revealing by-product. When the Government was compelled by the vote in the House of Commons to concede a Royal Commission into opium, there was an immediate protest: why single out opium when there were other drugs in common use in India? For many years, the opium lobby had contended that hemp was the more dangerous of the two. In 1840 the banker W. B. Baring had told the Commons that if the traffic were suppressed, it might simply lead to the adoption in the Far East of drugs 'infinitely more prejudicial to physical health and energy than opium', citing as an example 'an exhalation of the hemp plant, easily collected at certain seasons, which was in every way more injurious than the use of the poppy'. Reminded of hemp's existence, the Government decided on what appears to have been a diversionary tactic. On March 2nd, 1893 the Member of Parliament for Bradford East, W. S. Caine — a persistent anti-drug campaigner — asked for an enquiry into the use of hemp drugs in India; and the Under Secretary of State for India was able to assure him that the Viceroy was setting it up, and would be glad if the results 'show that further restriction can be placed upon the sale and consumption of these drugs'.

There was a mass of evidence available about their effects, but little of it which could be described as scientific, apart from some experiments conducted in the 1840s by Dr W. B. O'Shaughnessy, Professor of Chemistry in the Medical College of Calcutta. He had begun with animals, finding that they reacted in much the same way as humans. A middling-sized dog, given ten grains of hemp, 'became stupid and sleepy, dozing at intervals, starting up, wagging his tail, as if extremely contented; he ate some food greedily; on being called to, he staggered to and fro, and his face assumed a look of utter and helpless drunkenness. These symptoms lasted about two hours, and then gradually passed away.' Finding that no harm came to the animals, O'Shaughnessy next tried the drugs on patients suffering from disorders for which there was no effective remedy — rheumatism, tetanus, cholera, convulsions — with results which led him to claim in the *Transactions* of the Medical and Physical Society of Calcutta that 'in hemp, the profession has gained an anti-convulsive remedy of the greatest value'. With hemp, though, as with coca, it was difficult to make up pills or potions which were of consistent purity and strength; and the essential drug element in the plant eluded researchers. It remained in general use in medicine in India, particularly at the village level; but it did not elsewhere establish the reputation O'Shaughnessy expected.

In Britain, the drug — hashish, as it was loosely described — tended to be thought of as sinister; not on the basis of experience or experiment, but because of the reputation it had derived from legends. One had come down from Marco Polo, who had heard it on his voyage to China in the thirteenth century. The 'Old Man of the Mountain', he was told, had desired that his people should believe that a valley which he had enclosed, and made into a garden, was Paradise; 'so he had fashioned it after the description that Mahomet gave of his Paradise, to wit, that it should be a beautiful garden running with conduits of wine and milk and honey and water, and full of of lovely women for the delectation of all its inmates'. A selected youth would be given a drug to put him to sleep, and carried into the valley, so that when he woke up he would find himself, as he thought, in Paradise, and would enjoy its sybaritic delights. He would then again be put to sleep, and transported back out of the valley, 'whereat he was not over well pleased'. All he had to do if he wished to return, the Old Man of the Mountain would tell him, was to perform the service required of him: 'go thou and slay so-and-so; and when thou returnest, my angels shall bear thee into Paradise. And shouldst thou die, nevertheless even so will I send my angels to carry thee back into Paradise.' So great was the desire to get back that the initiates would face any peril to do so; 'and in this manner the Old One got his people to murder any one whom he would get rid of'.

In Marco Polo's account, therefore, the drug featured only as a way to enable the Old Man of the Mountain to transport the youths to and from the valley. But the legend became embroidered in the telling; the drug used to put the youths to sleep was given a very different role. The murderers used it — the story ran — to nerve themselves to carry out the Old Man's commands. When, early in the nineteenth century, the French etymologist Sylvestre de Sacy identified hashish, the drug, with *haschishin* — assassin — this was taken to be conclusive evidence that the members of the Order of Assassins had derived their name from the drug they took before committing their atrocious crimes. And the idea that hashish could be taken for this purpose appeared to be confirmed when it was learned that the 'whirling dervishes' used it, and when Livingstone reported that the 'pernicious weed' was used by African tribes to help them work themselves up into 'a species of frenzy'.

It was difficult, though, to reconcile the effects of the drug in the legend, with the effects of the drug as actually observed in most of the countries of the Middle and Near East, where it was in common use. The drinks which the Arabs made from the hemp plant, the French traveller C. S. Sonnini noted on his tour in the late eighteenth century,

> throw them into a sort of pleasing inebriety, a state of reverie that inspires gaiety and occasions agreeable dreams. This kind of annihilation of the faculty of thinking, this kind of slumber of the soul, bears no resemblance to the intoxication produced by wine or strong liquors, and the French language affords no terms by which it can be expressed. The Arabs give the name of *kif* to this voluptuous vacuity of mind, this sort of fascinating stupor.

Most observers echoed Sonnini; but this did not do much to redeem the reputation of the drug. To the English, as they entered upon the Victorian era, it was no recommendation to say that hashish induced 'voluptuous vacuity', the secondary reputation it now began to acquire — nourished, doubtless, by Dumas's account of its effects on the Baron Franz d'Epinay, in *The Count of Monte Christo*

> . . . there followed a dream of passion like that promised by the Prophet to the elect. Lips of stone turned to flame, breasts of ice became like heated lava, so that to Franz, yielding for the first time to the sway of the drug, love was a sorrow and voluptuousness a torture, as burning mouths were pressed to his thirsty lips, and he was held in cool serpent-like embraces. The more he strove against this unhallowed passion, the more his senses yielded to the thrall, and at length, weary of the struggle that taxed his very soul, he gave way and sank back breathless and exhausted beneath the enchantment of his marvellous dream.

The translators of *The Book of the Thousand Nights and a Night* confirmed the reputation of hashish, not simply as a drug by which husbands could be put to sleep so that lovers could enjoy their wives, but also as an aphrodisiac — as illustrated in the translation by Sir Richard Burton in the story of the lover who was about to consummate his design when he woke up to find that it was all a hashish-induced dream, and that he was surrounded by a crowd of people laughing at him, 'for his prickle was at point and the napkin had slipped from his middle'. The versions which circulated in England might omit or bowdlerise such episodes, but the reputation of hashish spread by hearsay, leaving the impression that even if some doubt might remain about what precisely its effects were, they were certainly deplorable.

Perhaps because of this reputation, the British Raj tended to be more suspicious of Indian hemp drugs, as they were described there, than of opium. They had been subjected to an enquiry on more than one occasion in the past, the latest investigation having been conducted as recently as the 1870s. Its report had claimed that hemp drugs were less dangerous than their reputation suggested, and that in any case prohibition was impracticable. The Liberal

Government decided to ignore these inconvenient findings, and set up a fresh enquiry.

The members of the Commission were appointed in July 1893, under the Chairmanship of the Hon. W. Mackworth Young, first Financial Commissioner for the Punjab. Their terms of reference indicated what was expected of them. They were to examine the trade in hemp drugs; its effect on the social and moral condition of the people; and 'the desirability of prohibiting the growth of the plant'. The Commission was composed of three British colonial officials, three 'native non-official gentlemen', and a Secretary, H. J. McIntosh — to whom much of the credit for the eventual report was probably due.

### Hemp drugs: enquiry

The Commission had been warned that it might have difficulty in finding witnesses willing to come forward and tell what they knew about the use and abuse of hemp drugs. No such difficulty was experienced. Civil servants, army officers, magistrates, doctors, lawyers, and business men filled in the questionnaire which was circulated, and a gratifying number of them agreed to give verbal evidence in amplification. One group only, the Commission was surprised to find, appeared reluctant to offer their services. A significant proportion of the missionaries who were sent the questionnaire returned it without their answers. Their common excuse was that they did not have a sufficient knowledge of the matter. This was in striking contrast to the attitude of the missionaries to opium, particularly in China, where they had been in the forefront of the agitation to suppress the traffic. Why — the Commissioners wondered — should the Indian missionary show such little concern? Pondering that question, they picked up an early clue. If the missionaries, of all people, disclaimed knowledge of the effect of hemp drugs, the drugs could hardly be a very serious threat to the social and moral condition of the Indian people.

The terms of reference had referred to 'drugs' in the plural; and the Commissioners' first task was to try to sort them out — which was not easy. There was *ganja*, made from the dried flowering tops of cultivated plants; *charas*, the resinous matter scraped off them; and *bhang*, the dried leaves. But as Watt had just pointed out in his study of Indian plants, and as witnesses were to confirm, the distinctions in practice had little meaning. One man's *charas* was another man's *ganja*, and the drink made out of either was commonly called *bhang*. The Commissioners heard witnesses who assured them that smoking *bhang* was more dangerous than smoking *ganja*; 'but there are many others whose experience is precisely the reverse'. Some witnesses thought smoking less harmful than drinking; 'but there is a great deal of evidence to a precisely opposite effect'. In the end the Commission cautiously accepted the common opinion that the flowers and resin might produce a more powerful drug than the leaves, but for the purposes of its enquiry it seemed simpler to take them together under the general label, hemp drugs.

How extensively — the Commissioners next had to consider — were hemp drugs consumed? Putting this question to witnesses revealed just how sparse the information was on the subject, even among those whose duties were 'believed to bring them into close and constant contact with the people'. It was possible to make a tentative estimate of the minimum quantity of *ganja* and *charas* used, because a duty was payable on the manufactured product; but it could safely be assumed that far more was used illicitly. As for *bhang*, made from the leaves, much of it came from the wild hemp plant, and there was no way of telling how much of it was smoked, eaten and drunk, except observation — and observation, the Commissioners found, was a highly unreliable guide. Men who offered themselves as knowledgeable witnesses might turn out to be relying on hearsay; and those who claimed to have observed their use and effects had often derived their information only from visits to shops and shrines where smokers congregated — the equivalent, the Commissioners felt, of a man claiming to be knowledgeable about the use and effects of alcohol in England, who had derived all his knowledge from visits to pubs.

From the evidence, however, one thing was obvious; that hemp drugs were far more extensively used than the average British, or even Indian, official realised. They were taken as medicine, not only for specific disorders, on prescription, but as tonics, and aids to digestion. Drunk with meals, *bhang* was the equivalent of the English labouring man's glass of beer. They were also generally

taken among the Hindus on family party occasions, and in connection with religious observances — particularly those linked with
Shiva who, according to legend, had greatly appreciated the effects
of hemp. But by far the commonest use was by workers to give
them staying power. 'Gymnasts, wrestlers and musicians, palki-
bearers and porters, divers and postal runners are examples of the
classes who use the hemp drugs on occasions of especially severe
exertion . . . all classes of labourers, especially such as blacksmiths,
miners and coolies, are said more or less generally to use the drugs,
as a rule in moderation, to alleviate fatigue.'

A medicine; an aid to endurance; a drink on family or religious
occasions: in none of these capacities, the Commissioners felt,
could the effects of hemp drugs be regarded as menacing. Even
when used as an intoxicant, its consequences generally appeared
innocuous — where they could be assessed: the *Report* quoted an
unnamed writer as saying, 'the action of hemp on a man is so
various that when we read the several descriptions given, differing
so widely, we would scarcely suppose we were considering the
same agent'. In so far as they could be summarised, though, the
immediate effect of a hemp drug was

> refreshing and stimulating, and alleviates fatigue, giving rise to
> pleasurable sensations all over the nervous system, so that the
> consumer is 'at peace with everybody' — in a grand waking
> dream. He is able to concentrate his thoughts on one subject; it
> affords him pleasure, vigour, ready wit, capacity for hard work,
> and sharpness for business; it has a quieting effect on the nervous
> system and removes restlessness and induces forgetfulness of
> mental troubles; all sorts of grotesque ideas rapidly pass through
> the mind, with a tendency to talk; it brightens the eyes and, like
> a good cigar, gives content.

In young men, too, it might give rise to sensual thoughts. But
considering the drugs were so widely used, there was no evidence
to justify their ugly reputation. How had it spread? The reason,
the Commissioners decided, was because the drugs had no
observable effects when they were taken in moderation. Even
those witnesses who most disapproved of them had had no
conception just how extensive that consumption was. It was only

the rare examples of immoderate use that were seen by doctor or magistrate; 'the ruin wrought in certain cases by excess has alone attracted their notice. They feel towards drugs as a man feels towards alcohol, whose experience has been mainly gained among the social wrecks of the lowest parts of a great city.'

The evidence obtained from replies to the questionnaires revealed that the proportion of men who took hemp drugs immoderately must be very small. It was nevertheless desirable, the Commissioners decided, to investigate the allegations that had been made about their effects on this minority; in particular, that the drugs were responsible for much of the insanity in India, and for much of the crime.

*Hemp drugs and insanity*

There was no shortage of witnesses to testify to the way hemp drugs caused insanity; a few even expressed the view that to re-open this particular line of enquiry was stupid, implying 'wilful blindness to what has been abundantly proved'. And so the evidence at first suggested. Statistics sent in from mental hospitals all over India showed that for years, hemp drugs had been one of the chief causes of mental breakdown. The foremost expert on the subject, Surgeon Lt. Col. Crombie, had already shown in an article in the *Indian Medical Gazette* that a third of the inmates of the Dacca hospital of which he had been Superintendent had smoked *ganja*; and in a very large proportion of cases, he believed, it had been 'the actual and immediate cause of their insanity'. The 1871 Commission, which in other respects had tended to play down the danger of the drugs, had accepted that their habitual use did tend to produce insanity; and the Government of Burma had just put a ban on hemp drugs largely for that reason.

There was no reason to doubt the validity of the statistical evidence; nor was it challenged. Nevertheless the Commissioners decided that it ought to be checked. Taking the last year for which full statistics were complete, they ordered a re-examination of the records of every patient admitted to a mental hospital in India, where that admission had been attributed to hemp drugs, in order 'to ascertain how far the statistics were reasonably correct, and, if possible, also to arrive at some conclusion as to whether hemp drugs have any real connection with insanity'.

The first discovery the check provided was that what was entered in the asylum records of admission as the 'cause' of insanity was not derived from a diagnosis made at the asylum. It was simply taken down by a clerk from the description given by the policeman or whoever was responsible for bringing the patient to the asylum, at the time. Examining magistrates, whose duty it was to check the admissions book, insisted that some specific cause should be shown; and it had become standard procedure — Major Willcocks, of the Agra asylum, admitted — to enter 'hemp drugs' as the cause, wherever it was found that the patients took them; 'I cannot say precisely why it has come down as the traditional practice.' He had seen no reason to worry about the attribution, he explained, as he had assumed the drugs were poisonous; 'my ordinary medical practice did not bring me into contact with them at all. I only came into contact with them in the asylum. I had no idea they were used so extensively as I find on enquiry to be the case.'

Of all the asylum superintendents, only three claimed responsibility for the diagnosis entered in the admission books — one of them being the acknowledged authority, Surgeon Crombie. But when they examined the admissions book for the Dacca asylum in the last full year when he had been superintendent there, the Commissioners found that it did not bear out his claim. In Dacca, as elsewhere, the entries had been based on whatever explanation had been given by the people who brought the man to the asylum. The Commission therefore decided to check each individual patient's record. In nine out of the fourteen cases of insanity attributed to hemp drugs that year, and accepted as such by Crombie, the check showed that hemp drugs could not have been responsible, as Crombie himself, confronted with the results, had to admit. The idea which he had publicised from his original figures — that hemp drugs were responsible for a third of the insanity cases in asylums in India — had therefore to be revised; the proportion was fewer than one in ten. Crombie had apparently formed the view, the Commission observed, that his experience had given his evidence about the danger of hemp drugs a special value. This view had not been borne out by their enquiry. Charitably, however, they ascribed his lapse to 'a mistake of memory'.

When the follow-up was complete, it was found that insanity could be related to hemp drugs in only forty cases from the whole of India, in the year chosen — less than seven per cent of admissions; and even then, there was usually another possible cause. And 'cause', the *Report* added, was a risky term to apply; 'intemperance of any kind may sometimes be not the cause of insanity, but an early manifestation of mental instability'. In such cases, over-indulgence in hemp drugs could be regarded not as a cause but as a symptom of some underlying predisposition to insanity.

Here, then, was evidence given by expert witnesses, accepted for years, used as the justification for campaigns in other countries to ban hemp drugs — in the case of Burma being accepted as responsible for the success of such a campaign — now shown to be worthless. How had the mistake been made? The explanation, the Commissioners decided, was simple. There was a natural tendency to look for, and blame, a specific physical cause. Hemp drugs had been an obvious choice, because as intoxicants they could sometimes produce symptoms similar to those of insanity.

> This popular idea has been greatly strengthened by the attitude taken up by asylum superintendents. They have known nothing of the effects of the drugs at all, though the consumption is so extensive, except that cases of insanity have been brought to them attributed with apparent authority to hemp drugs. They have generalised from this limited and one-sided experience. They have concluded that hemp drugs produce insanity in every case, or in the great majority of cases, of consumption. They have accordingly without sufficient enquiry assisted, by the statistics they have supplied, and by the opinions they have expressed, in stereotyping the popular opinion and giving it authority and permanence.

### Hemp drugs and crime

There remained the other charge to be considered: that hemp drugs bred crime. They did so, witnesses assured the Commission, in three ways: by driving men to steal so that they could afford to buy the drug; by releasing criminal instincts; or by destroying a man's self-control, so that he 'ran amok'.

Hemp drugs users, some witnesses explained, progressed inexorably from moderation to excess; excess made them too lazy to earn their living; and when addicted, they had to steal to maintain their supply. The Commissioners were unimpressed. The evidence they had collected had established that of the vast number of hemp drug users, only a tiny proportion used them immoderately. How, then, could it be claimed that the slide from moderation to addiction was inexorable? As for releasing criminal instincts, hemp drugs appeared to have precisely the opposite effect; they 'tended to make a man timid, and unlikely to commit a crime'. But the idea that the drugs could cause men to run amok was not so easy to dispose of, based as it was on common knowledge.

Witness after witness confirmed its truth. R. D. Lyall, with over thirty years of varied experience as an official and as a magistrate in India, told the Commission about the cases of such temporary homicidal frenzy, which he had personally had to deal with. So did W. C. Taylor, a veteran of almost half a century's experience of Bengal. Surgeon Crombie treated the Commission to a description of how a Bengali babu, 'as the result of a single debauch, in an attack of *ganja* mania slew seven of his nearest relatives in bed during the night'. And an Assam tea planter described another such *ganja*-induced frenzy which he had good reason to remember vividly, as it had happened on his own estate.

Again, the Commissioners decided to check the information, and asked the witnesses to provide the relevant records or references. Some immediately admitted that their information had been at second-hand, and could not be checked. Others promised to send along the details, from newspaper files; and then could not find them. R. D. Lyall was unable to trace a single case of those he had had to deal with; and the only one which W. C. Taylor was able to recall of the 'numerous cases' he had claimed to have been concerned with, turned out when checked to have had no connection with hemp drugs. An investigation of the records about Crombie's babu disclosed that he had indeed been taking *ganja*, but he had also been taking opium; that he had a history of insanity before drugs were implicated; and that he had not been on a debauch before the murder, which had been committed in a state of 'mere insane despair'. And when the records of the case which the

Assam tea planter had described were re-examined, it was found that his account to the Commission differed materially from the one he had given at the time; not least in that he had made no mention, at the time, of *ganja*.

In the end, the Commission were able to find only twenty-three cases of homicidal mania which it was possible to check; and in eighteen of them there was nothing to suggest that hemp drugs had been responsible. 'It is astonishing', the *Report* commented,

> to find how defective and misleading are the recollections which many witnesses retain even of cases with which they have had special opportunities of being well-acquainted. It is instructive to see how preconceived notions based on rumour and tradition tend to preserve the impression of certain particulars, while the impressions of far more important features of the case are completely forgotten ... the failure must tend to increase the distrust with which similar evidence, which there has been no opportunity of testing, has been received.

### Hemp drugs: verdict

The *Report* concluded with the Commission's verdict on the issue which they had been brought together to consider: should hemp drugs be banned, in India, as they were in Burma? The answer was an emphatic no. The drugs were not a serious hazard — except for a tiny majority of the idle and dissolute whose excessive consumption endangered only themselves. Banning them would be politically dangerous, because it would constitute an unpopular interference with Hindu religious and family observances. In any case, prohibition would be unworkable — for reasons which Watt had just pointed out; it would be impracticable to hold a man responsible for the existence of a wild plant growing near his hut, 'and it would be impossible to prohibit him from gathering, from such a plant, the daily quota used by him and his family'. And even if prohibition could be enforced, it would lead only to the increased consumption of more dangerous drugs, opium and alcohol. Why — a Madras missionary had asked — should the Government of India be concerned about hemp, rather than about 'the widespread and rapidly increasing and much more injurious habit of alcoholic drink?' Other witnesses had suggested an answer: it was a plot on the part of the liquor manufacturers. Graphs of sales figures, the Commission found, lent confirmation to the view that consumption of the hemp drugs and of alcohol were intermeshed. If hemp drugs ceased to be so readily available, the sales of alcoholic liquor could be expected to rise.

Summing up, the Commissioners in their *Report* could claim that they had carefully examined the physical, mental and moral effects of hemp drugs used in moderation, and that no observable adverse effects had been discoverable. There was no evidence that hemp drugs were habit-forming, in the way alcohol and opium were. A man who consumed the drugs even in moderation might feel uneasiness, or even a sensation of longing, if deprived of them. But that was not in itself a reason for depriving him of them — any more than it would be in the case of tobacco.

The *Report of the Indian Hemp Drugs Commission* was later to be rescued from oblivion by the campaigners against the prohibition of cannabis in America and Britain, in the 1960s; but its verdict on that drug of 'not guilty' is of less importance than its analysis of the remarkable irrelevance of accepted opinions about a drug, even when they are supported by men who are supposedly experts on the subject. Surgeon Crombie was a notable example of the kind of man who has so often helped to translate public preconceptions and prejudices on to Statute Books by lending the weight of his authority to them, when in fact he has never bothered to examine the evidence in front of him, in his job; he has simply rationalised it to fit those preconceptions and prejudices.

By painstakingly going behind such opinions, and scrupulously checking the records, the Commission were able to acquit hemp drugs of the charges laid against them — as they were used in India. It does not follow that a similarly honest committee would have come to the same conclusion in, say, the Cameroons, where German officers in the 1880s reported that they found hemp being taken for its 'stimulating effect on the nervous system, so that it is highly valued on long tiring marches, on lengthy canoe voyages, and on difficult night watches' — where, in other words, it was being used for the same purpose as coca in Peru, or opium in Formosa. And Livingstone may perhaps have been right when he reported that certain tribes in Africa took it to work themselves up into a suitable state of frenzy before going into battle — though this is more doubtful, because his description of the process suggests that they may have been taking it to calm their nerves. Indian hemp drugs were taken for very different purposes, in different parts of the world; and they appear to have performed whatever service was expected of them.

# 8

# *The Poet's Eye*

DRUGS DID NOT SIMPLY SATISFY EXPECTATION; ON OCCASION, THEY could nourish it. In the 1790s Samuel Taylor Coleridge, who had been prescribed laudanum — opium in an alcohol solution — for the relief of pain, found that it altered his perception; it could give him optical illusions — about distances, say:

> The poet's eye in his tipsy hour
> Has a magnifying power
> Or rather, the soul emancipates the eyes
> Of the accidents of size

Laudanum could also start reveries in which his imagination appeared to carry him away, as if in a dream, but leaving him with sufficient consciousness to be able to direct, to some extent, the course they were taking. In one of them, he composed *Kubla Khan*.

### Laudanum and laughing gas

Why comparable experiences had not been familiar before, remains a mystery. Opium had been used in Europe since medieval times; chiefly as a sedative, but doctors had come to realise that its effects could vary greatly. 'It causes sleeping, and watching' — Dr John Jones wrote, in a treatise published at the beginning of the eighteenth century — 'stupidity and promptitude in business, cloudiness and serenity of mind. It excites the spirits, and yet quiets them; it relaxes, and weakens, yet it enables us to undergo labours, journeys, etc.; it causes a furious madness, yet composes the spirits above all things.' But its vision-inducing potential was not grasped until Coleridge's experience, and not generally known until the publication in 1822 of Thomas de Quincey's *Confessions of an English Opium Eater*, with his description of what happened when he first took laudanum — tincture of opium in alcohol — for rheumatic pains in the head:

> in an hour, O heavens! What a revulsion! what a resurrection, from its lowest depths of the inner spirit! What an apocalypse of the world within me! That my pains had vanished was now a trifle in my eyes; this negative effect was swallowed up in the immensity of those positive effects which had opened up before me, in the abyss of divine enjoyment thus suddenly revealed. Here was a panacea . . . here was the secret of happiness, about which philosophers had disputed for so many ages, at once discovered; happiness might now be bought for a penny, and carried in the waistcoat pocket; portable ecstasies might be had corked up in a pint bottle; and peace of mind could be sent down by the mail.

Agony of mind was soon to follow — as Jones had warned; 'great and even intolerable distresses, anxieties and depression of spirits'. So intolerable were the withdrawal symptoms that many respected citizens who had begun to take opium as Coleridge and de Quincey had done, for the relief of pain, were unable to break the habit. Some, laudanum destroyed; others, like William Wilberforce and Wilkie Collins, managed to come to terms with it, taking large but not increasing doses. But laudanum did not provide them with visions. It merely kept the distresses, anxieties and depressions at bay.

Might there not be other drugs, though, which could expand an artist's horizon, without enslaving him? Shortly before the turn of the century Humphry Davy, the discoverer of nitrous oxide, found that 'sniffing' gave him a feeling of ecstasy; 'nothing exists but thought' he told himself as he awoke; 'The universe is composed of impressions, ideas, pleasures and pains!'. Soon, 'the laughing gas' and ether were being dispensed at 'frolics', which became a popular pastime. In parts of Ulster, ether became so popular that its consumption took on the proportions of an epidemic, whose consequences were entertainingly described by K. H. Connell in his *Irish Peasant Society*, from contemporary accounts. The atmosphere of some towns 'was "loaded" with ether. Hundreds of yards outside Draperstown, a visiting surgeon detected the familiar smell; market days smelt "not of pigs, tobacco smoke or of unwashed human beings"; even the bank "stove" of ether, and its reek on the Derry Central Railway was "disgusting and abominable".'

The Ulstermen appear to have been using ether as a cheap alternative to alcohol; a tablespoonful — enough on which to get pleasantly, though briefly, inebriated — cost one penny. But some people used it as a vision-inducer. 'You always heard music, and you'd be cocking your ears at it', as an ether-taker put it; or you would 'see men climbing up the walls and going through the roof, or coming in through the roof and down the walls, nice and easy'. What a man experienced after taking it was limited, apparently, by his capacity for experience. As De Quincey put it, if a man took opium whose talk was of oxen, he would dream about oxen — 'if he were not too dull to dream'. For a few individuals, though, ether or laughing gas provided sensations which they would treasure throughout their lives. In his *Varieties of Religious Experience*, William James was to recall how they could 'stimulate the mystical consciousness to an extraordinary degree', and though the truths might fade, 'the sense of a profound meaning having been there persists'.

### The forbidden game

The gases, however, could be dangerous in inexperienced hands; and many experimenters could get little but hilarity out of them. An alternative possibility as vision-inducer was Indian hemp, introduced into France by the men of Napoleon's army of the Nile, and taken up for experimental purposes in the 1840s by Jacques Moreau, a Parisian doctor who thought it might help in the treatment of patients suffering from mental illness. Trying it out on himself, he found it put him into paroxysms of uncontrollable laughter, and then gave him visions of an entirely pleasurable kind. 'It is really happiness which is produced', he wrote,

and by this I mean an enjoyment entirely moral, and by no means sensual, as might be supposed — a very curious circumstance, from which some remarkable inferences might be drawn . . . for the hashish eater is happy, not like the gourmand or the famished man when satisfying his appetite, or the voluptuary in the gratification of his amative desires — but like him who hears tidings which fill him with joy, or like the miser counting his treasures, the gambler who is successful at play, or the ambitious man who is intoxicated with success.

Dr Moreau shared the delights of his discovery with the members of the *Club des Hachichins*, founded in 1844, Dumas, Gautier and Baudelaire being among its members. Gautier described his reactions to the drug two years later in the *Revue de deux mondes*: 'frenetic, irresistible, implacable laughter' succeeded by grotesque hallucinations,

> fantasies of droll dreams confusedly danced about; hybrid creations, formless mixtures of men, beasts and utensils; monks with wheels for feet and cauldrons for bellies: warriors, in armours of dishes, brandishing wooden swords in birds' claws; statesmen moved by turnspit gears; kings plunged to the waist in salt-cellar turrets . . .

Baudelaire's account was more clinical. People trying hashish for the first time, he observed, would complain that it had little effect, which might be attributed to their resistance. But it would suddenly hit them with 'a sort of irrelevant and irresistible hilarity . . . as painful as a tickle'. Occasionally this led on to weakness and stupor, but for some people, 'a new subtlety or acuity manifests itself in all the senses', and this was when hallucinations set in. 'External objects acquire, gradually and one after another, strange new appearances; they become distorted or transformed. Next occur mistakes in the identity of objects, and transposals of ideas. Sounds clothe themselves in colours; and colours contain music.'

Such experiences could be very satisfying; 'the universality of all existence arrays itself before you in a new and hitherto un-guessed at glory'. But in the end, for Baudelaire, they were re-gressive in their effects. The hashish-eater, he decided, 'completely confounds dream with action, his imagination kindling more and more at the spectacle of his own nature corrected and idealised, he substitutes this fascinating image of himself for his real individuality — so poor in strength of will, and so rich in vanity'. And,

> the morrow! the terrible morrow! All the body's organs lax and weary, nerves unstrung, itching desires to weep, the impossibility of applying oneself steadily to any task — all these cruelly teach you that you have played a forbidden game . . . The especial victim is the will, that most precious of the faculties. It is said, and it is almost true, that hashish has no evil physical effects; or, at worst, no serious ones. But can it be said that a man incapable of action, good only for dreaming, is truly well, even though all his members may be in their normal condition?

Other experimenters with hashish were to reach a similar conclusion; among them the American Fitzhugh Ludlow — though he stressed that it was not the drug, but man's reliance on it, that caused the problems: 'the soul withers and shrinks from its growth towards the true end of its being beneath the dominance of any sensual indulgence', so that though the bondage might continue to be golden, there was all the while erosion of strength.

Not all the devotees of hashish experienced Baudelaire's 'terrible morrow'. A few were able to smoke it and examine its effects as dispassionately as they might have examined the effects of tobacco; among them the young Charles Richet, later to be a Professor of Physiology in Paris, and a Nobel prizewinner. Richet observed, as others had done, that for anybody under the influence of hashish, time could appear to stand still — or at least to pass more gradually; and in 1877 he presented a plausible explanation. Man's mind, he pointed out, is full of indetermined and incomplete ideas, intertwined. Disentangling them took time; and 'as time is only measured by the remembrance of ideas, it appears prodigiously long'. What hashish did was speed up the process:

> in the space of a minute we have fifty different thoughts; since in general it requires several minutes to have fifty different thoughts, it will appear to us that several minutes are passed, and it is only by going to the inflexible clock, which marks for us the regular passage of time, that we perceive our error. With

hashish the notion of time is completely overthrown, the moments are years, and the minutes are centuries; but I feel the insufficiency of language to express this illusion, and I believe, that one can only understand it by feeling it for himself.

But such detachment was rare among the members of the *Club des Hachichins* and their successors; and they had given hashish a reputation as a vision-inducer which experience, for the majority of people who tried it, failed to justify. It had been the atmosphere of the *Club des Hachichins,* and the personalities of its members, which had lent Indian hemp its potency, rather than any quality in the drug.

# 9

# *Science*

---

THE INVESTIGATIONS OF MEN SUCH AS MOREAU AND O'SHAUGHNESSY reflected a growing interest in pharmacology during the century, stemming from the results of the research of Davy, Priestley and Lavoisier, towards the end of the century before. Their discoveries had begun to elevate chemistry to the status of an exact science; and pharmacologists had naturally begun to look forward to the day when their branch of the faculty would share in the distinction.

For a while it looked as if their ambition was going to be realised. One by one, plant drugs began to deliver up their secrets — the alkalis which, it was assumed, constituted the essential drug element. Morphine was derived from opium in 1803, and other similar discoveries followed: caffeine, quinine, nicotine. More reliable evidence began to be available, too, about the purposes for which drugs were used throughout the world; and it became possible to investigate the subject not, as before, primarily from the standpoint of the botanist or the chemist, but with a view to assessing the role of drugs in society. And the first serious attempt at a general survey was made by James Johnston in his *Chemistry of Common Life*, which was published in 1854.

## James Johnston

Johnston, who was Professor of Chemistry at the University of Durham, had the breadth of outlook of a Benjamin Franklin or a Humphry Davy; he was interested in chemistry not for its own sake, but for what it provided for mankind. He was not thinking in terms simply of the chemical processes by which bread, or wine, were provided, but of what gave bread its flavour, and wine its bouquet. How significant he felt drugs were can be gauged by the fact that he devoted almost half the book to them; a chapter each to tea and coffee; two chapters to alcoholic liquors; and no fewer than eight chapters to 'the narcotics we indulge in', ranging from tobacco to deadly nightshade.

Johnston was disturbed by what he felt was the irrational prejudice against the use of narcotics of any kind, reflected in the efforts that had been made in countries all over the world to suppress them. It was absurd, he argued, to think of them as strange and sinister, considering the vast number of people who regularly took them. Precise estimates of the number of drug-takers were impossible to come by; but tobacco, he estimated, was used by 800 million people; opium by 400 million; Indian hemp by 200–300 million; betel by 100 million; and coca by 10 million.

No nation so ancient but had its narcotic soother from the most distant times; none so remote and isolated but has found within its own borders a pain-allayer and care-dispeller of native growth; none so savage which instinct has not led to seek for, and successfully to employ, this form of physiological indulgence. The craving for such indulgence, and the habit of gratifying it, are little less universal than the desire for, and the practice of, consuming the necessary materials of our common food.

Nor was it any more reprehensible; on the contrary, Johnston argued, man's recognition of the value of narcotics should be considered as forming 'one of the most wonderful chapters in his entire history'. In the first of the three stages of that history, man had found how to provide for his material needs — 'beef and bread'. In the second, he had sought ways to 'assuage the cares of his mind and banish uneasy reflections', which he did with the help of alcoholic beverages. And in the third, his object was

to multiply his enjoyments, intellectual and animal, and for the time to exalt them. This he attains by the aid of narcotics. And of these narcotics, again, it is remarkable that almost every country or tribe has its own, either aboriginal or imported; so that the universal instinct of the race has led, somehow or other, to the universal supply of this want or craving also.

Johnston cited tea and coffee as examples. Tea, in particular, could be a dangerous drug; 'green tea, when taken very strong, acts very powerfully on some constitutions producing nervous tremblings and other distressing symptoms, acting as a narcotic, and in inferior animals even producing paralysis'. But men had learned to use it more discreetly, so that 'it exhilarates without sensibly intoxicating'. Even the poorest took it, preferring the 'luxury' of a cup of tea to an extra potato or a larger loaf — a choice which Johnston wholeheartedly approved; 'he will probably live as long under the one regimen as the other; and while he does live, he will both be less miserable in mind, and will show more blood and spirit in the face of difficulties, than if he had denied himself this trifling indulgence'.

It was not the chemical properties of the plant — Johnston argued — but the uses to which man put it, that mattered; a point which comes across even more forcibly when his book is read today, as many of the plants which he included are no longer considered to be drugs. The English beer drinker esteems hops for imparting flavour; to Johnston, the hop was 'the English narcotic', justly celebrated as a sleep inducer, and 'unquestionably one of the sources of the pleasing excitement, gentle narcotic intoxication, and healthy tonic action which well-hopped beer is known to produce on those whose constitutions enable them to drink it'. Even more surprising is Johnston's description of lettuce.

The juice of these plants, when collected and dried, has considerable resemblance to opium. If the stem of the common lettuce, when it is coming into flower, be wounded with a knife, a milky juice exudes. In the open air, this juice gradually assumes a brown colour, and dries into a friable mass. The smell of this dried juice is strongly narcotic, recalling that of opium. It has a slightly pungent taste but, like opium, leaves a permanent bitterness in the mouth. It acts upon the brain after the manner of opium . . . eaten at night, the lettuce causes sleep;

eaten during the day, it soothes and calms and allays the tendency to nervous irritability.

There are other reminders in the *Chemistry of Common Life* that the classification of what is, and what is not, a plant drug may vary from country to country, and from period to period. But even more significant, in the light of what was to happen later, was Johnston's realisation that drugs could not be classified by their observed pharmacological action on man, because that action varied so greatly. Moslems, for example, took tobacco because it soothed the mind to sleep, while leaving the body alert and active. But,

that such is not its general action in Europe, the study of almost every German writer can testify. With the constant pipe diffusing its beloved aroma around him, the German philosopher works out the profoundest of his results of thought. He thinks and dreams, and dreams and thinks, alternately; but while his body is soothed and stilled, his mind is ever awake. From what I have heard such men say, I could almost fancy that they had in this practice discovered a way of liberating the mind from the trammels of the body, and thus giving it a freer range and more undisturbed liberty of action. I regret that I have never found it act so upon myself.

To some extent, Johnston realised, individual reactions to a drug could be accounted for by observing how the individual took it. A glass of whiskey would have a different effect if it were tossed off neat than if it were sipped, with water, for an hour. But this, he felt, was not enough to account for the remarkable differences in the effects of the same drug on different individuals — and even on different communities. Could it be, he wondered, that the use of a particular drug over a long period gradually changed the disposition and temperament of a people — in turn changing their reactions? There was no way of telling, with any certainty; but 'the fate of nations has frequently been decided by the slow operation of long-acting causes, unthought of and unestimated by the historian, which, while the name and the local home of the people remain the same, had gradually changed their constitution, their character, and their capabilities'.

In view of all this evidence, Johnston argued, to think in terms of trying to prohibit drug-taking by legislation was futile:

> A tendency which is so evidently a part of our general human nature, is not to be suppressed or extinguished by any form of mere physical, fiscal, or statutory restraint. It may sometimes be discouraged or repressed by such means, but even this lesser result is not always obtainable ... an empire may be overthrown by inconsiderate statutory intermeddling with the natural instincts, the old habits, or the growing customs of a people, while the instincts and habits themselves are only strengthened and confirmed.

### Francis Anstie

Johnston's thesis made an impression on Francis Anstie, a physician at the Westminster Hospital who had been specialising in toxicology, hoping — as he explained in his *Stimulants and Narcotics*, published in 1864 — to be able to remove the study of the subject from the metaphysical to the physical level. To this end he had experimented on himself, and on some patients, with a variety of drugs; his original intention being to put them into categories, such as the one suggested by the title of his book. To the patient, as well as to the doctor, the distinction seemed clear; some drugs were 'stupefying poisons' — narcotics; others, 'grateful restoratives' — stimulants. But the result of his researches had upset his expectation that he would be able to clarify the distinction for textbook purposes. 'To the philosophic student', he ruefully admitted, 'who desires to arrange in orderly classification the weapons of his art, and thereby to multiply his resources, the accurate definition of these two classes of remedies offers a problem at once of great interest and of extreme difficulty.' Chloroform, for example, was regarded as a narcotic. But his experiments had shown him that in certain circumstances, it could be a powerful stimulant. The action of alcohol was even more confusing. At first sight, it appeared to be a stimulant; 'but on analysing the symptoms we are at no loss to perceive that it is the emotional and appetitive part of the mind which is in action while the in-

tellect, on the contrary, is directly enfeebled'. It was at least possible, Anstie speculated, that the outbreak of the passions which
alcohol could induce was due, 'not to any stimulation of them, but
to the removal of the check ordinarily imposed by reason and will'.

To most Europeans, Anstie went on, opium was a narcotic; to
Orientals, a stimulant. They were able, 'sometimes without any
previous practice, to take large quantities of opium without suffering stupefaction; on the contrary, they appear much exhilarated in
spirits, and their minds work with much freedom. In some cases,
muscular power and the disposition for exertion seem actually to
increase'. The likely explanation, Anstie thought, was that opium
prevented other activities from interfering with mental processes,
which gave the appearance of an increase of intellectual power.
And this could also be an explanation of another mystery. Pain,
he suggested, was not relieved by sedatives and depressants —
except where they poisoned the system, as when a man took enough
alcohol to render himself insensible. What relieved pain was the
*stimulating* effect of opium, or other drugs, in small doses. It
was the stimulus, he concluded, that mattered, and that might be
given by some substance which was not, in the strict sense, a drug,
but which had the appropriate effect; 'I have seen one patient
suffering from severe agony with peritonitis who developed rapid
relief from the careful and gradual injection of a pint of rich soup
into the rectum'.

Like Johnston, Anstie had been compelled to recognise what a
minor part the pharmacology of a drug might play in determining
man's reactions to it, compared with the part played by man's
responses. It was a matter of common observation that the same
amount of alcohol which would enliven one man, would depress
another; or, according to his circumstances make the same man
jolly, one evening, and sad, the next. But to the new generation of
scientifically-minded chemists, toxicologists and pharmacologists
this was a thoroughly unsatisfactory state of affairs. It left their
discipline uneasily suspended, like a hammock slung between one
solid tree — chemistry — and some young saplings — biology,
neurology, psychology — which bent and swayed in every scientific breeze.

Throughout the century, therefore, pharmacologists continued
to engage in a search for certainties; and in this they were naturally

encouraged by further discoveries of alkalis. These, it continued to be assumed, represented the essential drug element in a plant. When they were extracted they would obviate the wastage involved in consumption of the rest of the plant; when refined, impurities would be removed. And it would be easier to measure out the prescribed strength of dosage. So it came about that morphine, the derivative, began to replace opium and laudanum as a sedative and a painkiller.

The outcome was the first of a succession of cruel disillusionments. So long as morphine continued to be taken strictly on prescription, for specific medical purposes, it fulfilled expectations. But some of the people for whom it was prescribed came to rely on it for release from everyday cares, and others took it for a 'lift'. It began to enslave addicts as effectively as laudanum had enslaved de Quincey. The medical profession — the doctors by this time had formed themselves into a profession, and had begun to exercise a closer supervision of drugs — reacted with alarm, and for a time addicts were treated by enforced deprivation. The withdrawal symptoms, though, could be dangerous, as well as painful; cases were reported of addicts, deprived of morphine, who had had hallucinations and delirium, and some of them died under the treatment. What was needed, clearly, was some drug which would do the work of morphine, but without creating addiction. Any medical scientist who found one would have his fortune made — as the young Sigmund Freud realised, when he first began to experiment with the alkali which pharmacologists had extracted from the leaves of the coca plant: cocaine.

## Cocaine

Unlike tobacco, coca had not established itself as a drug in Europe — or even in South America, among the colonists. For a young Spaniard to begin to take it was regarded as a sign that he was rebelling against his class; he would be repudiated, and forced either to leave or to live with the Indians, and adopt their ways. Occasionally travellers would return from voyages in the Andes with stories of the feats of endurance which the Indians performed under its influence; but although they were noted by Abraham Cowley (in whose mind, Dr Johnson was to recall, 'botany turns into poetry')

> Endowed with leaves of wondrous nourishment
> Whose juice succ'd in, and to the stomach ta'en
> Long hunger and long labour can sustain

its possibilities do not appear to have been recognised until the Jesuit Don Antonio Julian lamented in his *Perla de America* that it was not used in Europe alongside tea and coffee ('it is melancholy to reflect that the poor of Europe cannot obtain this preservative against hunger and thirst; that our working people are not supported by this strengthening plant in their long continued labours'). The author of a treatise published in 1793 suggested that the sailors in European navies would benefit from a coca ration; and in 1814 a writer in the *Gentleman's Magazine* elaborated on the proposition. It was not yet clear how the South American Indians achieved their feats of endurance, he admitted; but

> it is certain they have that secret, and put it into practice. They masticate coca, and undergo the greatest fatigue without any injury to health or bodily vigour. They want neither butcher, nor baker, nor brewer, nor distiller, nor fuel, nor culinary utensils. Now, if Professor Davy will apply his thoughts to the subject here given for his experiments, there are thousands even in this happy land who will pour their blessings upon him, if he will but discover a temporary anti-famine, or substitute for food, free from all inconvenience of weight, bulk and expense, and by which any person might be enabled, like the Peruvian Indian, to live and labour in health and spirits for a month now and then without eating.

With the coming of the Industrial Revolution, and the employment of men, women and children in the mills twelve hours a day, six days a week, there was an incentive to examine the claims for coca more seriously; especially after von Tschudi's observations in the 1830s convinced him that coca's reputation was well-founded. When he took an infusion of the leaves of the plant, while he was on a hunting expedition at 14,000 feet up in the Andes, he found it worked for him, too: 'I could then during the whole day climb the heights, and follow the swift-footed wild animals.'

Taken in excess over a protracted period, Tschudi realised, coca could have unwelcome effects; the inveterate chewer could be detected from 'his unsteady gait, his yellow-coloured skin, his dim and sunken eyes encircled by a purple ring, his quivering lips, and his general apathy'. But this was unusual. Ordinarily, the drug appeared to have no adverse effects. Even when it was taken in very large amounts, there was no loss of consciousness; and many of those who took it every working day (and doubled their intake on festival occasions) lived on to a great age, in perfect health. 'Setting aside all extravagant and visionary notions on the subject', he concluded, 'the moderate use of coca is not merely innocuous, but it may even be conducive to health.'

Tschudi's *Travels in Peru* was followed by accounts from other travellers, most of them in agreement with him; and in the 1850s an Italian doctor, Paolo Mantegazza, experimented on himself by chewing dried coca leaves. He experienced an increase in physical and mental energy, and when he tried an infusion of the leaves, he found that not merely did the inclination to take exercise become irresistible; he also had an odd feeling of becoming isolated from the external world, which would enable him to perform feats which ordinarily he would not have attempted. On an impulse he jumped up on his writing table, without smashing the lamp or other objects on it. Nor did he suffer any reaction, comparable with a hangover: following the activity he felt only quiet comfort. And increasing the dose — to the amount commonly consumed by the natives of Peru — only increased his sense of exhilaration. Joyously he told his colleagues that he preferred 'ten years with coca to a million centuries without'. In a treatise on the subject published in Milan in 1859 he wrote, more sedately, that the principal property of coca, 'not to be found in any other remedy, consists in its exalting effect, calling out the power of the organism without leaving any sign of debility'; and he recommended its use for nervous disorders.

Gradually, coca began to win adherents in other countries. In the early 1870s Sir Robert Christison tried it out on medical students in Edinburgh, and was impressed by the results; the chewing of coca leaves, he reported, 'not only removes extreme fatigue, but prevents it', and the only effect it had on the mental faculties was to eliminate the dullness ordinarily associated with fatigue.

In France racing cyclists began to take it, to increase their powers of endurance; so did the Toronto Lacrosse Club, in Canada, who with its assistance won the title 'Champions of the World'.

From the time of its foundation half a century before, the *Lancet* has enjoyed exposing nostrums as quackery; and the budding reputation of coca gave it yet another opportunity to live up to its reputation. In 1876 it carried a report of an investigation by G. F. Dowdeswell, a member of the staff of the University College Physics Department, into the properties of coca and its action on the human body. Dowdeswell claimed that he had been concerned solely with the measurable effects on a human subject — changes in pulse rate, temperature, and so on; and he had demonstrated they were negative. But consumption of coca had also failed to produce any of the subjective effects 'so fervently described, and ascribed to it, by others; not the slightest excitement, not even the feeling of buoyancy and exhilaration which is experienced from mountain air, or a draught of spring water'. Although Dowdeswell was not prepared to claim that coca, in this capacity, was pharmacologically inert, his experiments, he argued, demonstrated that its action was so slight 'as to preclude the idea of its having any value either therapeutically or popularly'. Whatever might be the virtue of the coca leaf in South America, the *Lancet* commented editorially, 'it seems to have lost much of its marvellous virtue when used in this country.'

Laboratory trials of that kind had not then acquired the authority they were later to command; and even the *Lancet*'s reputation was not sufficient to stem coca's growing popularity as a stimulant. The following year, it was admitted to the U.S. *Pharmacopeia*; soon afterwards, to its British counterpart; and from the variety of disorders for which it began to be prescribed it looked as if it might be following the same triumphant clinical course that tobacco had taken three centuries earlier. But it was just too late. Pharmacologists succeeded in identifying what was assumed to be the narcotic element of the coca leaf: cocaine. It seemed self-evident that it would be absurd to ask a patient to chew coca leaves, or drink infusions of them, when it was possible to give him accurately measured doses of its essential ingredient.

But first, it was necessary to demonstrate that cocaine worked; and in 1883 a German army doctor tried the drug out on soldiers to see if it did the same for them as the leaves did for the natives of Peru. It did. Cocaine, Dr Theodor Aschenbrandt was able to report, greatly increased their energy and endurance. The report attracted Freud's attention. He had just become engaged to Martha Bernays, and was looking for some medical discovery which would make his name, and his fortune, so that they could afford to marry. 'I am procuring some myself', he wrote to tell her, 'and will try it with cases of heart disease and also of nervous exhaustion, particularly in the miserable condition after withdrawal of morphine', a possibility which had been suggested in an American medical journal. Having taken some cocaine — it altered his mood from depression to cheerfulness, he was delighted to find, without impairing his ability to work — he tried it on his friend Dr Fleischl, a morphine addict, with immediately gratifying results.

'The temperament of an investigator' — Freud had told Martha in the letter describing his reseach into cocaine — 'needs two fundamental qualities: he must be sanguine in the attempt, but critical in the work'. He failed to heed his own advice. Cocaine, he decided, was 'a magical drug'. He took it himself against depression and indigestion; sent some to Martha; recommended it for a variety of disorders; and wrote an essay on it published in 1884, which was an extended eulogy. Cocaine provided 'exhilaration and lasting euphoria'; 'an increase of self-control'; 'more vitality and capacity for work'. Whether mental or physical, work could be performed without any fatigue; there were none of the unpleasant after-effects associated with alcohol; and 'absolutely no craving for the further use of cocaine appears after the first, or even repeated, taking of the drug; one feels, rather, a curious aversion to it'.

The following year, the first warnings were sounded. To some persons, nothing was more fascinating than indulgence in cocaine — a writer commented in the *Medical Record* for November 28th, 1885 —

It relieves the sense of exhaustion, dispels mental depression, and produces a delicious sense of exhilaration and well-being. The after-effects are at first slight, almost imperceptible; but continuous indulgence finally creates a craving which must be satisfied; the individual then becomes nervous, tremulous, sleepless, without appetite, and he is at last reduced to a condition of pitiable neurasthenia

By the spring of 1887 a Brooklyn doctor, J. B. Mattison, had compiled a formidable dossier to show that cocaine was highly addictive — as Freud himself, who had passionately defended cocaine, now realised. He had to watch Fleischl suffering from the agonies of chronic intoxication, delirium tremens, and 'white snakes creeping over his skin'.

There was no reason, in theory, why the unmasking of cocaine should have had an adverse effect on the reputation of coca — any more than the discovery that tobacco's alkali, nicotine, was highly poisonous had deterred people from smoking. But because the early experimenters with cocaine had argued that, as Freud put it, cocaine was 'the essential constituent of coca leaves', there was an understandable tendency for coca to be found guilty by association; and it had not been on the market for long enough to become established in the way that tobacco had been before nicotine was found.

Coca had its defenders: chief among them W. G. Mortimer, a Fellow of the New York Academy of Medicine. In 1901 he published his history of the 'divine plant of the Incas', a rambling, repetitive, but exhaustively researched defence of the use of the plant, as distinct from its alkali. The pharmacologists, he asserted, had deceived the public; cocaine no more represented coca than prussic acid, found in minute quantities in peach stones, 'represents that luscious fruit'. The analogy might not be precise, but the proposition he derived from it was of fundamental importance: that the action of cocaine on the human system, though in some respects similar to that of coca, must not be considered as identical: 'each gives a peculiar sense of well being; but cocaine affects the central nervous system more pronouncedly than does coca; not — as commonly presumed — because it is coca in a more concentrated form, but because the associated substances present in coca, which are important in modifying its action, are not present in cocaine'. As proof he was able to cite the discovery of Dr Henry Rusby that the Andean natives, making their careful selection of leaves for chewing, did *not*, in fact, choose the leaves with the ighest cocaine content. And in the entire literature on the subject, Mortimer claimed, before the attacks on cocaine, there had been no serious criticism of coca. Nor was there any known case of coca addiction or coca poisoning ('What it does for the Indian at fifteen', one authority had asserted, 'it does for him at sixty; a greatly increasing dose is not resorted to.') Not merely was it as innocent as tea or coffee, 'which are commonly accepted popular necessities — but it is vastly superior to those substances'.

But how was it — if the authorities Mortimer cited were correct — that the findings of scientific experimenters like Dowdeswell had been negative? Perhaps, Mortimer surmised, they had used the wrong kind of leaves. Or the explanation might be along the lines put forward in 1881 by a New York physician, W. S. Searle: that not only was coca's action so gentle that it could escape detection: it might not take place at all in experiments, because the appropriate mechanism would not be brought into action.

> While no other known substance can rival coca in its sustaining power, no other has so little apparent effect. To one pursuing the even tenor of his usual routine, the chewing of coca gives no special sensation. In fact the only result seems to be a negative one, viz.: an absence of the customary desire for food and sleep. It is only when some unusual demand is made upon mind or body that its influence is felt. And to this fact is to be attributed much of the incredulity of those who have carelessly experimented with it and who, expecting some internal commotion or sensation, are disappointed.

Mortimer himself felt that the explanation probably also lay in the different circumstances in which coca was consumed in South America, where it affected the body's capacity for work by more efficient conversion of food into energy. Coca helped the Andean Indians to avoid fatigue by acting upon the stored-up carbohydrates to which they were accustomed. It might have no affect — the implication was — on a Westerner accustomed to a different diet.

Whatever the explanation — Mortimer concluded — the evidence from clinical experience was irrefutable. He had himself circularised doctors all over America about their experiences with coca; over 350 had replied and a large majority of those expressing opinions were agreed that coca improved the digestion, strengthened the heart, stimulated the mind, and improved sexual performance. All doctors who agreed with him, he urged, should accept the need for a long and persistent campaign to explain coca's value, 'and so reflect credit upon themselves through the advocacy and use of a really marvellous drug'.

It was to no purpose. Coca might be all that Mortimer claimed, but it lost caste; the medical profession gradually losing interest. Cocaine, like morphine, continued to have a limited range of clinical uses; but they would soon, it was hoped, be replaced for most purposes by a new drug. Heroin had been derived from opium in 1898; soon it was being enthusiastically promoted by manufacturers, and enthusiastically welcomed by doctors, as more effective than its predecessors, and carrying — the assurance was — no risk whatsoever of promoting addiction.

*Mescaline*

After the disappointments with laudanum and Indian hemp, the search for a safe and effective vision-inducing drug had languished for a time; but towards the end of the century it was revived, largely through the efforts of a young Berlin pharmacologist, Louis Lewin. Lewin first made his reputation by some research into morphine; then, he went on to make the first scientific study of kava. Missionaries, Lewin had read, were inclined to regard kava as a powerful intoxicant which ought to be banned; yet Europeans who took it generally found that it had little or no effect on them. Why? Lewin decided to find the active chemical principle, test it, and settle the issue one way or the other. The tests convinced him that kava was a mild stimulant, improving muscular efficiency and endurance; and though it could be taken as an intoxicant, its effects were relatively gentle, compared with alcohol. At least people under its influence did not become noisy and aggressive.

Up to this point, Lewin was following Anstie's course; but whereas Anstie's findings compelled him to give up the attempt to distinguish drugs by their effects on man, Lewin remained sublimely confident that it was only a matter of time before he could unravel the strands sufficiently to allow him to categorise drugs according to their effects. And he was greatly encouraged in this view by peyotl, which came into his possession on a visit to America. The botanical Museum in Berlin decided the cacti were a new species; four alkaloids were extracted from them, including mescal — mescaline; and Lewin had his monument — the sub-species was named after him, *anhalonium lewinii*.

In Lewin, however, peyotl induced no vision. He found it only toxic (as did William James. It made him vomit; 'I will take the visions on trust', he told his brother Henry). But another American, the pioneer psychiatrist Weir Mitchell, was delighted with the results, when he tried peyotl in the 1890s, finding it a powerful physical and emotional stimulus. He could climb to the fourth floor of his hotel two steps at a time without puffing; and later — 'deliciously at languid ease, I was clearly in the land where it is always afternoon' — he had a sense of heightened intellectual power. In retrospect he had to admit that a reading of what he wrote under the influence failed to justify it; but he could not find words to express the 'beauty and splendour of what I saw'.

After reading Mitchell's account in the *British Medical Journal*, Havelock Ellis took mescaline, with very similar results. His first symptom was an access of energy, and of intellectual power; then visions, the colours indescribably vivid and delightful, so reminiscent of Monet's paintings that Ellis decided to offer some mescal to an artist he knew, to observe the effect. The artist duly had fantastic visions — but they were accompanied by paroxysms, pain, and the fear he was dying. 'It may at least be claimed,' Ellis wrote, 'that for a healthy person to be once or twice admitted to the rites of mescal is not only an unforgettable delight but an educational influence of no mean value.' But he realised that more research was needed; and the fact that Weir Mitchell had also had unfortunate results when he tried it out on a colleague did not encourage more orthodox medical scientists to carry it on.

Mescaline had been discovered at the wrong time. Pharmacologists were looking for drugs which had measurable effects; not drugs which induced unquantifiable delight. And Lewin, though he had no doubt that divine inspiration could account for such visions as that of the prophet Ezekiel — 'a great cloud, and a fire unfolding itself, and a brightness was about it, and out of the midst thereof as the colour of amber' — felt that visionary experiences were ordinarily 'transitory states caused by substances produced in the organism'. This was a view that was becoming increasingly popular among scientists: that the visions of the alcoholic, the schizophrenic and the mystic reflected biochemical changes in the body. The chemical processes interested them. The visions, they felt, were of no significance.

# 10

# Prohibition

THE EXPLOITATION OF DRUGS FOR PROFIT AND FOR REVENUE; THE
re-discovery of their vision-inducing qualities; and the impact of
scientific advances provided three separate, though sometimes
inter-locking, strands during the nineteenth century. There was
also a fourth, of a rather different nature; the mounting campaign
to have alcohol categorised as a dangerous drug, and banned
from general consumption.

The gin plague had compelled recognition of the dangers of
'ardent spirits' as they were commonly described, and though
it had been realised that prohibition did not work, and licensing
did, a widespread belief remained — particularly among the followers of Wesley, and in the Evangelical movement — that ways
should be found to reduce consumption still further. As spirits
were obviously an acquired taste, the simplest way to deal with
them would be to check the process by which the taste was
acquired; and it was with this in mind that a campaign began
against tobacco.

## The weed

The arguments used were similar to those which had been employed against hashish in Moslem countries — and to those
which were to be employed against beer, and later against cannabis. Tobacco was condemned on various grounds, as unhealthy
and as anti-social; but the main ground of criticism was that,
though smoking might be relatively harmless when indulged in
moderation, it led on inexorably not merely to excess, and

addiction, but also to the consumption of 'hard' liquor. This was the theme of a treatise published in America in 1798: *Observations upon the influence of the habitual use of tobacco upon health, morals and property*, by the formidable Dr Benjamin Rush — one of the signatories to the Declaration of Independence. Tobacco's influence on all three, Rush felt, was pernicious; and its most sinister feature was that the usual consequence of smoking or chewing was thirst.

> This thirst cannot be allayed by water, for no sedative or even insipid liquor will be relished after the mouth and throat have been exposed to the stimulus of the smoke, or juice, of tobacco. A desire of course is excited for strong drinks, which when taken between meals soon lead to intemperance and drunkenness. One of the greatest sots I ever knew acquired a love for ardent spirits by swallowing cuds of tobacco, contrary to the commands of his father. He died of dropsy under my care.

Rush's denunciation helped to promote an alliance between the anti-tobacco campaigners and the temperance movement, when it got under way a quarter of a century later. 'Rum drinking will not cease', the Rev. Orin Fowler prophesied in 1833, 'till tobacco-chewing, and tobacco-smoking, and snuff-taking shall cease'; and he went on to estimate that at least a tenth of the drunkards in the United States and throughout the world were made so by the use of tobacco — a piece of guesswork which was picked up and repeated again and again until, as Joseph Robert complained in his history of tobacco in America, it became a 'sort of sanctified census'. Other campaigners traced the route by which an innocent youth would be lured to perdition: having smoked, he would naturally resort to a soda fountain, from which it was an easy step 'to beer, and then brandy, and finally whiskey'.

Tobacco was also attacked in the mid-nineteenth century as a dangerous drug in its own right, causing — Dr Joel Shew alleged — a wide variety of disorders, including insanity, delirium tremens, and epilepsy. He accused it of causing impotence, too; but this was a minority view. The more general opinion among its detractors was that it represented a threat to American womanhood. 'No man can be virtuous as a companion', the eugenicist Orson S. Fowler claimed,

> who eats tobacco; for, although he may not violate the seventh commandment, yet the feverish state of the system which it produces necessarily causes a craving and lustful exercise of amativeness. Just as alcoholic liquors cause such amatory cravings, and for the same reason. As alcoholic liquors and the grosser forms of sensuality are twin sisters, so tobacco-eating and devilry are both one; because the fierce passions of many tobacco chewers, as regards the other sex, are immensely increased by the fires kindled in their systems, and of course in their cerebellums, by tobacco excitement. Ye who would be pure in your love instinct, cast this sensualising fire from you.

Such denunciations of tobacco continued to appear until the Civil War. Then, the armies in the field demanded to be kept supplied with it; on the Confederate side, the soldiers had eventually to be provided with a ration. Hope of having tobacco banned on the ground of its moral and physical effects dwindled. Restrictions continued to be called for, but mainly to protect the public from the anti-social side-effects, rather than to protect the smoker from the consequences of his vice.

In Britain tobacco was assailed on a more serious clinical level, in the pages of the *Lancet*. After a few weeks of vigorous controversy, an editorial in April, 1847 had to admit that though tobacco was certainly a powerful and addictive drug, it was not quite clear what *kind* of drug. Whether or not moderate smoking was healthy also remained debatable. There were no two opinions — the *Lancet* insisted — about the evils of excessive smoking. The only problem here was: what constituted excess? The test, the editorial suggested, was 'smoking *early in the day*' — when 'unless a man be the victim of pernicious habits, he certainly requires neither a sedative nor stimulant'. Anything over one or two pipes or cigars a day must also be regarded as excessive. For youths, any indulgence in the drug was dangerous. Their minds would be emasculated if they were unable to face their comparatively small anxieties without having recourse to the daily use of such a narcotic. 'Listless minds and languid bodies, slake-less thirst and shaking hands, delirium tremens, madness — and death. We have distinctly and surely followed this unhallowed indulgence in youths who began their studies with bright promise of success, with fair characters, and honest purposes.'

But by this time it had become futile for the *Lancet* to pronounce such warnings. Tobacco, along with tea, had established itself as one of the drugs of the working classes. It was also in high favour with men of letters, as endless tributes had begun to show; in verse — Thomas Hood's

> How oft the fragrant smoke upcurled
> Hath borne me from this little world
> And all that in it lies . . .

and in prose — Lord Lytton's

> He who doth not smoke hath either known no great griefs, or refuseth himself the softest consolation next to that which comes from heaven. 'What, softer than woman?' whispers the young reader. Young reader, woman teases as well as consoles. Woman makes half the sorrows which she boasts the privilege to soothe. Woman consoles us, it is true, while we are young and handsome; when we are old and ugly, woman snubs and scolds us. On the whole, then, woman in this scale, the weed in that: Jupiter, hang out thy balance, and weigh them both; and if thou givest the preference to woman, all I can say is, the next time Juno ruffles thee — O Jupiter, try the weed!'

By this time, too, the defenders of tobacco had found a fresh argument. Even if it were addictive, they claimed, at least the consequences were less hideous than from other addictive drugs, opium, or alcohol; and they were able to cite E. W. Lane's popular *Manners and Customs of the Modern Egyptians*, published in 1844. Tobacco, Lane had argued, as well as affording cheap and sober refreshment, calmed the nervous system, thereby probably restraining the peasant 'from less innocent indulgences'. In his *Letters from Turkey* in the 1870s von Moltke went further; it had been tobacco, he suggested, which had changed the wild nomadic

Scythians, the scourge of their neighbours, into the quiet and all too sedentary Turk.

## The Maine Law

A parallel controversy was also in progress about drink. Ought beer, wine and cider to be considered as a safer alternative to hard liquors? Or should they be prohibited in case youths, lured into taking them because they were relatively mild, would be tempted to move on impetuously to gin, or whiskey, or rum?

For a time, supporters of wine and beer were dominant. In *An Inquiry into the effects of ardent spirits upon the human body and mind*, published in 1784, Benjamin Rush had argued that the consumption of beer and wine should be encouraged, in order to discourage dram-drinking. In Britain, even John Wesley had praised wine, 'one of the noblest cordials'; and in 1826 Sydney Smith, recommending ale and tobacco to the readers of the *Edinburgh Review* as 'the joys and holidays of millions, the greatest pleasure which it is in the power of fortune to bestow', warned that these were amusements 'which a wise and parental legislature should not despise, or hastily extinguish'. To his mortification the legislature was soon to go to the other extreme. In 1830 the Wellington Government, in its death throes, tried to court popularity with brewers and workers by reducing the cost of the licence to sell beer to £2 a year — a sum which was small enough to make it possible for any householder to take out a licence, as the brewers were delighted to advance the money. There was an immediate massive increase in the number of public houses — 50,000 in six years — and of facilities for cheap beer drinking. As a result, there was a repetition of what had happened a century earlier when similar encouragement had been given to gin — though on a less lethal scale. Again, the prevailing social conditions — with the lives of workers on the land being disrupted by enclosures, and of urban workers by the introduction of the factory system — encouraged the consumption of alcohol as a narcotic rather than a stimulant. 'Everybody is drunk,' Sydney Smith sadly observed, 'those who are not singing are sprawling. The sovereign people are in a beastly state.'

In 1832 James Teare stood up at a temperance meeting in Manchester and claimed that *all* intoxicating liquor was an enemy to God and man; 'the sooner it is put out of this world, the better'. Ten weeks later, seven men signed the first teetotal pledge, in Preston; and in 1835 a national society of teetotallers was formed. The movement grew rapidly in Britain — and still more rapidly in Ireland, where Father Mathew's preaching persuaded tens of thousands to take the pledge. In this period the campaign was for voluntary abstinence; and although it became known that the sister movement in the United States was for legislative intervention, it came as a complete surprise when a prohibition Bill was debated in the Maine Legislature in 1850, and as a still greater surprise when, the following year, it was passed. No attempt was made to stop people bringing liquor into the State for their own consumption, and the fruit-growers' lobby was influential enough to prevent apple cider being included in the ban. But 'the Maine Law' was generally regarded, and described, as prohibition; the first enactment based on the premise that all alcoholic liquors as such were dangerous drugs which ought to be taken, if at all, only on a medical prescription.

What happened in America had the effect of disrupting the movement in Britain. At first, the news of the Maine Law was enthusiastically received by all concerned. But it led some reformers to argue that what had been done in America could be done in Britain; and a split developed between those who continued to advocate voluntary abstinence, and those who wanted legal prohibition — the 'suasionists' and the 'suppressionists', as the two sides came to be described. In 1853 the United Kingdom Alliance was established 'to procure the total and immediate legislative suppression of the traffic in all intoxicating liquors'; and it was soon engaged in vigorous and sometimes embittered controversy with the suasionists, who objected to legal compulsion on principle and argued that there was no chance of such a measure passing in Britain.

The controversy started a public debate on the rights and duties of the State, in this context, and the arguments were considered by John Stuart Mill in his *Essay on Liberty*. Mill took as his text a letter which Lord Stanley had sent to *The Times*, replying to the views propounded by the Secretary of the U.K. Alliance. 'All matters relating to thought, opinion, conscience appear to me without the sphere of legislation,' Stanley had argued; 'all

pertaining to social act, habit, relations, subject only to discretion-
ary power vested in the State itself.' But there was another category,
Mill pointed out. Individual acts might have social consequences.
In that case, the Secretary of the Alliance in effect was arguing,

> If anything invades my social rights, certainly the traffic in
> strong drink does. It destroys my primary right of security, by
> constantly creating and stimulating social disorder. It invades
> my right of equality, by deriving a profit from the creation of
> a misery I am taxed to support. It impedes my right to free
> moral and intellectual development, by surrounding my path
> with dangers, and by weakening and demoralising society, from
> which I have a right to claim mutual aid and intercourse.

What this amounted to, Mill thought, was a new theory of
social rights; 'that it is the absolute right of every individual that
every other individual shall act in every respect exactly as he ought'.
So monstrous a principle, Mill felt,

> is far more dangerous than any single interference with liberty;
> there is no violation of liberty that it would not justify; it
> acknowledges no right to any freedom whatever except, per-
> haps, that of holding opinions in secret, without ever disclos-
> ing them; for the moment an opinion I consider noxious passes
> anyone's lips, it invades all the 'social rights' attributed to me by
> the Alliance.

Mill was being unfair. The Alliance were not claiming that
because they disapproved of the consumption of alcohol, they
had a right to stop other people drinking. They were simply
arguing that if an individual's drinking had social consequences of
a kind which affected other people's rights — by, say, making
the streets unsafe — they could then claim that right. As it
happened, the Alliance stated that they did not even want to stop
individuals brewing their own beer; it was the consequences of the
liquor traffic, rather than of liquor, to which they objected. But
here, they had put themselves on weaker ground, as the suasionist
Joseph Livesey pointed out. If the Alliance were going to tell a
man, 'you can brew your own beer', he argued — he failed to see

'how it can be wrong for your neighbour of the Royal Hotel to brew it for you, and take pay for it'.

Stanley had also uncovered a weakness in the Alliance's case. Their aim was to suppress the traffic in intoxicants; how were intoxicants to be defined? 'Is tobacco to be included? Is opium?' The Secretary of the Alliance, who was presumably well aware that any attempt to link tobacco with alcohol as a national menace would weaken his organisation's prospects, was forced to hedge. The tobacco traffic, he claimed, rested on the drink traffic 'and would fall with it, without any special enactment' — as also, he added, would the opium traffic. But he offered no evidence for this assertion.

### Fanshawe's travels

In Britain, though, the decisive factor — as Livesey realised — was not going to be philosophical disputation, but the composition of the House of Commons. 'Out of the 658 members,' he wrote, 'there are probably not a dozen who would claim to be abstainers. These gentlemen have their cellars stored with liquor, have it daily on their tables, and have it introduced on every social occasion as a mark of friendship — and is it likely that they would pass a Bill to prevent others enjoying the same, according to their means?' It was most unlikely; but the hopes of suppressionists were kept alive partly by the extension of the franchise in Britain, which brought in working class voters, and partly by the achievements of the movement in America. Twelve other States had followed Maine's example; and though there had been backsliding as a result of the Civil War, the movement had soon picked up again. A National Prohibition Party was formed in 1869; its candidates began to win seats in State legislatures; and in 1890, it won its first seat in the House of Representatives at Washington.

Was it possible that prohibition might be introduced, on a national scale? Could it work? Did it, in fact, work in the States which had introduced it? In 1892 an English lawyer, E. L. Fanshawe, was despatched on a tour of America and Canada to try to find out. In his report, he was to claim that his sponsors — he did not say who they were — had given him strict injunctions to preserve impartiality; and whatever his personal opinions may have been (he was no teetotaller, himself) he did not allow them to obtrude.

Fanshawe was intrigued, on his arrival in America, to observe the differences in drinking habits. They helped, he felt, to account for the different courses which the temperance movement had been taking. In public, American men drank only water — iced. Except in a few cities, he usually found himself the only person taking wine or beer with his dinner. The clergy were virtually compelled to be abstainers; and at public functions, drink was the exception. At gatherings at the White House, disrespectful persons said, 'water flowed like champagne'.

Fanshawe found, though, that if he went into a bar, at any hour of the day, he might meet friends who had been drinking water at dinner the night before, and they would be having a glass of whiskey, or a 'cocktail'. Worse (for once, Fanshawe could not repress his disapproval) they would be 'treating' each other; a practice so un-English, at that time, that he had to explain it in a footnote; 'two Americans go together to a bar; one treats the other who, feeling himself under an obligation, must have his revenge' (in Nebraska treating had been made illegal, 'but not prevented').

Even in States where there was no prohibition, Fanshawe found, drinking was regarded as a vice. Those who indulged themselves took care to do so in secret — or at least in privacy. And they did precisely the same in States where there was prohibition. He had arrived expecting to hear complaints about the way prohibition infringed the rights of the individual. Instead, all he heard was complaints about the difficulties of enforcing it.

This was due partly, he decided, to the fact that the prohibitionists, not being numerous enough to win on their own ticket, had concentrated on acquiring sufficient strength to hold the balance of power between Democrats and Republicans; which put them in a position to compel one or other party to pass 'dry' legislation, but did not necessarily compel them, when in office, to enforce it. Enforcement would depend on who was the successful party's nominee to run the police; and he might be in the pay of the brewers and distillers.

In any case, the problems confronting even those communities which were determined to enforce prohibition were formidable. It had been found relatively easy to enforce 'local option', where that was the law, because small communities were better able to winkle out illicit traffickers in their midst. When Fanshawe went to Cambridge, Mass., he could see just how efficiently it worked. But it worked efficiently only because Boston was nearby, with its 'high return of arrests for drunkenness, and its high percentage of non-residents among those arrested'. As for prohibition at the State level, Fanshawe's enquiries showed it to be almost farcical. In Maine, for example, there was nothing to stop citizens bringing in as much liquor as they could carry. They could even purchase it in hotels to drink in private rooms; and in Bangor it was openly sold in bars, and by chemists. In Kansas, the State usually cited as having done most to make a success of prohibition, he was told that it was legal for members of clubs to keep liquor; they could obtain it through 'bootleggers' or — again perfectly legally — by ordering deliveries from a nearby 'wet' State.

Fanshawe was not called upon by his English sponsors to pronounce a verdict: but the report spoke it for him. Prohibition could not hope to work. How could whiskey be kept out of 'dry' Kansas City (Kan.) when the 'frontier' was an imaginary line running down the middle of the street dividing it from 'wet' Kansas City (Mo.)?

Why, then, had the futility of prohibition not been recognised? One reason, Fanshawe showed, was that men who had the responsibility for enforcing the law naturally also had an interest in pretending that it worked, if necessary by deliberate falsehoods. In Kansas, for example, the attorney general had boasted that prohibition was 'depopulating the penitentiaries' by reducing violence and crime, a statement which had been gratefully repeated by the temperance reformers in England in a pamphlet, *Does Prohibition Prohibit?* When Fanshawe investigated the figures, however, he discovered that in proportion to the population, there were more prisoners in Kansas jails than there had been in 1860, the year prohibition had been introduced — a higher proportion, in fact, than in the adjoining 'wet' States.

The fundamental difficulty about enforcement was that the man in the street, whatever he might do in the polling booth, was on the side of the law-breakers, rather than of the law — as an enforcement officer he had met in Bangor had freely admitted. And this was having the unfortunate effect of bringing the law itself

into discredit, by engendering 'a spirit of disregard for its obser-
vance'. It was also corrupting American political life. In Rhode
Island, Fanshawe was told, a Republican attorney general had
tried to implement campaign promises by bringing over a hundred
offenders to justice. Their lawyers cleverly delayed proceedings
until after the next elections, to give time for 'wet' influence in
both parties to get to work. He was not re-elected — the only
Republican on the slate who failed to secure re-election; and the
proceedings were quietly dropped.

## The Anti-Saloon League

Fanshawe's report, published in England, was hardly likely to
make any impact in the United States. Even if it had been, a
different verdict could have been wrung from it; that prohibition
could never succeed unless it was extended to all States of the
Union, and backed by federal law and federal enforcement. And
while he was there, the movement which was eventually to succeed
in persuading the necessary proportion of the electorate to accept
that solution was getting under way: the Anti-Saloon League,
founded in 1893. For a time, however, there appeared to be a
possibility of a compromise plan, satisfying both suasionists and
suppressionists, derived from the Gothenburg experiment, begun
in Sweden in the 1860s. It was not prohibition, but it went some
way to satisfy the suppressionist aim of concentrating on the
traffic, rather than on drink, by taking control away from private
enterprise and putting it in the hands of 'disinterested management'. The manufacture, distribution and sale of drink were
looked after by a board, none of whose members was allowed to
have any pecuniary interest; the aim being not to stop consumption, but to ensure that it did the least possible harm.

To this end, alcoholic drinks became obtainable only through a
form of lay prescription. The hours at which they could be purchased, and the type of premises in which they could be consumed, were designed to discourage social drinking. The idea was
to favour beer at the expense of spirits, and the consumption of
beer rose rapidly; but as it had been very low before, and as the
consumption of spirits fell, the experiment was regarded as
successful, and the system became general through Sweden and
Norway.

For a while, the United Kingdom Alliance was attracted to the Gothenburg idea, thinking it might prove a handy stepping-stone on the way to ultimate prohibition. It also attracted Joseph Chamberlain, fitting in as it did with his view that all monopolies granted by the State should be managed by local authorities for the community, rather than for private profit. When he was elected to the Commons in 1876, he moved a resolution in favour of a scheme along Gothenburg lines, and it attracted fifty supporters.

In the United States, too, some interest was shown in the experiment; the Massachusetts legislature and the Federal Department of Labor in Washington sent investigators to Sweden, both of them making favourable reports on how the scheme was working. But by this time the movement for outright prohibition was gaining too much momentum to be thus side-tracked. The Anti-Saloon League established itself on a national basis, and it was to provide the organisation by which, over the next twenty years, prohibition became so powerful a cause that politicians were no longer able to exploit it for their own ends; instead, they found, the prohibitionists were able to exploit them. By the 1906 elections, the League was able to show that it could wreck the chances of a politician who opposed it; his name was sent for suitable treatment to the League's accredited speakers, and also circulated on a black list to all electors. The party bosses began to require their candidates to agree to pledge themselves not to oppose prohibition; better still, to endorse it.

There were some setbacks; but by 1913 the League showed its power when the Webb-Kenyon Bill, designed to assist States to enforce prohibition more effectively, was passed in spite of a Presidential veto. And to the frustration of the liquor interests, the war, when it came, did nothing to hinder the prohibitionists; it actually helped them, as economists demanded cuts in drink consumption to save cereals for the G.I.'s rations; and Congress agreed to sponsor an amendment to the Constitution to enable prohibition to be introduced.

## The d'Abernon Committee

In Britain, too, the war helped the suppressionist cause. If Lloyd George had been able to get his way, prohibition might have been introduced there, too, to assist the war effort. But opinion in Parliament and in the Cabinet was still hostile; and the cost of some variant of the Gothenburg system, which he also contemplated, would have involved astronomical sums to compensate the liquor interests. His colleagues were able to argue, too, that the consumption of alcoholic liquor was falling rapidly, helped by a voluntary abstinence campaign (King George V abjured drink for himself and the Court for the duration of the war) and by various restrictions imposed by 'DORA' — the Defence of the Realm Act, which among other things regulated the hours at which public houses could remain open. Although Lloyd George remained convinced that — as he claimed in 1916 — Britain was fighting Germany, Austria and drink, 'and the greatest of these three deadly foes is drink', he allowed himself to be persuaded that not enough was known about the enforced deprivation of drink on workers; and it was agreed that before any decision was taken, a Committee under Lord d'Abernon should investigate the whole subject of the effects of alcohol, and 'more particularly the effects on health and industrial efficiency produced by the consumption of beverages of various alcoholic strengths'.

The Committee's report, published in 1917, differed from those of earlier parliamentary investigations in one significant respect; it considered the action of alcohol as a drug. It was also, the Committee conceded, a common article of diet; and the habit of drinking was encouraged by the agreeable taste of fermented liquors. They insisted, nevertheless, that it was basically as a drug that alcoholic liquor was consumed.

The need to consider alcohol in this way had been stressed by Sydney Hillier in his *Popular Drugs*, published in 1910. He had devoted half the book to it, explaining that while statistics showed there had been a general decline in the consumption of alcoholic drinks in England, the news should not be welcomed unreservedly, because it did not necessarily mean any reduction in drug consumption; 'no statistics are available relating to morphinism or other drug habits, but there is a very general consensus of opinion, among those who are best able to judge, that there is an increase in the number of persons addicted'. Drink must never — Hillier insisted — be considered as a problem in its own right. The possibility must always be kept in mind that it might be the lesser of two evils.

Lord d'Abernon and his colleagues, however, were asked to consider only drink, and its effects on the war effort. The figures they collected were sufficient to warn the Government of the magnitude of the confrontation Lloyd George was contemplating. The amount spent annually on alcoholic liquor in the United Kingdom was half as much again as the entire receipts from the railway system, and more than double the expenditure on bread. Until the war, the amount spent had been almost equal to the entire revenue of the State; and in some countries it had actually been more. What was likely to happen if prohibition were introduced was not within the Committee's terms of reference; but the statistics were disturbing enough in themselves. Lloyd George decided it would be wise to rely on' DORA ' — reinforced by such occasional additions such as a 'No Treating' order, and reductions in the strength of beer. The expedients worked well enough. By the end of the war, consumption of beer had fallen by nearly a third, and of spirits by more than a half. The rate of 'drunk and disorderly' convictions, too, dropped from nearly 200,000 in the first year of the war to below 30,000 in the last.

## The Volstead Act

No similar inquiry was conducted in the United States. The required quota of States having announced their ratification, Prohibition was introduced in 1920. Three years later Roy Haynes, the Commissioner in charge of the enforcement of Prohibition (as it came to be called, with a capital 'P') gave an account in *Prohibition Inside Out*. It was designed to show that, appearances notwithstanding, 'the illegal liquor traffic is under control'. But Haynes was also anxious to defend himself and his subordinates from criticism, already mounting. To do so, he had to describe the difficulties that had confronted them; and the book turned into a treatise on why the illegal liquor traffic had not been, and could not be, brought under control.

To begin with, there had been the unwelcome discovery that the demand for hard liquor was — in the economists' new jargon — inelastic. A high proportion of the spirit drinkers of the pre-Prohibition era were prepared to continue to buy their supplies, even if the price doubled or trebled. As expected, some were men and women from all classes who had become so dependent on drink that they could not bear to do without it. But much more serious was the number of respectable citizens who were drinkers in moderation, and who had no intention of drinking any less, whatever the law might say. 'One finds upon the Roll of Dishonour proud old names long worn without stain or blemish, now close-linked with names that have been a by-word with the *demi-monde* of half a hundred cities', Haynes lamented. 'One finds names that once epitomised honour and power and community esteem, steeped in the same befouling brew with the names of thieves, thugs and murderers.' Nor was it only the rich man who must have his drink. It was also the industrial worker, especially the immigrant; the German steel worker in Milwaukee, who had always regarded his beer as part of his life; the New York Italian who had never been drunk, yet could not conceive of a meal without wine.

To cater for this demand there were six main sources of supply; genuine liquor, in stock; genuine liquor diluted or mixed with synthetic varieties; synthetic liquor made from grain alcohol, with colour and flavour added; 'moonshine' — liquor distilled from vegetable substances; 'denatured' alcohol, redistilled; and wood alcohol. This variety of sources would have made Haynes' task difficult enough; what made it impossible was the variety of uses for which alcohol could still legally be manufactured. In the event of any attempt to stop the use of communion wine, the Rev. E. A. Wasson had announced in 1914, 'we would do as our Lord told us to do — "all of you, drink of this" — if we had to go to jail for it'. The threat had sufficed: Communion wine was exempted from the law, and many a consignment so labelled found its way to the dinner, rather than the altar table. An even more abundant source was medical prescription. Whiskey and brandy had been dropped from the *Pharmacopeia* in 1916, but alcohol remained an essential ingredient in prescriptions for a wide range of diseases; and although prescribing habits were subjected to scrutiny, any doctor who was prepared to break the law, either for cash reward or for the benefit of himself and his friends, ran little risk. Chemists, too, licensed as they were to sell alcohol in certain forms, found the law easy to evade.

The most prolific source of alcohol, though, was industry, which had so great a need for it that considerable quantities could be siphoned off without exciting suspicion. Industrial alcohol was 'de-natured' — rendered unfit for human consumption; but it could easily be re-distilled. Firms were set up ostensibly to produce commodities which required an alcohol base, but in reality to divert the alcohol into illicit channels. A State Governor, Giffard Pinchot, estimated in 1924 that the 150 firms which had been authorised in his State to purchase de-natured alcohol to manu-facture perfumes and hair tonics had ordered enough of it to fulfil the needs of the population of the entire world.

What with 'moonshine' — easy enough to make and, in a country the size of the United States, extremely difficult to check — Haynes had been unable to stem the flow of illicit spirits manu-factured *in* the United States. But he had also to deal with smuggling; and the difficulties that presented, as set out in his book, and as expressed by other law enforcement officers at the time, read like a weird parody of what had happened in China with opium, a century before. Vast quantities of liquor — James Beck, a Washington law officer, complained in an article in the London *Sunday Times* on July 15th, 1923 — were being taken out from British possessions

with a full knowledge that they were to be used to violate the laws of the United States and break down this policy of pro-hibition. Our requests that clearance papers should be refused to notorious rum-runners were denied. They persisted, and wholesale lawlessness virtually challenged the right of the U.S. to be master within its own household, for it has never been challenged by any competent authority on international law that each sovereign nation, notwithstanding the comity of nations, has entire right to assert full police power over any foreign merchant vessel within the territorial limits of the sovereign.

William Jennings Bryan made the same complaint. 'There is no more excuse for the use of adjacent territory for conspiracies against the Prohibition Law . . . than for the use of such territory for conspiracies against any other law of the land. Piracy would not be given protection under the British flag. Why should smuggling?' British merchants were as little disposed to listen to such arguments as they had been to listen to Commissioner Lin. The Scottish distillers even found a way of expanding their market. Distillers in the United States had been permitted to continue to export their spirits, provided they were sold for 'non-beverage purposes'. The Scotch distillers, buying them in bulk, could truthfully claim they had no intention of drinking them; the whiskey they made out of them was sent back across the Atlantic, for the Americans to drink.

The Canadian distillers were soon on to the same ruse. As Haynes sarcastically commented, the residents of British Columbia, who had previously shown no enthusiasm for American whiskey, suddenly become so enamoured of it that they required 200,000 gallons. They, too, had been careful to honour the pledge that they were not going to drink it; they had promptly re-exported it to California.

The French, too, had not been disposed to let their wine and brandy trade to the United States be terminated. The islands of St. Pierre and Miquelon became the equivalent of Lintin. There were only about 4,000 inhabitants and they were soon buying 1,000 gallons per head, annually, of various liquors. Their harbours were thronged with depot ships, supplying schooners designed to carry 50,000 gallons, which could cruise in safety outside the three-mile limit for weeks at a time, waiting for smuggling craft which came out from the shore, or taking with them their own equivalent of the 'fast crabs' — speed boats which were faster than anything the American customs possessed, and which could run a consignment ashore, land it, and return to the parent ship in the course of a night. If it were too risky to put it ashore, they would dump it on the seabed, with a buoy to mark its position, and leave the vendor to collect it when he judged it safe to do so (a standard wine drinkers' joke was that the test whether a bottle of wine was a genuine import was the mud on the bottle).

There was also piracy. Prohibition had not been many months in force before Haynes received a report that pirate ships were beginning to operate along the Atlantic coast. 'Their method of operation is to learn of the destination and route of a boat regularly engaged in smuggling from the Bahamas and then overtake it, overpower the crew, and remove the cargo of liquor to the pirate boats.' Piracy even came to the Great Lakes, where men in 'swift little motor boats' waited just out of sight of land to intercept the smugglers, knowing the smugglers could not call on the law to protect them.

In one respect, Haynes was worse off than Lin had been. He had the land frontier with Canada to protect — as long as the distance from England to India, he ruefully noted. For much of its length it was marked only on the map; and, as somebody had put it, 'you cannot keep liquor from dripping through a dotted line'. The American enforcement officials could actually watch the liquor arriving, and being put into warehouses across the border; but they were themselves being watched, and no move would be made until at a signal from the American side, small boats or lorries would run the consignments across. It was more difficult — one of Haynes' men who had been a G.I. complained — than trench warfare in France; 'over there we could shoot them or grab them where we saw them, or go right in and get them; but over here we've got to wait till they come over to our side of no man's land.'

So, bootlegging had already become a major industry; and the consequences, Haynes did not attempt to hide, had been catastrophic. As there could be no legal redress if inferior, or even poisonous, liquor was passed off as gin or whiskey, the consumer had no protection. In Chicago, coroners' verdicts revealed that a hundred people had died in the first five months in 1923 from drinking 'bootleg hooch'; and the real figure, he felt, must certainly have been far higher.

Equally serious was the way in which Prohibition was breeding corruption. Forty-three of Haynes' agents had been found guilty of illegalities in Philadelphia alone; and although he claimed that this represented only a small proportion of the total force, he was careless enough in another part of his book to stress that the number of such offenders caught was 'doubtless but a fraction of those who are guilty'. Nor was it only his men who became involved. Reports of a trial in an Indiana town disclosed that liquor had been freely on sale there in saloons — and even in soft drink establishments; the proprietor of one of them complained that he had had to mortgage his premises, in order to pay the protection money demanded of him. This was the result of a conspiracy which

> included the mayor, the sheriff, a judge of the city court, the prosecuting attorney of the county, a former sheriff, a former prosecuting attorney, a detective sergeant, a justice of the peace, an influential lawyer, and former deputy sheriffs, detectives, policemen, petty lawyers, bartenders, cabaret singers and notorious women.

Haynes naïvely believed that the publicity given to the Indiana trial would lead to increasing respect for the law. But the sentences passed on the conspirators, considering the enormity of their offence, had been derisory; and he had to admit that the light fines often imposed in such cases had 'contributed in no small way to the spirit of defiance in which bootleggers hold the law'. Although there had been a fair haul of little fish, the big-time violators had found little difficulty in avoiding prosecution — or, if they were prosecuted, in escaping conviction.

*Repeal*

The story of Prohibition has been told too often to need repeating. It was to last for another ten years, with the forces of the law becoming annually more disillusioned, more ineffectual, and more corrupt, while the bootleggers became richer, more powerful and — as Sidney Whipple was to show in his *Noble Experiment* — more ingenious; especially the smugglers. They would arrange for consignments to be periodically intercepted by a customs man who was in their pay, so that he could lull suspicions; perhaps even get himself written up as a hero in the local newspapers. So much a matter of course did the traffic from Canada become that the prices obtainable for consignments in the nearest United States city would be available in bars — as the price of opium had been listed in Jardine's Canton newspaper.

The initial reaction to Prohibition's failure was a demand for higher penalties, as a deterrent; and these were duly imposed in many States. In Michigan, a mandatory scale of penalties was laid down, culminating at the fourth offence with imprisonment for life. When the first life sentence was imposed, the culprit turned out to be not the local Al Capone but Mrs Etta May Miller, mother of ten, whose fourth offence was being found in illicit possession of a bottle of gin. That was an extreme example: but because it was so rare for any of the men who ran the bootlegging industry to be convicted, the policy of high penalties fell into disrepute; as did Prohibition.

Even in 1923, Haynes had lamented, there had been those who undermined the law by criticising it; particularly the smartly dressed men and women, in fashionable drawing rooms or restaurants,

> The colour deepens on milady's cheek; the voice of her escort grows thick.
> What are they saying as the pocket flasks run low?
> 'Prohibition is a joke ... it can never be enforced ... it's dead easy to get all you want ... they can never make this city dry ... popular opinion's against the law.

As the 1920s went by, such opinions came to be more often heard, until even President Hoover was forced to realise that Prohibition's effects were destructive — and embarrassing, in terms of the international reputation of the United States (with the possible exception of the Prince of Wales, Capone was the world's best known public figure). As Hoover had described Prohibition as 'this noble experiment', and had won election with the help of 'dry' votes, he could not very well demand that it should be repealed; instead, he resorted to the traditional expedient of a Commission of Enquiry — ten men and the President of Radcliffe, Ada Comstock. They studied the subject for eighteen months, and in spite of the fact that they had a built-in conservative Republican bias, they had to concede in their report, published early in 1931, that Prohibition had failed. There was a mass of evidence, they had found, of drinking 'in homes, in clubs, and in hotels; of drinking parties given and attended by persons of high standing and respectability; of drinking by tourists at winter and summer resorts; and of drinking in connection with public dinners and at conventions'. There was similar evidence of drinking by women, and by the country's youth: 'votes in colleges show an attitude of hostility to or contempt for the law on the part of those who are not unlikely to be leaders in the next generation'. The same

attitude was also to be found in the views and the conduct of well-
off citizens in the average community, and 'in the tolerance of
conduct at social gatherings which would not have been possible
a generation ago'. Taking the country as a whole,

> people of wealth, business men and professional men and their
> families, and, perhaps, the higher paid working men and their
> families, are drinking in large numbers in quite frank disregard
> of the declared policy of the National Prohibition Act.

One reason, the Report continued, was people's irritation with
State interference in a matter where they felt the State had no
business interfering.

> In consequence, many of the best citizens of every community,
> on whom we rely habitually for the upholding of law and order,
> are at most lukewarm as to the national Prohibition Act. Many
> who are normally law-abiding are led to an attitude hostile to
> the statute by a feeling that repression and interference with
> private conduct are carried too far. This is aggravated in many
> of the larger cities by a feeling that other parts of the land are
> seeking to impose on them.

As a result, crime had become rampant, the huge profits
enabling bootleggers to defy attempts to enforce the law; and
there were 'revelations of police corruption in every type of
municipality, small and large, throughout the decade'.

The report alarmed Hoover, less for its depressing verdict than
because of the implications for his forthcoming Presidential
campaign, when he would need the 'dry' vote. He held meetings
with the Commission, and managed to persuade them that however disastrous the consequences of Prohibition might be, this
was not the time to end it; which enabled him to claim that 'by
a large majority' the Committee 'does not favour the repeal of the
18th Amendment as a method of cure for the inherent abuses of
the liquor traffic. I am in accord with this view.' Collectively, as a
Committee, this was what they had agreed. But only three of
them, as individuals, had supported the continuance of the Act.

The rest, for their own reasons, had recommended either that it should be repealed, or substantially revised.

As it happened, there was by this time a further argument against Prohibition, which may have been decisive; the need to provide more employment, and more revenue, following the great crash. The prices of illicit liquor in general had held so steady during the whole Prohibition period that it was actually possible to assess, with a reasonable expectation of accuracy, what the Government could expect to get from duties if the trade was again legalised; roughly the same, it was found, as it got from income tax. 'Dry' influence was still sufficiently feared for Franklin D. Roosevelt to refrain from actively denouncing Prohibition in the 1931 Presidential campaign; but he pledged himself, if elected, to put the Prohibition issue to the individual States. By the end of the year following his election, enough of them had ratified repeal to bring the noble experiment to an end.

# 11

# *The International Anti-drug Campaign*

IT HAD NOT NEEDED THE FAILURE OF PROHIBITION TO TEACH THE Americans that if drugs were to be controlled in domestic use, the need would arise for international regulation, too. Half a century before, there had been alarm at the spread of opium smoking introduced by the Chinese who came to work in California; and also at the more insidious form of opium consumption indulged in by the growing numbers of Americans who were persuaded to take tonics or cordials which had the drug as a prime constituent. After the Americans took over the Philippines, too, they became concerned about opium consumption there. Measures to check the traffic proving unsuccessful, the idea of imposing international control was mooted; and by a fortunate chance, the opportunity suddenly presented itself to secure international agreement.

## *The Shanghai conference*

For some years, the improvement in the quality of the opium produced in China had been reminding the British in India that their hold on the Chinese market could not last much longer. Indian opium — the Hong Kong *Daily News* had warned in the 1880s — was becoming a drug on the market 'in more senses than one'; the day would soon come when the native Chinese article would be exported. Exports from India to China, which had risen decade by decade for so long, began to fall, the quantity of home produced opium in China surging rapidly past the quantity imported.

In December 1905 the Conservative Government in Britain, which had held power for a decade, resigned; and the following spring, the House of Commons unanimously adopted a resolution 'that this House reaffirms its conviction that the Indo-Chinese opium traffic is morally indefensible, and requests His Majesty's Government to take such steps as may be necessary for bringing it to a speedy close'. The new Liberal Government, urged on by its backbenchers' humanitarian zeal, opened negotiations with the Chinese by offering to reduce opium exports annually, provided they reduced home production, step by step, and did not import from other countries. If all went smoothly, in ten years' time the traffic could cease. The Chinese unhesitatingly accepted. 'It is hereby commanded,' the imperial edict ran, 'that within a period of ten years the evils arising from foreign and native opium be equally and completely eradicated.'

The American Government, alerted by the authorities in the Philippines, realised that if India and China really did reduce production there was a chance that the United States' problems could be solved, too, provided that other countries did not expand production. Through the prompting of the State Department, an International Conference was convened in Shanghai in 1909 to study the whole opium problem. All the major countries with an interest in the traffic were invited and only one, Turkey, did not send a representative, owing to her domestic upheavals — a valid enough excuse, as they were to lead to the victory of the Young Turks, and the deposition of Abdul the Damned. The representatives of the remaining thirteen states met, conferred, and agreed in principle that there was a need for greater effort on the part of their Governments to control the traffic in opium and its derivatives, particularly morphine.

The Shanghai Conference had been arranged only for an exchange of views; but its success prompted President Taft to call for a Conference of Delegates with plenipotentiary powers. It met at The Hague in 1911, attended by the representatives of China, France, Germany, Great Britain, Italy, Japan, the Netherlands, Persia, Portugal, Russia, Siam and the U.S.A. And again, a heartening measure of agreement was reached. In future, it was agreed, the production and distribution of raw opium should be carefully regulated, and its export to other countries permitted only to duly authorised persons, through duly authorised channels. The production, distribution and consumption of prepared opium — the kind normally used for smoking — was gradually to be suppressed altogether, so that trade in it would cease. The production and distribution of opium derivatives was to be restricted to the amounts required for medical and scientific purposes. The necessary licensing arrangements, the delegates agreed, would be introduced by their respective States, when they ratified the agreement.

Crucial to the success of the whole enterprise, clearly, was the satisfactory working of the Anglo-Chinese agreement. And it had far surpassed expectations — as even the sceptical British Consul-General in China, Sir Alexander Hosie, was compelled to admit. As he had toured the poppy growing areas of China in the 1880s, he could make the necessary comparisons; and touring them again in 1910, he found that poppy cultivation in some provinces had virtually ceased, and in most others had been greatly reduced. Public opinion, it appeared, had been roused against opium, in much the same way as it had been aroused against spirits in Ireland by Father Mathew, but with the added element of patriotic fervour, opium still being identified with foreign oppression. And in a country as heavily populated as China, it was easy to detect and prevent poppy cultivation, when the will was there. Although the revolution in the central provinces in 1911, and the subsequent breakdown of the central Government's authority, meant that the drive finally to eliminate opium production lost momentum, enough had been accomplished to show that it might be possible to achieve that purpose, when order was restored.

In India, too, opium production was being steadily reduced — or so the authorities claimed. But on a visit to Japan in 1916 the young American writer Ellen La Motte met a Hindu, who assured her that the authorities were lying. They had reduced production only so long as there was no alternative, because the Chinese market was slipping from their grasp; but they were still deeply involved in the traffic. At the time, La Motte assumed his allegations were the product of his nationalist fervour; but in the year which she spent touring Eastern countries, she came to realise that they were wholly justified.

As soon as the agreement to reduce exports of Indian opium to China had been entered into, she discovered, every effort had been made to evade it. The simplest way had been to send opium to the International Settlements in the Treaty Ports, which were not 'China' for export purposes. As a result — a Shanghai missionary had shown — the number of licensed opium dealers in the International Settlement there had risen from 87 before the agreement, to 663 in 1914; and the value of opium imports into the Settlements had nearly trebled. The figures published showing the reduction in exports of opium to China also concealed the fact that much of it was finding its way there in a different, derivative, form. Board of Trade returns disclosed that exports of British morphine to the Eastern countries had been rising rapidly; from five and a half tons in 1911 to fourteen tons in 1914.

Although the acreage under poppy cultivation in India had fallen following the agreement with China, Ellen La Motte was able to show that the fall had stopped by the time war broke out, and output had begun to rise again. Such confidence did the British Government have that the market, so far from continuing to contract — as the Hague Convention envisaged — would remain buoyant, that a loan made to Persia was guaranteed from the Persian opium revenue. Although the Persian delegate had signed the Hague Convention, La Motte recalled, his Government did not ratify it: 'no wonder!'

## The League of Nations

By the time the first of La Motte's exposures of the duplicity of the British Government's opium policy appeared, however — in 1920 — the League of Nations had been established; and one of its functions was to take over the supervision of international agreements such as the Hague Convention. At the League's first meeting, an advisory committee on opium and other drugs was set up, with two functions; to collect and analyse information on the drug traffic, and to try to persuade member States to keep the regulations laid down to control it. The information collected, when analysed, revealed that La Motte's strictures had been justified.

The Hague Convention was revealed as no more than a string of aspirations.

The contracting nations, for example, had pledged themselves to control the output of raw and prepared opium; but they had been careful not to say how, or when. They had promised to manufacture no more opium derivatives than were required for scientific and medical purposes; but they had not settled how much was required. And even when specific pledges had been made — for example, to end the trade in prepared opium — there had been nothing to stop merchants in the countries which had previously imported it ordering, instead, the equivalent amount of raw opium, and processing it themselves.

Britain, as the chief opium producer, was the chief beneficiary; but firms in many countries shared in the profits, particularly in Switzerland, already providing a haven for those who were evading their own country's fiscal laws. The Dutch merchants were also well placed. Although their Government had been host to the Hague Conference, and had been nominally in charge of securing adherence to the Convention until the League took over, it had neglected to make any regulation requiring returns from Dutch companies of their output of morphine or cocaine. There was consequently no legal means of telling whether they were conforming to the Hague code. Nor would the figures, had they been supplied, necessarily have been reliable. The Hague Convention, in requesting that relevant statistics should be furnished, had neglected to make any provision to ensure that the statistics would be accurate. At their fifth session, the members of the Opium Committee of the League were presented with, among other documents, two sets of figures; one from the British, purporting to be the amounts of morphine exported from Britain to Japan

| Year | British exports of morphine to Japan lb | Japanese imports of morphine from Britain lb |
| --- | --- | --- |
| 1916 | 7,257 | 37,898 |
| 1917 | 1,825 | 41,509 |
| 1918 | 0 | 7,749 |
| 1919 | 0 | 4,716 |
| 1920 | 1 | 11,741 |

between 1916 and 1920; the other from the Japanese, purporting to be the amounts of morphine imported from Britain in the same period.

No satisfactory explanation could be found for the discrepancies — or for the one pound of morphine exported in 1920; but at least they alerted the League to the futility of relying on information provided by interested parties.

The British blandly used such evidence to justify their policy of keeping opium a government monopoly. British governments, the implication was, could not lie, nor could they cheat. In reply to La Motte and others who accused them of exploiting the drug for revenue, they reverted to the old excuse that, on the contrary, they were keeping the duty high to discourage consumption. She had shown that in the Straits Settlements, in the first decade of the century, opium duties had sometimes provided the bulk of the revenue — a fact which, as it had been reported to Parliament by a commission of enquiry, the Government could not easily dispute. But — the League's Opium Committee was told — this was precisely why the Colonial Government had acquired monopoly powers in 1910 — for the purpose of 'gradual and effective suppression'. The Government had implemented that policy by drastically reducing the number of licensed opium dens, which had fallen from 500 in 1909 to 200 in 1922, and by putting up the price. It was only later that the statistics, when they were published, revealed that so far from the suppression policy being effective, the State monopoly had actually contrived to sell more opium, in spite of the reduction in the number of licensed dens. Coupled with the higher price, this had meant a most gratifying increase of revenue; in 1918 opium still accounted for sixty per cent of the Straits Settlements' entire income.

In India, too, the Government was doing its best to recoup some of the losses following the agreement with China by encouraging the sale of opium under licence; when in 1921 the young Gandhi called for a campaign against 'that other oppressor' — as he described the drug — his followers were arrested on charges of 'undermining the revenue'. So little concerned were the British about the views of the League of Nations that after a Commission under Lord Inchcape had investigated India's finances in 1923, its report, while recognising that it might be necessary to reduce opium production again if prices fell, went on to warn against diminishing the area cultivated, because of the need to safeguard 'this most important source of income'.

## The 1925 Convention

By this time, public opinion in the United States had been roused; and in February 1923 a Resolution was put before the House of Representatives in Washington by Stephen Porter, Chairman of the Foreign Affairs Committee, arguing that the crucial factor was overproduction of opium. At the very most, the world needed 125 tons of opium for medical and scientific purposes — less than one-tenth of what was currently being produced. All the evidence, he said, went to show that in such circumstances, 'habit-forming narcotic drugs, by reason of their extraordinary nature, will overcome all barriers, even the bars of prisons' — and he quoted Sir John Jordan, by this time a member of the League of Nations Opium Committee, 'Whatever and wherever opium is produced it will reach the consumer.' To try to control the traffic by even the most drastic of laws was futile; the only hope for effective control was to get the producing nations to cut production. Both Houses of Congress unanimously agreed to ask the President to request the producer nations to accept the necessary regulations. In the autumn, the Assembly of the League called a fresh conference, with delegates from interested member countries (and from the United States, though she was not a member) with plenipotentiary powers, to see what could be done to improve upon the Hague Convention.

To Ellen La Motte, who came to Geneva from America to report on its deliberations, it was a heartening experience. Here were delegates from most of the great nations of the world coming together to grapple with one of the greatest of man-made evils; and the most impressive feature of all, she felt, was the integrity and dedication of the representatives of the countries which had suffered most. 'One fact emerged clearly', she wrote in her first report to the *Nation* magazine. 'The whole Orient is anxious to put down opium.' But some of the European nations were equally anxious to keep it up. Britain, as the European country which controlled the major source of opium, would be the key; 'if Britain yields, the rest will collapse'.

At the first meeting, the British delegates showed themselves apparently ready and anxious to yield. They raised no objection to the proposal, backed by the Americans and the Chinese, that opium production and distribution should in future be limited by international agreement. The only question — the British delegates suggested — was how? The answer, the Americans replied, was simple. An estimate should be made of the quantity of opium and its derivatives required for medical and scientific purposes, and production limited to that amount by international agreement. Again, the British agreed, merely stipulating that the term 'legitimate' should be added to 'medical and scientific'.

It seemed reasonable; but as the Americans soon realised, it effectively sabotaged their proposal. One by one the delegates of the colonial powers rose to explain what uses for opium, in their own colonies, they would consider 'legitimate'. The Dutch pointed out that allowance must be made for custom; smoking opium might be evil, but it had been eaten from time immemorial in the Dutch East Indies. The French found it difficult to understand why it should be considered any better to eat opium than to smoke it; if consumption was going to be permitted at all, there was no reason to suppress it simply because of the way it was taken (in French Indo-China, opium was usually smoked). The British agreed. What mattered was not how the drug was taken, but for what purpose; they could not regard the use of opium as a 'family drug' as illegitimate (in India, opium was licensed for sale as a family drug). Each delegate assured the Americans of his country's willingness to accept their proposal, so long as it was understood that each country had the right to decide what form of consumption was legitimate in its own colonies, and how much could be produced to cater for it. The Americans, disillusioned, quit the Conference, the British explaining that it was all the Washington Government's fault, for giving them firm instructions which left no room for compromise. But La Motte was sure that the instructions which the British delegates had received had been just as firm — 'make it as difficult as you like for a person to buy a grain of heroin, but don't hamper an "authorised person" from ving a ton, from time to time, as he pleases'. The British, though, had been careful not to reveal their policy.

The British had certainly behaved as if 'don't touch production' had been their brief. When the Chinese urged them to introduce restrictions in their own colonial territories, they fell back on the argument they had adopted a century before: what would be the use? Some other country would simply move in on the market, and keep the colonies supplied by smuggling. The British delegates scarcely bothered to conceal which 'other country' they assumed would do the smuggling: China. For a hundred years they had argued that they could do nothing to prevent opium from British colonies being smuggled into China. Now, with exasperating logic, they were claiming they would be able to do nothing to prevent Chinese opium from being smuggled into British colonies. Following the American example, the Chinese delegation departed.

The colonial powers, however, were careful to avoid giving the impression that they were blocking reform. An impressive-looking list of proposals for control of the opium traffic was adopted before the Conference adjourned.

Coca and Indian hemp were added to the list of substances which were to be restricted. The contracting countries were to 'undertake' to enforce the regulations — rather than, as the Hague agreement had put it, to 'use their best endeavours' to enforce them. A permanent Central Narcotics Board was to be established, to which the contracting countries would be required to make returns of all imports and exports of the listed drugs, and also to show, separately, the estimated amounts required for medical and scientific purposes. When there was evidence of excessive production or importation, the country concerned could be asked to give an explanation. An international accounting agency, with powers to investigate, was also to be set up; and the contracting parties agreed to accept compulsory arbitration in any dispute arising out of the new Convention which could not be settled by other means. Considering the difficulties which the Conference had faced, not least through the withdrawal of the Americans and Chinese, its achievements appeared very creditable, on paper.

American observers were not deceived. A former Editor of the *New York Evening Post* and Chief of the Washington Bureau of the Associated Press, John P. Gavit, had been covering the meetings; and he asked himself, when they were over, what steps the Conference had taken 'reasonably calculated to limit the manufacture of these substances or the production of the raw material from which they are made'. The answer, he felt bound to emphasise, was 'none whatsoever'. Only two of the decisions, he felt, had held out any promise: that relevant information would be more carefully scrutinised and correlated: and that the permanent Central Narcotics Board was to be composed of men who 'by their technical competence, impartiality, and disinterestedness will command general confidence' — they were to be given five-year contracts, further to reduce their dependence on their own governments. But Gavit was obviously not the only person to have realised that a strong independent central board, by publicising the relevant information, would be able to expose which States were failing in their duty. Switzerland, whose pharmaceutical industry handled much of the European narcotics traffic, promptly served notice that if the information she forwarded to the Board was disclosed to her disadvantage, 'she would forthwith cease to furnish any'.

The Swiss need not have worried; the central board was never set up, its place being taken by an advisory committee. Only one of its members, La Motte reported, was dedicated to controlling the opium traffic; the representative of China. The rest were dedicated to preventing control from becoming effective, with the help of ingenious procedural techniques. One British delegate would insist upon open sessions, on principle. Another would agree, but put the reasons why, in practice, this or that particular issue ought more properly to be discussed in private; a proposition which would be gratefully accepted by the other colonial powers. At public sessions of the Opium Advisory Committee, the Chairman would proceed with remarks like

'Gentlemen, you have read Document 418? I take it there is no discussion? Good. We will now pass on to Document 419.'

Sometimes, too, the reference would be to a numbered paragraph in a document which had not been made available to the press. As a result the 'open' sessions were productive mainly of gibberish.

La Motte was, however, able to unearth one news story of interest: that the British Government was proposing to extend its opium operations in India. When criticised for over-production there, the British had long replied that at least the opium was going up in smoke; it was highly esteemed for that purpose, but no good for extracting derivatives like morphine. Now, the League heard that this was incorrect. Indian opium could produce admirable morphine — and the British had decided to go into morphine production in India for themselves.

## Alexander's travels

La Motte's conviction that the British were pretending to support the League only to mask their own design — the extraction of the maximum revenue possible from opium — was soon to be given confirmation. In 1927 H. G. Alexander was offered a travelling fellowship to investigate the drug problem in the Far East; and after his return to England he published an account of what he had found. He made no secret of his own view, derived from the time when his father had been Secretary of the Society for the Suppression of the Opium Traffic; this, he claimed, had simply made him more careful to rely only on sources which could not be regarded as prejudiced against the traffic, such as the reports of the Indian Revenue, Customs and Excise Departments. And they revealed that it was still Government policy to encourage the production not merely of opium, but also of Indian hemp — even when there were complaints about the effects. Thus, in the report of the Excise Department of the United Provinces for the financial year 1926–7, the inhabitants of the Benares region were criticised as 'most depraved in respect of the use of intoxicants, although it is the very centre of the sacred soil of the Hindus'; yet the same report boasted that 'the downward tendency in the sales of *charas* has now been arrested', and disclosed that consideration was being given to a proposal for the cultivation of more hemp to produce more *ganja* and, therefore, more revenue. The sales of hard liquor were also growing. When any suggestion was made that they ought to be reduced, the reply would be along the lines given in the Excise Report for the Bombay Presidency for 1925–6; attempts to curb legal sales merely increased illicit traffic, so that there was 'no improvement in temperance, increasing contempt for law and

authority, and demoralisation of the inadequate excise staff' —
as well as, of course, 'loss of revenue'.

So while the British Government was professing to be taking
measures to reduce consumption of opium and hemp drugs, its
agents in India were in fact busy pushing sales in order to increase
the colony's revenue. Alexander did not know what should be done
— or could be done. Control, he admitted, would not be easy,
and might require a different approach in different circumstances;
as between town and country, say. But of one thing he was certain:
whatever policies were adopted, they should not be left to Britain
or to any other colonial power to decide or enforce, or the situation would get worse: with, in all probability, destructive consequences — for the colonial powers, as well as for their colonies.

> Even in the limited sphere of drug and drink habits, the main
> guilt of the West, for which sooner or later, the East will call
> us to account, arises from the export of manufactured habit-
> forming drugs, such as morphine and cocaine, and from the
> export of spirits. So long as we go to the East with these things
> in our hand, Chinese and Indians and Malays are not likely to
> have much use for the programmes of social reform that we carry
> in the other.

### 'The Smugglers' Reunion'

In the meantime, Ellen La Motte had been trying to keep the
American public informed about what was going on at 'The Smugglers' Reunion', as the disillusioned newspaper correspondents in
Geneva dubbed the League's Opium Committee. She had found
an ally: the Italian delegate, Signor Cavazzoni. He was probably
simply there to make mischief for Mussolini's amusement; but he
made it entertainingly. The Opium Committee's only response was
to find a new way to make things more difficult for correspondents;
it was agreed to cut down on the number of their proceedings
printed — 'to save paper', they claimed. La Motte was sure it was
to enable them to doctor the records. Events were to show she
was right.

At this point the British delegates created a surprise, by proposing that the League should send a fact-finding mission to the
Far East to investigate the opium situation there. This proposal,

they could claim, showed they had nothing to hide. But as Gavit had already warned in his *Opium*, published in 1925, it was part of the colonial powers' game to keep the general public under the impression that drug taking was an exotic Oriental vice, slipping into Western countries through the docks and slums; whereas in fact the real danger lay not in opium or hashish from the 'depraved' East, but in the drugs which were coming from the expensively equipped, skilfully and scientifically conducted pharmaceutical laboratories of the 'civilised' West — Britain, the United States, France, Holland, but chiefly from Switzerland and Germany. The fact-finding mission was being deliberately sent to the wrong place. And the British had another motive, as one of their delegates admitted to La Motte: 'what we really want is independent proof of our inability to carry out our obligations under the Hague Convention'. The British memorandum on the project emphasised that in spite of the vigilance of their customs officials in colonies like Malaya and Hong Kong, smuggling had greatly increased, and now 'seriously embarrassed the Governments of those territories'. Smuggled opium or morphine were indeed embarrassing: they reduced the colonial revenue.

Having proposed the Commission, the British were in a good position to limit its terms of reference, which they did by insisting that only the distribution and consumption of opium — not production — should be studied. Three Commissioners were chosen: a Belgian economist and two members of the diplomatic corps, from Czechoslovakia and Sweden. Their qualifications for selection remain obscure. They held sittings in more than thirty different centres within the space of seven months, which precluded any possibility of investigation in depth — though as they were careful to explain, staying longer would not have helped, as the kind of information they were looking for was not available. They had hoped to be shown the results of research; but

> in this field little has been done. Even the question of how much morphine a smoker or an eater of opium absorbs is unsolved. Practically every question connected with the opium smoking problem needs scientific study. A few examples of problems requiring investigation are the actual effects of opium smoking on the individual, the effect of dross upon the consumer, the

relative harmfulness of smoking and eating, the question of heredity . . . and the possibility of finding harmless substitutes.

The Commissioners, however, found no difficulty in collecting evidence in the form of personal views about opium; and what they heard surprised them. They had all three come out — they explained in their report — with the prevailing Western notion of the deleterious effects of opium on health, expecting to have it confirmed. But among the witnesses they examined, members of the indigenous races as well as the Chinese, they had found a widespread opinion that opium smoking was not harmful, the arguments in its favour 'reaching sometimes to a superstitious belief in the medicinal value thereof'. They also repeatedly came in contact with the opinion, based on personal experience, that opium used in moderation acted as a useful mental and physical stimulant, the physical stimulus being particularly valuable where people had to work hard under difficult climatic conditions. Even those notorious establishments, the 'opium dens' — or 'opium divans', as they were sometimes known — were far from being the haunts of depravity that Western fancy had depicted. They were 'often the only available resting places for the poor, and though they are not attractive, they are scarcely, even at their worst, more repulsive than the localities where the corresponding classes of the Western people consume beer or stronger alcoholic beverages'.

In general, the Commission's report did just what the British had hoped it would do. It fed doubt into the minds of members of the League whether opium should be regarded as a social menace; and it actually conceded that the system of government monopolies which had been established in British possessions was the best solution, because it presented the only means by which price and consumption could be controlled. Their policies, the British could boast, had been vindicated. But their scheme, as things turned out, had worked rather too well. It was not opium — the report went on to argue — that was the real trouble. It was opium's derivatives, morphine and heroin, 'a far more serious menace to the world'.

It had not taken long before heroin's pretensions to be a non-addictive drug had been exposed; and experience had shown that it was far more addictive than cocaine. The timing of the recommendation, too, was unfortunate for the manufacturing countries, as there had just been a succession of embarrassing scandals in connection with the statistics which each member nation was required to send to the League. Between 1925 and 1926, the returns had revealed, at least a hundred tons of morphine had disappeared — in other words, had been diverted from legal into illicit channels.

The countries concerned had manufactured the morphine, and declared it, as bound by the 1925 Convention to do; the morphine had then simply vanished. Some idea of what this disappearance involved could be gauged from the fact that the world requirements of morphine for medical and scientific purposes were put at less than forty tons a year.

A search promptly began for a scapegoat, and it was conveniently provided by Turkey, which had refused to ratify the Convention. If the Turks were to disclose their figures — the rumour ran — they might prove revealing. The Turks thereupon disclosed them, and they were indeed embarrassing; but not to the Turks. They showed that Turkey had exported more than two tons of morphine and four tons of heroin to European countries which had ratified the Convention. Under the Convention, they were required to declare all such imports. Assuming that Turkey would not disclose the deals, none of the countries involved had made the required declarations. Those consignments, too, had slipped into the illicit market.

For still better measure, the Turks threw in the information that in 1928 a single Alsace factory had manufactured nearly 9,000 lb of heroin — rather more than two and a half times the world's estimated medical and scientific needs, that year, and 8,920 lb more than the amount which the French had declared, in the production figures they provided to the League, for the three years 1926–8. The French Government, protesting its innocence, closed down the factory. The Turks were apparently expecting this move, as the chemists who lost their jobs were offered work in new heroin factories in Turkey,

How had the morphine and heroin been diverted? The 'Naarden Case' helped to clear up part of the mystery. Naarden, a Dutch firm, had been ordering huge consignments from other countries, including over 1,500 kg of heroin from a Swiss firm, and re-exporting them — but describing them as 'in transit', so that the

Dutch Government would not need to declare them in its returns to the League. But there were no statistics to reveal the drug's ultimate destination.

### The Blanco formula

These scandals attracted hostile publicity. It could no longer be pretended that the Hague Convention, even as 'strengthened' by the 1925 reforms, was working satisfactorily. But how could it be improved? The obvious solution was the one the Americans and Chinese had urged on the other States at the Geneva Conference; limitation of production of opium to the amount needed for medical and scientific purposes. The delegates of the manufacturing countries now announced that they were prepared to accept limitation, provided agreement could be reached on how it was introduced.

They were very careful to ensure that agreement would not be reached. It was accepted that each of the manufacturing nations should have a production quota; but none of them was prepared to accept a smaller share of the market than it already enjoyed; and the idea of simply freezing the share of each, at the level at which it had been on some agreed date, satisfied nobody, because, it was claimed, it would destroy freedom of choice for the purchaser in the future, and infringe national sovereignty.

The apparent deadlock had been broken by a member of the League Secretariat. A. E. Blanco, son of a Spanish father and a British mother, had been in the British-run Chinese Customs Service; he had given much thought to the matter. In future, he proposed, any country which wished to use a dangerous drug for medical or scientific purposes should declare in advance what supplies would be needed, and where it proposed to obtain them. In this way it would be possible to allocate quotas in advance, the world over, but without freezing the levels or restricting choice; so that if some manufacturer made a particularly good brand of medical heroin or morphine, he would be able to benefit the following year from increased demand.

The Blanco formula was the simple answer to the objections raised by the manufacturing countries: altogether too simple for their comfort. The Opium Advisory Committee — the 'Smugglers Reunion' — unable to think of any objection to the proposal, decided simply to ignore it. Blanco resigned in disgust, and there the matter would have ended, had his scheme not been brought to the notice of the influential American philanthropist, C. K. Crane.

Crane, struck by what he felt was the scheme's beautiful simplicity, recommended it in a letter to the State Department. It would automatically disclose the volume of the legitimate drug market in every country, he pointed out; yet it would leave producers free to compete for a larger share of the market, thereby minimising the need for government intervention to apportion quotas. At the same time, States' rights would not be infringed, as States could each decide what supply of a drug they needed. Prompted by Crane, the State Department drew the scheme to the attention of the Advisory Committee. The committee reacted as before. As the delegates could think of no valid objection, 'the only thing to do with the Scheme', the British representative suggested, 'is to bury it'; and on the motion of the Indian delegate, that 'the matter should simply be dropped', it was.

### Russell Pasha

But it was soon revived, and from an unexpected quarter: Egypt, then a British Protectorate, suffering from an uneasy sense of thwarted nationality.

Towards the end of the nineteenth century the authorities there had become increasingly worried by the number of young men who took to smoking opium or hashish, deserting families, jobs and society. Various measures had been adopted to control drug-taking. Hashish had sometimes been subjected to a heavy duty; sometimes prohibited, with heavy penalties, even death, for anybody caught with it. The frequent alterations of policy, though, were an indication of how ineffective the laws were; largely because they rarely applied to foreigners. The better the law was enforced in Egypt, the higher rose the price of opium or hashish; and the greater the profit would be to foreigners who could import the drugs with impunity and sell them through illicit channels, until the price came down again.

Malcolm Muggeridge was to describe in his autobiography how, when he went to teach at a school in Egypt in the 1920s, he observed that the students at Cairo University often seemed to be 'faraway, lost in some dream of erotic bliss; a consequence no doubt, in the case of many of them, of their addiction to hashish, widespread among the *effendi* class, and prevalent among the *fellahin*, particularly the ones who had moved into the towns'. The deleterious effects of this addiction, Muggeridge recalled, were then universally taken for granted,

> and the Egyptian authorities, following a plan of modernisation and national revival on the general lines of Kemal Ataturk's in Turkey, spent a lot of money and effort in an attempt to stamp it out. Russell Pasha, the head policeman and the last Englishman to hold the post, was particularly active in trying to prevent hashish getting into the country, and in reducing indulgence in it . . . if anyone had suggested that all this endeavour was misplaced because hashish did little harm, and was anyway nonaddictive, the suggestion would have been received with incredulity and derision.

And Muggeridge went on to use the recollection as the text for a sermon denouncing the apologists for cannabis half a century later; 'I know of no better exemplification of the death wish in the heart of our way of life than this determination to bring about the legalisation of hashish, so that it may ravage the West as it has the Middle and Far East.'

The passage in his autobiography happens also to be an interesting exemplification of the way in which moral attitudes can colour memories. 'Russell Pasha' — Thomas Wentworth Russell — did indeed devote a great deal of time and energy to trying to keep hashish out of Egypt. Those were his orders, and he carried them out with intelligence and integrity. But he did not think hashish was a menace. He divided drugs into two categories, 'white', and 'black'. Hashish — 'the vice of the city slums' — was in the white category; it did 'comparatively little harm', he felt, and could not be held responsible for the country's addiction problem. It would be more sensible, he believed, to legalise the white drugs. According to his friend and biographer Baron d'Erlanger, he announced that 'he was seriously considering some form of government monopoly whereby hashish would be grown domestically, and its smoking would be licensed and made to produce revenue for the Egyptian Government, instead of costing

̤̤ormous sums for the prohibition and, in addition, draining the country of the money which was sent abroad to pay for the foreign grown raw material'.

The idea proved unacceptable to his superiors; Russell had to continue to try to prevent hashish smuggling into Egypt. But his main preoccupation was with the black drugs, heroin (which a missionary, Herbert Hayes, identified as the main threat as early as 1922) and cocaine (according to a report from the American consul in Cairo in 1923, fashionable men and women could be seen stopping their automobiles so that they 'could buy their stuff, and sniff it on the sidewalk'). It was heroin, though, Russell recalled in his autobiography, 'which nearly killed Egypt'. D'Erlanger agreed; by 1929, when Russell was appointed Director of the Egyptian Central Narcotics Bureau, it had pushed opium, hashish and cocaine into the background. Heroin not merely provided 'a sensation of pleasant stupefaction, of happy contented drunkenness, of deadening comfortable drowsiness', which was what people had originally taken it for, but also 'a buoyancy of spirits, increased imagination, temporarily enlarged brain power, and a capacity to think of things which they would not otherwise have imagined'. But the price was a disturbing addiction rate. One in four of Egypt's adult male population, Russell estimated, became a black drug addict.

His first task had been to find how the heroin was coming into the country; something that had baffled the customs officials. From the start, according to d'Erlanger, 'a certain unromantic and sordid aspect was recognised and faced squarely; namely that the obtaining of reliable information is overwhelmingly a matter of money'. It was decided to pay informers so liberally that giving the required information would be more profitable than smuggling. There was an immediate and gratifying response, revealing where the heroin was to be found; 'in cases of olives; in tins of powdered glue, of butter; in barrels of tomato sauce, of oil, and of wine; in sacks of prunes; in millstones; in stoves with false bottoms: in carpenters' lasts; in the soles and heels of shoes; and even by means of tubes concealed in what Mrs Grundy might have called 'the most intimate recesses of the person' (a method which, d'Erlanger observed, 'starts quite an amusing line of thought when one remembers which was the most usual way of taking heroin for its pleasurable effects').

But as Russell soon realised, the men who were running the traffic were never caught, because they took good care that the actual smuggler, who might be caught, did not know who they were. As soon as they found their consignments were being intercepted, they switched them into different channels; and any temporary reduction in the supply of heroin available in Egypt actually helped them, by raising its price, to afford the increased outlay in payments to couriers, and in bribes to customs officials. And Russell found, as Commissioner Lin had done, that informers would realise they could again make more money by assisting the smugglers than by assisting the police; or, they could have it both ways by tipping the police off to the occasional consignment, while helping the bulk of the heroin to go through.

Russell was right; it was 'overwhelmingly a matter of money'. There was more than enough money in a single small tin labelled beans, but containing heroin, to persuade many officials to do no more than wink, as the crate full of tins of beans went through; and the financial resources of the traffickers stretched much further than those of the police. For Egypt to try to suppress heroin on her own, Russell realised, was a futile exercise. It could only be got rid of through an international agreement. It was with that objective that he went to Geneva to put Egypt's case to the League. Largely by the force of his personality, he finally goaded the delegates into activity.

For all his achievement, though, in alerting public opinion to the limitations of international control over the drug traffic, Russell did not disguise from himself the limitations of the general policy which he had been called on to carry out in Egypt. Whenever by energetic measures he succeeded in limiting for a while the supply of 'black' drugs, thereby pushing up the price beyond the means of many Egyptians who ordinarily took them, the enforced abstinence, he found, did them little good. They turned, instead, to a mixture of tobacco and henbane — impossible to deal with effectively by police measures, as tobacco was too well established to ban, and henbane grew wild. They even started to drink 'stewed' tea, in the quantities required to intoxicate them, with lamentable consequences 'to both their pockets and health'. So worried did the Egyptian authorities become that in the 1930s they closed the teashops, and smashed the utensils used to make and serve the tea. The addicts found other ways to get it. 'They are always searching for a stimulant', an Egyptian landlord told a committee of enquiry in 1933; and as they could no longer afford the harder drugs, or hashish, 'they are now finding it in this vile brew, to the damage of their health'.

The reason people became addicted in this way, the landlord suggested, would make an interesting subject for social and medical research. Russell would have agreed. He was a shrewd enough observer to realise that it was not the drugs, but the disposition to take them, that mattered. Why, he wondered, were the Egyptians so susceptible? Might the responsibility lie with the spread of parasite-carried diseases like bilharzia, following the changes in the level of the Nile as a result of the construction of the Aswan Dam? Whatever the cause, a drug or drugs was invariably found to assuage the craving. Coffee, hashish, opium, heroin . . . and now, stewed tea; 'and so it goes on'.

## The 1931 Convention

And so it went on; at Geneva, too, though not quite so smoothly as before for the members of the Opium Advisory Committee. When Russell arrived in Geneva in 1930 as Egypt's delegate to the Committee, the scene there was quickly transformed: internally, by his energetic efforts to find ways round the obstacles they had put up, and externally by the world-wide publicity his ideas and speeches attracted. When a meeting of delegates from the manufacturing countries that autumn failed to reach agreement, because of their unwillingness to accept quotas, the Blanco formula was revived, and in the summer of 1931, a modified version of it was at last accepted. In future, estimates of production and importation were to be made by each member country, based on medical and scientific needs and submitted, with explanatory memoranda, five months in advance. All exports of heroin were to cease; all illicit heroin seized was to be destroyed or rendered harmless; and all important cases of illicit trafficking were to be reported to the League.

From the legal point of view, the 1931 Convention was unique; the first not merely to apply the principles of a controlled economy to a group of commodities by international agreement, but also to regulate all phases of the production of dangerous drugs from the time the raw material entered the factory to the final acceptance of the finished product by hospital, laboratory, or chemist's shop. Its impact appeared to be instantaneous; by 1932 the price of raw opium was down to a quarter of what it had been in 1929. The Advisory Committee, which for so long had resisted the introduction of any such controls, now proudly boasted how well they were working. The figures presented by the manufacturing countries showed that they had begun to put the scheme into effect even before it had been formally ratified; the amounts being manufactured had 'closely approximated to, or even fallen below, the amounts which appear to be required for legitimate consumption'.

Gradually it became clear, though, that the fall in the price of opium had little to do with the new Convention. It was the great slump that had drastically reduced demand; the resulting surplus of opium and its derivatives had pushed down the price; and some governments were restricting the production of narcotics mainly in the hope of keeping the prices from falling further. When the international drug traffic began to recover, it was seen that the Convention was of little help in controlling it. The few countries which had refused to ratify were able to cater for illicit demand, wherever it was to be found; and modifications to the Blanco formula reduced its effectiveness. The advance estimates which countries presented to the League of their drug requirements, it was agreed, did not have to be precise. Illicit narcotics, if seized, need not, after all, be destroyed. And there were no sanctions to employ against governments which failed to fulfil their pledges.

The collapse of the Convention was described by Ferdinand Tuohy in his *Inside Dope*, published in 1934, illustrated by the 'news flashes' which he had collected while writing it; ranging from the discovery that 251 carrier pigeons were being employed by the inmates of a U.S. prison to keep them supplied with narcotics, to the report of the discovery by the French authorities of a smuggling trick of the kind recorded a century earlier by Commissioner Lin; a zinc-lined coffin from the Levant had been found to contain heroin, as well as the corpse, the plan being to allow the committal service and the burial to proceed, and 'for those in the deal on this side to act the ghoul later'. In spite of the optimism generated by Russell Pasha's impact at Geneva, Tuohy claimed, 'the dope stream is experiencing small difficulty in finding new channels'. And worse would follow. Earlier drugs — he cited hashish — had at least been 'natural'; it was the alkaloids, the derivatives, which were disastrous. And now, they were being duplicated by chemists; one of his 'news flashes' concerned the invention of a new synthetic drug, far stronger than morphine.

Tuohy's fears were confirmed by S. H. Bailey's more academic survey of the international campaign against drugs, published in 1936. The third phase of the campaign, as Bailey described it — the first had been initiated at The Hague, and the second by the revised Geneva Convention in 1925 — had not, he felt, been operational long enough to be fairly judged; but already administrative difficulties were making themselves felt. Any scheme for the limitation of drugs had to be

grafted on to the diverse legal and administrative roots of more than sixty independent States with their numerous and widely scattered protectorates, colonies, and leased or mandated territories. Desirable international measures may be obstructed by constitutional barriers in one country, or public sentiment in another. Handsome allowance has to be made for the variations in the efficiency, experience and reliability of administrative agencies in different territories.

And by 1936, the chances that these administrative problems would be solved was small. The League's authority was everywhere crumbling. The Japanese had defied it by occupying China north of the Great Wall; and although they could claim that by setting up their Manchukuo opium monopoly they were only following the British colonial pattern, as accepted by the League's own fact-finding mission, it seemed improbable in view of their record that they would use their powers to reduce production. Visiting Manchukuo for *The Times* in 1935 Peter Fleming asked himself the question, 'is the monopoly a crusade or a racket?'. On the evidence, he decided, it was clearly a racket. Opium dens had been opened to all, even teenagers; consumption was increasing; and the monopoly was already making huge profits — as the Japanese authorities cynically acknowledged, by imprinting a flowering poppy on their Manchukuo coins.

But even if the Japanese and all other producing countries had been willing to co-operate, Bailey warned, the effort might be futile, because of the development of synthetic drugs; 'the infinitely varied and variable series of narcotic substances which competitive research continues to discover and the medical profession of the world to demand'. And it would never be easy to control such enterprises because they were highly mobile; 'operations can be begun with little preparation in one centre and, when economic, legal or administrative conditions become less favourable, transferred to another'. It was a prophetic statement; but for the time, the drug manufacturers of illicit drugs hardly needed such assistance. With Mussolini leaving the League, and Hitler ignoring it, its authority was further eroded, and even the semblance of international control of the drug traffic disappeared.

# 12

# Heroin and Cannabis

WHILE THE LEAGUE HAD BEEN WRESTLING WITH THE PROBLEM OF controlling the international drug traffic, its member States had been going their individual ways, some paying little attention to the League's requests. The nation which came closest to carrying out the League's recommendations was, ironically, not a member: the United States; and the consequences of the methods it chose to adopt to stamp out drug-taking were to prove even more disastrous, though on a smaller scale, than Prohibition.

### The Harrison Act

The Harrison Narcotics Act, passed in 1914, was chiefly designed to restrict the use of opium and its derivatives to medical purposes, the doctor being permitted to prescribe them 'in the course of his professional practice only'. But the limits of what would constitute professional practice were left undefined. Was the doctor allowed to prescribe heroin to addicts — the maintenance dose, as it came to be known? Or did this fall outside his professional competence? The law enforcement officers took the view that it was no part of the profession's duty to indulge the addict with his drugs. Doctors who continued to provide patients with the maintenance dose found themselves liable to be arrested — which, even if they were not jailed, meant that they would face professional ruin. So the addict — as *American Medicine* commented soon after the Act came into effect — is 'deprived of the medical care he urgently needs; open, above-board sources from which he formerly obtained his drug supply are closed to him, and he is driven to the underworld where he can get his drug'. The underworld had no difficulty in supplying him. By the end of the First World War, an investigating committee found, the problem of addiction was more serious than ever in American cities. The illicit traffic in opiates had increased until it just about equalled the legal traffic, and the number of addicts had risen to around a million.

Predictably, the committee recommended tougher laws, and tougher enforcement: and in 1924 an Act was passed prohibiting the importation of heroin — this being the policy the United States delegates were trying to persuade the League of Nations Opium Conference to accept. The effect was rapid, and striking. Hitherto the profession had made little distinction between morphine and heroin addicts, the general assumption being that though heroin was the more addictive, the two drugs were not significantly different in their effects. But — according to Edward Brecher in his survey of the period in *Licit and Illicit Drugs* — hardly had the law been changed than morphine, though easier and cheaper to get, almost disappeared from the black market. So far from stopping the traffic, the *Illinois Medical Journal* complained in June 1926, the 'well-meaning blunderers' who had passed the Act had ensured that those who dealt in heroin could now 'make double the money from the poor unfortunates upon whom they prey'. All that the United States Government was doing was ensuring the prosperity of the bootleggers of narcotics, in the same way as they had ensured the prosperity of the bootleggers of alcohol, at enormous cost to the nation.

## The Rolleston Committee

What would have happened — it was often asked — if the American Government, instead of denying addicts their maintenance dose, had allowed them to have it on prescription? The easiest comparison was with Britain, which had had a similar problem with addiction to opiates in the early part of the century, arising out of ill-advised prescribing habits and the boom in patent medicines; and which had also passed a law, the 1920 Dangerous Drugs Act, designed to bring them under control. When the issue came up whether the maintenance dose should be allowed, however, the decision lay not with the law officers, as in

America, but with the Ministry of Health. The Ministry decided to appoint a committee, under Sir Humphrey Rolleston, to advise on it; and the committee sent one of its members, Dr Harry Campbell, to the United States to observe how the Harrison law was working.

As a consequence of the law, Dr Campbell reported,

> a vast clandestine commerce has grown up in that country. The small bulk of these drugs renders the evasion of the law comparatively easy, and the country is overrun by an army of peddlers who extort exorbitant prices from their helpless victims. It appears that not only has the Harrison law failed to diminish the number of drug-takers — some contend, indeed, that it has actually worsened it; for without curtailing the supply of the drug it has sent the price up tenfold, and this has had the effect of impoverishing the poorer class of addicts and reducing them to a condition of such abject misery as to render them incapable of gaining an honest livelihood.

The Rolleston Committee was exclusively medical in its com-position. One of the most cherished tenets of the medical pro-fession was that the doctor had a right to prescribe whatever he thought suitable for his patients, with or without the State's sanction. Dr Campbell had given the Committee just the kind of evidence they needed to justify the continuance of this policy. They recommended that doctors should be allowed to prescribe heroin not simply in the course of treatment, but also to the patient who, 'while capable of leading a useful and fairly normal life as long as he takes a certain non-progressive quantity, usually small, of the drug of addiction, ceases to be able to do so when the regular allowance is withdrawn'. The medical profession in Britain having more prestige and more influence than the American, the recommendation was accepted. As a result, though there was always a black market in the opiates between the wars, it remained very small. The addict who could get his heroin for a few pence on prescription was not going to pay ten times as much to a peddler.

In the United States, heroin addiction grew progressively more serious; for reasons given in 1936 by August Vollmer, who had

been Chief of Police in Berkeley, California, and subsequently a
Professor of Police Administration in Chicago:

> Stringent laws, spectacular police drives, vigorous prosecution
> and imprisonment of addicts and peddlers have proved not only
> useless and enormously expensive as means of correcting this
> evil, but they are also unjustifiably and unbelievably cruel in
> their application to the unfortunate drug victims. Repression
> has driven this vice underground and produced the narcotic
> smugglers and supply agents, who have grown wealthy out of
> this evil practice and who, by devious methods, have stimulated
> traffic in drugs. Finally, and not the least of the evils associated
> with repression, the helpless addict has been forced to resort to
> crime in order to get money for the drug.

Drug addiction, Vollmer went on to argue, was not a police
problem — 'it never has been and never can be solved by policemen'; it was a medical problem. Instead of penal sanctions, 'there
should be intelligent treatment of the incurables in outpatient
clinics, hospitalisation of those not too far gone to respond to
therapeutic measures, and application of the prophylactic principles
which medicine applies to all scourges of mankind'.

### Marihuana: Harry Anslinger

Vollmer was a respected figure — he was a former President of
the International Association of Chiefs of Police. But how little
attention was paid to his opinions could be gauged from the fact
that the following year, Congress passed a law bringing yet another
drug under federal prohibition: Indian hemp.

Before 1900, hemp had hardly rated as a drug in the United
States. This was not because of any lack of availability; in the
South, it had long been one of the main cash crops — grown by,
among others, George Washington, and encouraged by later
administrators, chiefly to provide fibres. It was no more regarded
as a plant drug than the morning glory — at least by the whites;
they preferred their tobacco and alcohol. Only the Southern black
slaves took it; as Richard Burton, who liked to compare different
types of hemp as other men like to compare different wines,
observed when he visited the region. He was interested to discover

that 'few of their owners had ever heard of it'. So little were its
narcotic properties known, let alone worried about, that S. S.
Boyce's treatise on hemp, published in New York in 1900,
contained no reference to them; and that same year the U.S.
Department of Agriculture announced that it had decided to
import experimental quantities of 'superior varieties of hemp seed'
from the East, for experiments to see how they would grow in
America.

Drugs made from hemp were used to a small extent in medicines;
and the Department, worried by the growing cost of imported
drugs, and with a view to making the United States self-sufficient
in her requirements, also embarked on a systematic survey over the
next few years to find how much was needed of hemp and other
plant drugs, and how and where they could best be grown. Experimental farms were established, at which tests could be made; and
hemp was found to do very well in the Eastern and upper Southern
States. Farms to produce it commercially were accordingly started
in Pennsylvania, Virginia, and South Carolina. During the war,
farmers were encouraged to produce still more, until they almost
fulfilled the country's entire requirements; a feat which was held to
be greatly to their credit by Henry Fuller in his survey of American
drugs, published in 1922.

During the 1920s, however, marihuana — as it came to be
described when taken for non-medical purposes — began to
acquire a sinister reputation; partly owing to the stories coming
out of Egypt, where hashish was still getting blamed for the
addiction rate; partly because it began to spread north into States
of the Union where it had not been known before. Some of them
banned it; and at the time the Federal Bureau of Narcotics was
set up under the wing of the Treasury Department in Washington
in 1930, there was a move to get marihuana banned throughout
the country. The Treasury was unimpressed. 'A great deal of public
interest has been aroused by newspaper articles,' its report claimed
in 1931, 'appearing from time to time on the evils of the abuse of
marihuana, or Indian hemp. This publicity tends to magnify the
extent of the evil and lends color to the inference that there is an
alarming spread of the improper use of the drug, whereas the
actual increase in such use may not have been inordinately large.'

The Chief of the new Narcotics Bureau, however, did not share the Treasury's view. Harry Anslinger had been Assistant Commissioner of Prohibition, and was understandably anxious to wipe out the memory of his failure to make it work. He was young — still in his thirties — ambitious; and filled with a deep repugnance for drugs dating back, by his own account, to an episode in his childhood. He had been born in Pennsylvania, near a township in which one adult out of ten was reputed to be an opium addict; and as a twelve-year-old, he heard a woman screaming in agony for the drug, a sound he never forgot. He had come to feel the same horror of marihuana.

The Federal Bureau of Narcotics, however, was originally drawn into the campaign against marihuana less by Anslinger's antipathy to the drug than for administrative simplicity. It had become obvious that narcotics could not be adequately controlled so long as each State had a different set of regulations, and a national Conference of Commissioners on Uniform State Laws had been considering how best to unify them. In 1932 they put forward a draft narcotics law which, it was hoped, all States would introduce, imposing prohibition except for medical purposes. At this stage, the decision whether or not to classify hemp as a narcotic within the meaning of the Act was left optional. Anslinger, regarding this as unsatisfactory, determined to arouse public opinion to the marihuana menace. His Bureau therefore prepared a brochure in which it was claimed that, 'those who are accustomed to habitual use of the drug are said eventually to develop a delirious rage after its administration during which they are temporarily, at least, irresponsible, and prone to commit violent crimes'; and that prolonged use was 'said to produce mental deterioration'.

'Said to' was a favourite Bureau phrase when there was no evidence who had done the saying. Anslinger had other devices, too, to rouse fear of marihuana. It had dropped out of general medical usage, he claimed, because its effects were too unpredictable. This was true; doctors did not find it easy to prescribe the appropriate dosage, because individual reactions were so varied. But Anslinger's interpretation of 'unpredictability' was his own. A patient, he explained, might not react at all; but he might 'go beserk'. And the young were particularly at risk; much of the prevailing crime, vice and gang warfare were due to the drug.

The Bureau's report for 1933 promised a propaganda campaign against marihuana. For a while, it did not 'take'; *The Reader's Guide to Periodical Literature*, Brecher was later to find, listed no article on the subject in the ten years 1925–35 — itself an indication of how little alarm the drug had been causing. Then, the flow began; and most of the articles either acknowledged the help of the Bureau, or showed internal evidence of having accepted it. Anslinger himself gave network radio broadcasts to arouse, as he put it, 'an intelligent and sympathetic public interest, helpful to the administration of the narcotic laws'. They emphasised marihuana's close relationship with hashish, and attributed to it 'a growing list of crimes, including murder'.

Anslinger's main aim was to shake Congress into action; and in this he succeeded. When in 1937 the Treasury introduced a Federal Marihuana Bill, putting the drug into the same category as the narcotics controlled by the Harrison Act, Congressmen were so little concerned to dispute the Bureau brief that the only serious opposition came from representatives of the bird seed industry. They managed, just in time, to put over their case that hemp seed, whatever it might do to humans, did only good to birds, upon whom it had no observable narcotic effects, and whose health — and plumage — suffered without it.

Having committed himself to prohibition of marihuana, Anslinger was aware he would need to justify himself by making a better job of enforcement than he had been able to do with either alcohol or heroin. The Bureau's campaign through the press intensified. In the same month — July — that the Act went through, an article by Anslinger appeared in the *American Magazine* purporting to recount some of the crimes committed under the influence of marihuana, which bore an interesting resemblance to those which had been described to an Indian Hemp Drugs Commission, including a murder in Florida:

> When officers arrived at the home they found the youth staggering about in a human slaughterhouse. With an axe he had killed his father, mother, two brothers and a sister. He seemed to be in a daze. . . . He had no recollection of having committed the multiple crime. The officers knew him ordinarily as a sane, rather quiet young man; now he was pitifully crazed. They

sought the reason. The boy said he had been in the habit of smoking something which youthful friends called 'muggle' a childish name for marihuana.

Anslinger omitted to provide any evidence that the smoking of muggle had been in any way responsible for the crime; but with his authority for it, the incident was to be used again and again, in later articles, by journalists who had found it among the files.

In one respect, the campaign was a little too successful for Anslinger's peace of mind. He had secured a fervent supporter in Earle Albert Rowell, a hot-gospeller, who had been touring America lecturing audiences on marihuana's effects. The drug, according to Rowell's thesis:

1 Destroys willpower, making a jellyfish of the user. He cannot say no.
2 Eliminates the line between right and wrong ...
3 Above all, causes crime, fills the victim with an irrepressible urge to violence.
4 Incites to revolting immoralities, including rape and murder.
5 Causes many accidents, both industrial and automobile.
6 Ruins careers for ever.
7 Causes insanity as its speciality.
8 *Either in self-defence or as a means of revenue, users make smokers of others, thus perpetuating evil.*

The italicised part of Rowell's creed was an embarrassment to the Narcotics Bureau, because it related to another of Rowell's beliefs; that in order to stamp out marihuana, it would be necessary also to ban tobacco, because smoking cigarettes led young people on to smoking marihuana. 'Slowly, insidiously', Rowell claimed,

for over three hundred years, Lady Nicotine was setting the stage for a grand climax. The long years of tobacco-using were but an introduction and training for marihuana use. Tobacco, which was first smoked in a pipe, then as a cigar, and at last as a cigarette, demanded more and more of itself until its supposed pleasures palled, and some of the tobacco victims looked about for something stronger. Tobacco was no longer potent enough.

It was no part of Anslinger's strategy to add to his difficulties with a campaign against tobacco: Rowell was repudiated.

Marihuana was now officially a 'black' or 'hard' drug. What this was going to mean was forecast by Dr Henry Smith Williams in 1938.

> With the aid of newspaper propaganda already started, an interest will be created in the alleged allurements of marihuana smoking; and the army of inspectors sent out to explore the millions of fields in which the weed may be grown need only apply, with slight modifications, the methods learned in the conduct of the narcotics racket, in order to develop a marihuana industry that could eclipse the billion dollar illicit narcotics racket of today. Racketeers ... should have no difficulty at all in developing a five billion dollar racket with marihuana — provided only that the press can be induced to stimulate curiosity by giving the drug publicity.

And the press, fed with more horror stories by Anslinger, duly did its worst.

### The La Guardia Report

Up to this point, there had been no attempt seriously to investigate the effects of marihuana in the United States. But when the Mayor of New York, Fiorello La Guardia, was urged to initiate a campaign against the drug, he recalled that many years before he had been impressed by a report on the subject by an army board in Panama, 'which had emphasised the relative harmlessness of the drug and the fact that it played a very little role, if any, in problems of delinquency and crime in the Canal Zone'. In 1939, with the help of the New York Academy of Medicine, La Guardia set up a committee consisting of twenty-eight doctors, pharmacologists, psychiatrists and sociologists, who were allowed the time and the facilities to do what half a century earlier the Indian Hemp Drugs Commission, for all its thoroughness, had not attempted: scientific tests of the drug, in controlled conditions.

The outcome of the enquiry was remarkably similar to that of its predecessors. The behaviour of marihuana smokers — the Chairman of the Committee, Dr George B. Wallace, wrote in his summary of its conclusions — was ordinarily 'of a friendly, sociable character. Aggressiveness and belligerency are not commonly seen.' No direct relation had been found between marihuana and crimes of violence. There was no evidence that it was an aphrodisiac. Smoking could be stopped without any resulting mental or physical distress comparable with withdrawal symptoms after opiates; and there was no sign that smokers acquired tolerance of its effects, compelling them to take more. On the contrary, an excessive dose reversed the usually pleasant effects. 'Marihuana does not change the basic personality structure of the individual. It lessens inhibitions and this brings out what is latent in his thoughts and emotions, but it does not evoke responses which would otherwise be totally alien to him.' No mental or physical deterioration of a kind which could be attributed to it had been diagnosed even among those who had taken the drug for years. So far from its being a menace, 'the lessening of inhibitions and repression, the euphoric state, the feeling of adequacy, the freer expression of thoughts and ideas, and the increase in appetite for food brought about by marihuana, suggest therapeutic possibilities'.

The American Medical Association reacted angrily to the implication that it had failed to recognise cannabis's potential. 'Public officials will do well to disregard this unscientific, uncritical study', the AMA *Journal* urged on April 28th, 1948, 'and continue to regard marihuana as a menace wherever it is purveyed'. The damage, it feared, had already been done — to judge by the account of some 'tearful parents' who had noticed a mental deterioration in their son, 'evident even to their lay minds' and found he had been smoking 'tea' (the then current slang); when taxed with it, he had cited the committee's report — which he had read about in a pop music magazine under the heading '*Light up! Report finds "tea" a Good Kick!*' — as his justification. Anslinger was of the same mind. The report's 'giddy sociology and medical mumbo-jumbo', he was later to complain in one of his autobiographies, 'put extra millions in the pockets of the hoods'.

*Marihuana: the second phase*

Following the report of the La Guardia Committee, voices were heard periodically in the United States suggesting that even if its research had not been perfect, the results at least confirmed that there were no known serious hazards from marihuana to the individual or to society. Would it not be as well, then, to give up the apparently futile attempt to ban it, and to concentrate instead on the campaign against heroin and the other hard drugs?

Anslinger found the proposal intolerable. To block it, he began to advance a new argument, contradicting views he had himself held earlier. In 1937 he had assured Congress that marihuana did not lead on to hard drug addiction, because he wanted to prove that marihuana addicts were, as he put it to Congress, 'an entirely different class', who were made violent by the drug, rather than by the need to find money to pay for it. They knew nothing of heroin, he asserted, and 'did not go in that direction'. But by 1956, when new forms of drug control were being debated, Anslinger realised that he could no longer rely on Congressmen accepting his link between marihuana and violence, exploded by the La Guardia findings. He would have to find some fresh reason for maintaining prohibition of the drug. Marihuana, he now admitted, was not a 'controlling factor' in crime; the real danger was 'that marihuana, if used over a long period, does lead to heroin addiction'. His expert advice was accepted.

When it began to become obvious, later in the 1960s, that the campaign to stamp out marihuana was not succeeding, and that the habit was spreading rapidly throughout the country, particularly among the youth, State legislatures displayed the by now reflex action. They passed laws to intensify enforcement, and to increase penalties. Edward Brecher has since listed them in his *Licit and Illicit Drugs*, including:

Alabama: mandatory sentence for the possession of a marihuana cigarette: five years. Second offence, up to forty years. No suspended sentences or probation permitted.

Illinois: for first offence of selling marihuana, ten years to life.

Louisiana: mandatory sentence for possession, first offence, five to fifteen years hard labour.

Missouri: life sentence for first offence of sale, second of possession.

Rhode Island: mandatory ten years for possession with intent to sell.

And in Massachusetts anybody found in a place where marihuana was kept, or in the company of anybody possessing it, could receive a five-year sentence. At the same time, the campaign was intensified on the federal level. In 1960 there had been 169 arrests in connection with marihuana; in 1965 there were 7,000, and the following year, 15,000.

The campaign was a humiliating failure, for two main reasons. One was that it proved impossible to stop smuggling. The long border with Mexico, in particular, was easily breached — often by the owners of the 80,000 cars which, by the late 1960s, were passing into Mexico and back into California every weekend (at one checkpoint there were eighteen lanes, which did not make for secure customs enforcement). But the main reason was the same as under Prohibition forty years earlier: that enforcement lacked solid support from public opinion. The young were often on marihuana's side; and parents were gradually learning to live with the knowledge that their children were not going to be stopped from breaking the law.

It was also becoming apparent that none of the terrible consequences Anslinger had forecast were manifesting themselves. Marihuana caused no deaths, and no addiction of the kind which afflicted takers of the opiates or of alcohol; nor were its takers more prone to mania, to violence, or to crime than the rest of the community. By the time President Nixon, whose views reflected Anslinger's, set up his own enquiry — which he took care to 'load', appointing nine of the thirteen members himself, and leaving them and the public in no doubt as to what he expected of them — the campaign against marihuana was disintegrating. 'There is increasing evidence,' Dr James Carey of the University of California told them, 'that we are approaching a situation similar to that at the time when the Volstead Act was repealed.' On the one hand, there were the savage penalties; on the other, a breakdown of enforcement. The police, though willing enough to make raids on hippy camps, did not relish the idea of making sweeps through the massed ranks of fans at pop festivals; still less, of raiding the homes of the G.I.s — sometimes officers — who had brought the habit back with them from Vietnam.

Politicians, too, could no longer be so sure that a hard line on drugs would win them electoral support. In some States, tacit agreements were reached to leave University campuses to discipline themselves over marihuana; fines for possession become nominal. In the winter of 1972 the Consumers' Union pronounced 'marihuana is here to stay. No conceivable law enforcement programme can curb its availability', and called for a new Act to introduce orderly controls on cultivation, production and distribution. In 1973 Oregon took a tentative step towards legislation, by converting possession of small quantities of marihuana into a 'violation' — comparable to a parking offence — rather than a crime. And when the Shafer Committee reported, to Nixon's disgust it recommended that possession of small quantities of cannabis should cease to be a criminal offence.

### Britain and cannabis

It might have been expected that the British, aware of the good fortune in escaping the consequences of the United States' heroin policy, would have taken care not to ban cannabis themselves. But the drug was rarely used socially in Britain, and as the plant had continued to resist conversion into a standardised potion, or pill, it had been falling out of medical use. When it was introduced by the West Indian immigrants after the Second World War, it was known only through the lingering legends of the Arabian nights, and the Assassins. And for a time, it was allowed to circulate in what became semi-ghettoes where the immigrants lived.

Around 1950, it began to spread out through much the same channels as it had in the United States, chiefly through musicians and their fans; and stories about the way the drug was corrupting the nation's youth began to appear in the newspapers. They were loaded with menace: readers were reminded that cannabis was really hashish, the drug of the Assassins, and told that it was being pushed by coloured dope peddlers. Britain had no Narcotics Squad, and no Harry Anslinger; but it had Dr Donald McIntosh Johnson, later to be Conservative M.P. for Carlisle, whose *Indian Hemp: a Social Menace* sounded the alarm in 1952. In it he described how the respectable 'Mr A' had been slipped a 'Mickey Finn', which had driven him into so manic a mental condition that he had had to be certified, and incarcerated for a few days in a mental hospital. The drug used, Dr Johnson claimed, was cannabis; and he went on to explain that it had also been responsible for the outbreak of hysteria which had afflicted the citizens of the Provençal town of Pont St. Esprit, not long before.

The Pont St. Esprit outbreak was soon traced to ergot poisoning; but the explanation of 'Mr A's' disorder did not come until several years later, when Dr Johnson revealed in an autobiography that he was 'Mr A' himself (thus qualifying, perhaps, as the only man to have been elected an M.P. after having been certified). He was unable to show that cannabis had been responsible. By then, however, the combination of the press campaign and the propaganda of the Society for the Study of Addiction (whose Hon. Secretary's views were given in the introduction to Johnson's book; distinguishing between drunkards and cannabis users, he claimed that 'alcoholism, for all its attendant degradation, does not usually poison one's nature; drug addiction does') had led the Government to determine to ban sales of the drug. As the medical profession disclaimed any desire to use it, it ceased to be available even on prescription.

What followed was a repetition of what had been happening in the United States, though with the additional complication that the police activity was initially directed against the West Indians. A number of respectable citizens, who had taken cannabis all their adult lives in much the same way as their white neighbours took beer, found themselves given long prison sentences, coupled with judicial homilies on their wickedness in corrupting British youth. The effect the campaign had was greatly to increase the demand. By driving it underground, the authorities succeeded in making 'pot' a secular cult, combining the attractions of a rebel conspiracy against parental and civil authority, and a secret society. White teenagers took to the drug in rapidly growing numbers, so that by 1964 more whites than coloureds were being convicted of cannabis offences. Inevitably, the demand grew for tougher enforcement, and higher penalties. But cabinet ministers or stockbrokers who applauded the searches of a pop singer's suitcases by the Customs, or his flat by the police, became less enthusiastic when they found that most of the white malefactors were from the aristocracy and the professional classes — including their own sons and daughters.

This was an embarrassment, because by the Dangerous Drug Act of 1965, designed to implement United Nations' policy, penalties had been raised. In theory, anybody found in possession of cannabis could receive as long a sentence as a convicted murderer. In 1967 the Labour Home Secretary, Roy Jenkins, sought a way out of the difficulty by appointing a committee of enquiry into the whole subject under Lady Wootton, the leading British authority in the area where sociology, criminology and psychiatry overlap. Its report, published in 1969, followed those of earlier enquiries. There was nothing to suggest that cannabis was responsible for aggressive social behaviour, or crime, or ill-health. Physically-speaking it was 'very much less dangerous than the opiates, amphetamines, and barbiturates, and also less dangerous than alcohol'. Nor was there any evidence that cannabis-takers were led on to take heroin; 'it is the personality of the user, rather than the properties of the drug, that is likely to cause progression to other drugs'.

James Callaghan, Jenkins' successor as Home Secretary, was no more disposed than Nixon to accept the committee's verdict. He excused himself from taking action by claiming — as Nixon was to do — that the committee had allowed itself to be bamboozled by the cannabis lobby. But whatever the disagreements on the committee's findings there was no disputing one of its assertions; that in spite of campaigns to stamp it out, cannabis use was on the increase. Doubtless encouraged by the report, the users continued to multiply, as an investigation undertaken by the *Sunday Telegraph*, revealed in 1972. Previously, the cannabis had entered the country chiefly in small consignments, often amateurishly brought in. But the demand had now put up the price to the point where it attracted a smuggling network of the sophisticated kind hitherto associated with the heroin traffic:

Ingenuity shown in disguising cannabis in freight is endless. It has been found concealed in crates of foodstuff, the handles of badminton racquets, padded ice-hockey gloves, sub-aqua air bottles, surf boards, hippie beads, sculptured busts, contraceptives, antiques, Moroccan pouffes and ornamental bricks.

Other expedients employed by the traffickers included the use of radio-controlled model aircraft, launched from motor-boats in the English Channel, and — most serious of all — of the diplomatic bags addressed to members of the Embassies of the poorer countries, who had learned how they could enjoy high living in London with no trouble, and rarely any risk. A senior member of the staff of the Indian High Commission had been detected, the *Sunday Telegraph* report claimed, smuggling 50,000 grains of cannabis into Britain in a consignment of chutney.

Faced with such evidence, the reaction of the Customs was to boast that larger quantities of cannabis were being intercepted. But this, as Timothy Green explained in his book about international smuggling, must be regarded as the measure of prohibition's failure. No large scale smuggling operation could afford to lose more than a small proportion of its consignments — around five per cent, Green estimated. It followed that if more cannabis was being intercepted, this could only mean that more was finding its way in. Only if interceptions began to *fall*, should the Customs claim they were succeeding. In much the same way, the rise in the number of convictions, which the police used to justify themselves — from around fifty in 1957 to over 10,000 in 1972 — could more sensibly be regarded as a reflection of a great increase in drug taking. The estimates of the number of cannabis users supplied to the Wootton Committee in 1968 had ranged between 30,000 and 300,000. The *Sunday Telegraph*'s investigators came to the conclusion that in 1972 'although the United Kingdom is in general a law-abiding country, anything up to two millions of its citizens use the drug'.

### Heroin: U.S.A.

If the authorities in Britain and the United States could not suppress the use of cannabis by banning it, the chances of the traffic in heroin, easier and vastly more profitable to smuggle, being effectively stopped by prohibition were remote. The British, realising this, held on to their policy of allowing doctors to prescribe a maintenance dose; and it worked — though they had some uneasy moments in the 1960s, when it was found that the number of new cases of addiction, though negligible by American standards, was rising with disconcerting rapidity. An investigation revealed the reason; a handful of doctors were prescribing heroin so lavishly that they were feeding the small black market in the drug. There had always been the risk that leaving it up to the individual doctor to decide who needed heroin might lead to trouble. The biggest category of morphinists in the world, Lewin claimed, were doctors; and there were ninety doctors among Britain's 300 known heroin addicts in the early 1950s. There were also a few who were concerned only to increase their incomes. Reluctantly, the medical profession had to agree to abrogate its members traditional right, and confine the prescribing of heroin to designated clinics. The expedient worked; the rise in the addiction rate was halted.

Why, then, was the British system not introduced in the United States? Partly because it would have meant passing control to the Department of Health and Welfare. It was Anslinger's boast that he blocked this proposal, because he preferred to work in liaison with the Coast Guard, the Customs, the Secret Service and the Department of Justice. When it was pointed out to him that control by the Department of Health in Britain had largely made it unnecessary for the Coast Guard, the Customs, the Secret Service and the Department of Justice to concern themselves with the heroin traffic, he insinuated that the British must be hiding the real addiction figures. Anyway, he added, Britain was a small island, which made it easier to prevent smuggling.

This was an unfortunate choice of argument, because it revealed why his policies had been foredoomed to failure — the smuggling of heroin into the United States could not be prevented. Neither stricter enforcement nor severer penalties were reducing it. Any standard textbook on drugs showed why. Many heroin takers acquired 'tolerance', needing larger amounts to enjoy the same effects. The more they took, the more difficult it was to stop taking the drug, because of the agonising nature of the withdrawal symptoms — even worse with heroin than with the other opiates: yawning, restlessness, irritability, tremor, insomnia, depression, nausea, vomiting, intestinal spasm, diarrhoea, chilliness alternating with sweatiness, gooseflesh, cramps, pains in the bones, muscle spasms. While undergoing these tortures, the addict knew — as a textbook listing them put it — that 'at any point in the course of withdrawal, the administration of a suitable narcotic will completely and dramatically suppress the symptoms'. To purchase this relief, he would pay any price, and risk any penalty. As a result, heroin became a profitable enough commodity for the traffickers to be able to afford to conduct their smuggling operations on a highly organised and efficient level.

### The blackest irony

So, by a savage paradox, the more determined the campaign by the United States Government to stamp out the drug traffic, the better it suited the traffickers. By the late 1960s, it was possible for a syndicate to offer $35 a kilo for raw opium — enough to ensure an abundant supply from impoverished peasants in Eastern and Middle Eastern countries, and to encourage them to cultivate land which had not been tilled before. The heroin manufactured from that kilo could be sold for $20,000; sometimes considerably more. Out of so spectacular a profit rate, the syndicate were able to afford to perfect their chain of operations so that at each stage, the carriers of the heroin could not betray the man who had consigned it to them, because they would not know who he was: nor could they be betrayed by the man they handed it over too, except through carelessness or bad management (a technique which Timothy Green likened in his study of smuggling to a system of electrical fuses so arranged that if one blew it could be replaced, and the rest could continue to function normally). The larger the difference between cost price and selling price, too, the better the syndicates were able to afford to bribe Customs Officers and policemen, and the greater the incentive for the 'pusher' to extend his market by attracting new customers. And they were thrown into his path by the Vietnam war, which introduced tens of thousands of G.I.s to heroin. In Vietnam they could buy the pure product at one-twentieth of its cost back home, where it was often heavily adulterated. What happened — as described by Frances Fitzgerald in her *Fire in the Lake* — reads like mimicry of what had happened to so many earlier efforts at prohibition.

The traffic in heroin was the final and perhaps the blackest irony of the war. The heroin came largely from Burma and Laos. Much of it was processed in or near Vientiane by those people for whose sake (it was to be supposed) the U.S. Government was demolishing the rest of Laos. It came to Vietnam either by air drop from Vietnamese or Lao military planes, paid for by the U.S. Government, or through the Customs at Tan Son Hut airfield. The Vietnamese Customs Inspectors earned several dozen times as much for not inspecting the bags and bundles as for inspecting them. When the American Customs advisers attempted to crack down on their 'counterparts', they discovered that the two key customs posts were held by the brothers of Thieu's Premier ... As this 'freely elected Government' would not prosecute the Customs Officials (heroin, the Vietnamese said, was 'an American problem'), the heroin continued to enter the country unimpeded. Once in Vietnam it was sold openly in the streets and around the American bases by young war widows and children orphaned by the American War.

The United States might leave Vietnam — Frances Fitzgerald remarked — but the Vietnam war would never leave the United States; 'the soldiers would bring it back with them like an addiction'. They did. The demand for heroin continued to rise until, as Frederick Forsyth unkindly noted in a survey of the heroin traffic in 1973, it became 'America's largest single consumer import', worth $4,000,000,000 a year.

The fact that the prohibition policy led to an increase in drug-taking, though, was less demoralising than its social side-effects; particularly crimes of violence. This was not because drugs unleashed criminal tendencies, as Anslinger had claimed; the criminal activity was largely the result not of the drugs, but of the prohibition policy. As the Le Dain Committee of enquiry into drug use in Canada put it, in their interim report,

> Because of the illegal nature of the drug the cost of a heavy heroin habit may run anywhere from $15.00 to $50.00 a day and higher, in spite of the fact that the medical cost of the drugs involved would be just a few cents. There are very few legitimate ways in which most individuals can afford to meet that kind of

expense. Consequently, when tolerance pushes the cost of drug use above what the user can afford legitimately, he is forced into a decision — either to quit the drug and go through withdrawal, or turn to easier, criminal, methods of acquiring the necessary money.

In 1972 the New York Health Department estimated that there were around 400,000 heroin addicts in the city; 15,000 of them in jails, 25,000 under treatment, the rest on the streets — where, according to the police commissioner Patrick Murphy, they were connected with seventy per cent of the city's crimes. In Washington that year, the city's Narcotics Treatment Organisation put the count of heroin addicts at 15,000; its head, Dr Robert du Pont, estimated that 'the annual value of property and services transferred because of addiction, through robbery, theft, prostitution, drug sales and so on, was $328,000,000.' And at the same time, prohibition was creating new criminals out of men and women who would not ordinarily have become law breakers — as the Le Dain Committee noted in its final report in 1973. The fact of a drug being unobtainable legally 'will often drive a person to seek support and reinforcement in a deviant or criminal sub-culture'; and a prison sentence tended to reinforce this bond, because there was 'a considerable circulation of drugs within penal institutions'.

With heroin, as with marihuana, enforcement officials were ready with what appeared to be evidence that they were doing their job — figures showing that they were improving the interception rate. The U.N. narcotics committee were told that seizures of heroin in the United States were up from 160 kg in 1969, to 221 kg in 1970. But in the same period, the United States narcotic authorities' own estimates for the illicit import of heroin, assuming they were correct, showed that the proportion which was being seized had actually fallen. And there was sufficient evidence of the involvement of Customs and police by 1966 to lead John M. Murtagh, a judge of the New York Criminal Court, to comment that the narcotics law 'corrupts more than it corrects'; a warning borne out three years later when, within twelve months, no fewer than thirty-nine New York narcotics agents who were under investigation for drug offences resigned.

*Control at source*

Although the attempt to stop drugs coming into the United States was not succeeding, there were hopes for a time that it might be possible to introduce an alternative method of control. In 1959 an American fact-finding mission was despatched to visit the countries of the Near East to investigate the drug traffic. It reported that the chief source of illicit heroin were the Turkish poppy fields. The opium was being smuggled through the Lebanon to Italy and France, where it was converted into heroin and exported to the United States. There was little prospect of interception, as the people involved were untouchables; the Mafia, in Italy, and unknown but evidently influential figures in France. But why wait until the opium was on its way? Why not cut off the supply at its sources?

The idea had the attraction of simplicity. The United States Government was paying huge sums annually in a futile effort to beat the smugglers; part of the expenditure could be diverted, in the form of aid, to induce the Governments of the countries where the poppy — or any other drug-producing plant — was cultivated, to prevent cultivators from growing crops to supply the illicit market. The problem would then solve itself, for there would be no raw material for the traffickers to work on. All that was needed was some new international agreement, of the kind that had been mooted in the old League days, but which the U.N. should be better able to enforce. Anslinger had himself appointed as the United States delegate to the U.N. Commission to promote the policy, and in 1961 agreement was reached on what became known as the Single Convention on Narcotic Drugs.

It proved to be as unworkable as the Hague and Geneva conventions, and for the same reasons; chief among them, the fact that some of the nations involved had promised more than they could perform, and others had never any intention of implementing their pledges. Typical of the unreality was the Convention's decision that 'the use of cannabis (hemp) for other than medical and scientific purposes must be discontinued as soon as possible, but in any case within twenty-five years'; a 'rather optimistic time-table', as Dr Norman Taylor — Curator of the New York Botanical Gardens, and author of a couple of refreshingly sane books on drugs — remarked, when 'matched against three thousand years of use by untold millions'. Taylor's scepticism was justified. Visiting Morocco eleven years later, a *Guardian* correspondent found that though the Government had pledged its support to the campaign to phase out *kif*, it had carefully refrained from interfering with the cultivation of hemp. The farmers were earning twice as much from it as they had earned from growing corn; so, as a tribesman explained, 'now we've all switched'.

The attempt to deprive the heroin traffickers of their main source, the poppy fields of Turkey, also failed. Tempted by the promise of American aid, the Turkish Government agreed to try to stop poppy cultivation for the black market; and for a while the production of opium was restricted. But as the illicit marketeers were able to offer higher prices, this only meant that it was the supply of legitimate — medical — opium which dwindled. By 1972 some nations were running short; the Japanese representative complained at the U.N. that his country could only get half its legitimate requirements. At the same time the Turkish peasants, who had been instructed to stop growing poppies, were becoming restive. The payments they had received out of the American funds, they felt, were insufficient to compensate them for the loss of so lucrative a crop. As their votes were at stake, the Turkish Minister for Agriculture in the Ecevit Government began, in 1974, to dismantle the controls his predecessors had introduced.

# 13

## The Collapse of Control

EVEN IF HEROIN AND CANNABIS COULD HAVE BEEN BANISHED, it had become clear by the 1970s that they would immediately have been replaced by other drugs. Some had already established themselves — occasionally with the active help of governments, or of the medical profession, or both.

When the amphetamines — 'pep pills' — were first marketed in the 1930s, doctors had begun to prescribe them for patients who felt tired or lethargic; and later as a slimming aid. During the war they proved a help to men in the forces who were required to stay alert on duty; and when it ended, vast quantities of them, surplus to requirements, were dumped on the open market. Sometimes they were employed as an adjunct to alcohol; when in 1947 'Chips' Channon held the dinner party which one of his guests, Somerset Maugham, told him was the apogee of his career (the guests included two queens), he described in his diary how he had 'laced' the cocktails with benzedrine, 'which I find always makes a party go'. But then it was realised that, injected intravenously, the amphetamines could produce an explosive bout of euphoria; and as they were cheap and easily available, they were soon being extensively used for that purpose, with destructive effects on the health of some of the addicts, ranging from brittle finger-nails to ulcers, chest infections, liver disorders, and cerebral haemorrhages. Governments banned sales, except on prescription; but so many people had acquired the habit of taking the drug, and so many doctors were willing to indulge them, that the black market was rarely short of supplies. Taking amphetamines, in Brecher's estimation, ranked 'among the most disastrous forms of drug use yet devised' — particularly in Sweden, where the attempt to impose total prohibition led only to a rise in the price, encouraging illicit manufacture and smuggling, and leading to a spectacular growth in the number of addicts.

Barbiturates took a similar course. In 1949 *Colliers* ran an article under the title 'Thrill pills can ruin you', alerting its readers to the fact that sleeping pills, if injected, were euphoric. The health authorities added their warnings which, as Brecher commented, ensured that 'throughout the 1950s and the 1960s, the relatively harmless sleeping tablets of the 1930s played their new role as one of the major illicit American drugs'. As with the amphetamines, the barbiturates were so widely prescribed that control was impossible; the black market could be fed from tens of thousands of family medicine cupboards. But when a committee of enquiry set up by the British Government recommended in 1972 that the barbiturates should be recategorised, to bring them under the same type of control as heroin, the British Medical Association's scientific committee successfully blocked the proposal, ostensibly because of the 'practical difficulties in implementing regulations', but really because it would further have eroded the doctor's right to prescribe.

Cocaine also made a come-back 'Sniffing' had enjoyed a vogue in the United States in the 1920s; in his *Drugs and the Mind*, Robert S. de Ropp surmised that the original 'dope fiend' peddled cocaine, rather than heroin. But it was expensive; the amphetamines, far cheaper and more easily obtainable, for a while replaced it. When the amphetamines proved an unsatisfactory substitute, cocaine began to return to favour in American cities. Its high price was less of an impediment to sales than it had been in the depressed 1930s, and provided an incentive to smugglers; Timothy Green estimated in 1969 that a yachtsman carrying 10 lb of cocaine to the United States could make £10,000 on a single trip; and by 1973, according to Thomas Plate in the *New York* magazine, 10 lb was fetching anything up to $160,000 on the market. With the raw materials, coca leaves, abundant and cheap, this left an ample margin to perfect smuggling techniques, and to bribe Customs or police. Once the cocaine had been brought in, there was no difficulty in selling it. What Plate called the iron law of drug marketing, 'supply determines demand', came into operation; whenever it was available, cocaine became

> ... the drug of choice, not only among whites but ever increasingly among affluent black drug users as well ... Among Latin Americans in New York, cocaine is often the preferred drug of entertainers, expensive prostitutes, very successful businessmen, and certain religious sects for whom cocaine use is literally an act of faith. And among white drug users, cocaine is especially popular with rock stars, writers, younger actors and actresses, and stockbrokers and other Wall Street types ...

And even if all these drugs could have been brought under some control — by, say, the discovery of some instrument on the lines of a geiger counter, capable of infallibly detecting them — it would not have solved the problem. Apart from synthetic variants, there were numerous substances which though not sold as drugs, could be used for that purpose — and frequently were. Benzine and glue had long been sniffed 'for kicks', and with the advent of the aerosol can, it was found that there were endless alternatives; 'literally hundreds of easily accessible sources', the Le Dain Committee found, including paints, paint removers, lighter fuel, and dry-cleaning fluids: 'it was recently observed that thirty-eight different products containing such substances were available from the shelves of a service station's highway store in Ottawa'. In the circumstances, the Committee pointed out, effective restriction was hardly practicable, 'except at considerable inconvenience to a large segment of the population'; and, as the large segment of the population was unlikely to accept that inconvenience, the existence of these 'substances' created a problem 'which clearly calls into question the potential of the crimino-legal system in controlling drug use'.

### The doors of perception

The crimino-legal system of control, whatever its defects, was at least theoretically relevant so long as there was agreement that drug-taking was a social evil, which ought to be suppressed. But by this time a different category of drug had come into widespread use, supported by testimonials from men whose opinions commanded respect, who claimed that it could bring great benefit to society.

During the war a Basle chemist, Dr Albert Hofman, took a minute quantity of an ergot derivative — four-millionths of a gramme — in his laboratory, and after cycling home with some difficulty ('my field of vision swayed before me and was distorted like the reflections in an amusement park mirror, I had the impression of being unable to move from the spot, although my assistants later told me that we had cycled at a good pace') he experienced startling symptoms, which he noted down when he recovered;

> vertigo, visual disturbances — the faces of those around me appeared as grotesque, coloured masks; marked motor unrest, alternating with paralysis; an intermittent feeling in the head, limbs, and the entire body, as if they were filled with lead: dry, constricted sensation in the throat; feeling of choking; clear recognition of my condition, in which I sometimes observed, in the manner of an independent, neutral observer, that I shouted half insanely or babbled incoherent words. Occasionally I felt as if I were out of my body . . .

By that time — 1943 — there was more of a disposition to investigate any drug capable of inducing such a reaction — not out of any feeling that the visions might be of value to the beholder, but because the Pentagon was looking for a drug which might be used to facilitate brainwashing, or for disorienting enemy forces in the field. And as the visions which Hofman's LSD induced sometimes bore a resemblance to those seen in psychotic states, a few psychiatrists began experimenting with it in the hope it might help in the treatment of schizophrenia. Although the military soon lost interest, and the psychiatrists' hopes were not realised, LSD was remembered when there was a sudden resurgence of interest in vision-inducing drugs, following the publication of Aldous Huxley's *The Doors of Perception* in 1954.

There was nothing strikingly new in Huxley's experience after taking mescaline. His description of looking at his bookshelves —

> Red books, like rubies; emerald books; books bound in white jade; books of agate, or aquamarine, of yellow topaz;

lapis lazuli books whose colours were so intense, so intrinsically
meaningful, that they seemed to be on the point of leaving the
shelves to thrust themselves more insistently on my attention

— might have come from Havelock Ellis, or from the case histories
provided earlier by Louis Lewin. But the general public, disillusioned with civilisation's materialist progress, was more willing
by the 1950s to listen to Huxley's argument that the heightened or
altered perception obtainable from mescaline was worth enjoying, not just in its own right, but for the new insights, the new
meanings, it could provide. 'I am not so foolish', he wrote

as to equate what happens under the influence of mescaline or of
any other drug, prepared or in the future preparable, with the
realisation of the end and ultimate purpose of human life;
Enlightenment, the Beatific Vision. All I am suggesting is that
the mescaline experience is what Catholic theologians call 'a
gratuitous grace', not necessary to salvation but potentially
helpful and to be accepted thankfully, if made available. To be
shaken out of the ruts of ordinary perception, to be shown for a
few timeless hours the outer and the inner world, not as they
appear to an animal obsessed with survival or to a human
being obsessed with words and notions, but as they are appre-
hended, directly and unconditionally, by Mind at Large — this
is an experience of inestimable value to everyone and especially
to the intellectual.

People who wanted to shake themselves out of the ruts of ordinary perception did not find it easy to obtain mescaline, for
which the raw material peyotl, was scarce; but LSD could be
manufactured in a laboratory, and it quickly became the standard
drug for that purpose. And scientific trials began to confirm — in
so far as such trials could — that it worked. In LSD — Dr Richard
Blum and his associates at Stanford University claimed in 1964 —
a means had been found 'for enhancing values or expanding the
self, a road to love and better relationships, a device for art
appreciation or a spur to creative endeavors, a means of insight,
and a door to religious experience'. For a few individuals, though,
researchers admitted, the consequence of taking LSD was a 'bad

trip', involving experiences which were disturbing and sometimes terrifying. Stories began to circulate about the destructive effect of these bad trips on promising youths, like those which had been heard about marihuana (or tobacco), but with some characteristic twists — in particular, the much-repeated tale of the girl who told her friends 'look, I can fly!' and stepped to her death from a fourth-floor window.

Inevitably, down came the ban — even, in the United States, on research into LSD. The outcome was the growth of a cult, catered for through a profitable black market. The formula was generally known; the materials available; the manufacturing process not difficult; and distribution ridiculously simple, as LSD, in addition to being tasteless, odourless and colourless, occupied negligible space in relation to its potency. Prohibition was immediately followed, Brecher wrote,

(a) by an increase in the availability of LSD, and (b) by an increase in the demand. The increased availability can be explained in part by the higher prices which law enforcement engendered, and which attracted more distributors. The increased demand can similarly be explained in part by the LSD publicity that legislative action engendered. As in the case of the opiates, the barbiturates, the amphetamines, glue and other drugs, the warnings functioned as lures.

*The peyotl cult*

It is possible from the available evidence to show how the attempt to suppress the vision-inducing drugs has failed, and why: because it has repeated the self-defeating pattern so often seen before. What is not yet possible is to assess the impact of the mescaline/LSD movement (or even, for that matter, of the influence of the cannabis cult) on those who came to take it, let alone on society as a whole.

Early on, the psychedelic movement split into two main groupings, though they were never clearly differentiated. Both derived from the views of Humphrey Osmond — who had introduced Huxley to mescaline: that these drugs 'provide a chance, perhaps only a slender one, for *homo faber*, the cunning, ruthless, foolhardy pleasure-greedy toolmaker, to merge into that other creature whose presence we have so rashly presumed, *homo sapiens* the wise, the understanding, the compassionate'. By some of Osmond's followers, this was taken to mean that the function of the drugs was simply to reveal, to anybody who took them, the limitations he had been imposing on himself; so that he would seek ways, not necessarily through drugs, to explore the potential within himself which he had not known existed. But there were others who, like Dr Timothy Leary, tended to invest the drugs themselves with almost magical powers, and to propagandise for them on a national — and eventually, on an international —scale. By the 1970s the Leary version was beginning to go out of fashion; LSD was being used, if not with more discrimination — its illegality made this difficult — at least with greater care, in recognition of the unpredictability of its effects. But the story of the movement which Huxley and Osmond sparked off, and which in their different ways William Burroughs, Allen Ginsberg and Carlos Casteneda, among others, pushed along, cannot yet adequately be told — not, at least, as history.

What can be told is the parallel story of how differently peyotl was handled in the Indian reservations; and how different the results. A century ago it was found that the peyotl cult had not, as had for many years been believed, been successfully put down by the Spaniards. After they were driven from Mexico, it began to re-emerge. The peyotl cactus, anthropologists found, was still worshipped, though the ceremonial had picked up Christian accretions, originally designed to deceive the Spaniards, but eventually establishing themselves in their own right, so that the ceremony took the general form of the Mass, and Jesus's name was involved. Peyotl was still taken, though, for the traditional vision-inducing purposes, as were the morning glory, and the psilocybe mushroom; the Mazatecs believed that Jesus had given the mushroom to them, and included him and his saints' names in their chants.

In the 1880s the peyotl cult began to spread north into the United States, alarming members of the Commission on Indian Affairs. The Commission's agent in charge of the Comanche reported in 1886 that they were getting a kind of cactus from Mexico 'which they eat, and it produces the same effect as opium, frequently putting them to sleep for twenty-four hours at a time'; he for-warded some specimens for analysis, adding that 'as the habit of using them seems to be growing among them, and is evidently injurious, I would respectfully suggest that the same be made contraband'. The Federal Government did not take his advice; but from time to time individual State legislatures, disturbed by reports that Indians in their reservations were going over to peyotism, would debate how to stop them getting supplies of the drug. The difficulty ordinarily was that peyotism was a religion, and that it had wrapped itself up in enough Christian doctrine to be able to liken peyotl to communion wine. How far this was originally deliberate policy is hard to tell; but it became so with the foundation of the Native American Church, whose expressed aims were

> to foster and promote religious beliefs in Almighty God and the customs of the several tribes of Indians throughout the United States in the worship of a heavenly Father, and to promote morality, sobriety, industry, charity and right living and cultivate a spirit of self-respect, brotherly love and union among the members of the several tribes of Indians throughout the United States and through the sacramental use of peyotl.

But to many Christians, the use of peyotl was not so much sacramental as sacrilegious; and to many respectable citizens, it was scandalous that the American Indians should be permitted to enjoy a notorious drug. A campaign after the Second World War to have it banned was only warded off with difficulty, largely through the efforts of two anthropologists who had studied the subject, Weston La Barre and J. S. Slotkin. It was amazing, Slotkin observed, to find that the expert evidence on which the campaigners relied — fantastic stories about the effects of the drug, and the nature of the ritual — was derived from white and Catholic officials in the reservations; 'none of them have had the slightest first-hand experience with the plant or with the religion, yet some fancy themselves to be authorities and write official reports on the subject.' From his own extensive experience, members of the cult were both more industrious and more temperate in their drinking habits than other Indians in the reservation.

With the renewal of interest in vision-inducing drugs in the 1950s, the campaign against peyotl started up again, this time for fear of what it might do to the white youth of America. In 1964 a California court ruled that it was a sufficient public danger to justify a ban on it, in violation of religious freedom, because it was gaining adherents among the hippies; and the rumour circulated that it was frequently the cause of insanity. Newspapers began printing some of the same kind of stories that had circulated about hemp drugs in India. An investigation was set up by Dr Robert L. Bergman, of the Public Health Services, to follow up the fifty-odd reports of peyotl-induced psychosis. The vast majority of the reports, it was found, were simply hearsay, and could not be traced to any source. Only one single instance was found which could be described as 'a relatively clear-cut case of acute psychosis', and that was of a Navajo who, in defiance of the cult's own injunction, had also consumed a quantity of alcohol. Although the cult did not always 'take' — the Apaches on their Reservations adopted it for a while, but went back to alcohol, their preferred drug — in general its effects appeared beneficial. 'We have seen many people come through difficult crises with the help of this religion', Dr Bergman commented,

> and it appears to me that for many Indian people threatened with identity-diffusion it provides real help in seeing themselves not as people whose place and way in the world is gone but as people whose way can be strong enough to change and meet new challenges.

The success of the cult, admittedly, does not prove that it would have been possible to establish anything similar among the white population of America, or of other Western countries. Nor would the obvious alternative — making LSD a prescription drug, to be dealt with by doctors — have worked; few doctors have the required interest or understanding. What the peyotl experience does suggest is that alternatives could have been found to the drug policies of Western governments, had there been a better appreciation of what was involved.

*Mao's way*

In retrospect, then, the lesson which emerges from the confused history of drugs is that though we have been unable to learn the right way to handle them, we have at least been shown what is the wrong way: prohibition. But there has been one striking exception to this rule: Communist China. It seems to be agreed, even by observers who have little sympathy with the rule of Chairman Mao, that opium has effectively been banished.

Three forces were at work to make this possible. Public opinion in China remained hostile to opium, as a foreign imposition. In so highly communalised a country, it was difficult for those who smoked opium to do so for long without being detected, and denounced; and even harder for farmers to cultivate poppies. Most important of all, smuggling became unprofitable because the ordinary commercial channels through which opium could be illicitly distributed ceased to exist.

In Western countries, though public opinion might be hostile to drugs, there was always sufficient privacy available to enable those who were able to obtain them to take them with relatively little risk; the commercial channels were geared to assist the smuggler, as was the freedom of movement between country and country; and there was far more purchasing power available to be spent on drugs. China's example, consequently, was irrelevant, and would remain so as long as the Western countries retained their traditional economic and social fabric.

# 14

# *Psychopharmacology*

IN THE WESTERN WORLD, THEN, BY THE 1970S, THERE COULD NO longer be any doubt that the attempt to control drugs through the crimino-legal system had failed; and though there was great reluctance to admit as much, there was more of an inclination to explore alternative possibilities. And science was at last beginning to help, by beginning to investigate the social effects of drugs.

### d'Abernon: the effects of alcohol

The first tentative exploration of this territory was made in the First World War, when the d'Abernon Committee was set up to advise the Government on the effects of drink on the war effort. Drink taken during the day, Lloyd George believed, made workers slower and clumsier; and drink taken in the evening was apt to cause absenteeism 'the morning after'. To what extent, the d'Abernon Committee were asked to estimate, was the war effort thereby disrupted?

In their report, the Committee had to admit defeat. It was not merely that scientists had not provided them with the answers; scientists had not even asked the relevant questions. They had conducted a great deal of research into alcohol in the laboratory, but none into alcohol in the pub, the factory, or the home. Did the drunkenness caused by beer or wine differ from that caused by spirits? Did mixing drinks tend to produce drunkenness? How far did the dilution of a drink — whiskey with soda, say — modify its action? What was the effect of taking food in conjunction with alcohol? Did fatigue alter the effect of alcohol on performance of skilled movements? Was alcohol more injurious in dry than in moist climates? To what extent was alcoholism caused by physiological disturbances? And did the psychological effects of alcohol — cheerfulness for example — improve resistance to adverse physical circumstances such as cold? None of these questions had been put.

Nor, the report continued, had there been research into an aspect of drug-taking about which a misconception was firmly rooted in the public mind. It was widely assumed that alcohol, like other drugs, caused addiction. Yet the great majority of drinkers did not become addicts. There must, presumably, be something in an individual which predisposed him to addiction; but what? Again, the scientists had evaded the question. As a result there was 'an almost entire absence of reliable data regarding the psychology of the drunkard, though adequate information on this point is obviously essential in devising rational methods of treatment of the inebriate. Little is known of the progress of the drinker from occasional excess to chronic alcoholism. Are the occasional drinker and the habitual drunkard two distinct types, or is the former an early stage of the latter?'

The reason scientists had neglected applied research, the Committee suggested, was partly that they were reluctant to involve themselves in social, as distinct from academic, issues (sociology was not yet accepted as an academic discipline); and partly that they did not care to venture into unexplored territory — the choice of subjects for investigation had 'often been determined by the ease with which they could be put to the test, or by their bearing on some theoretical controversy, rather than their intrinsic and practical importance'. This was a shrewd criticism; and the guidelines which the Committee offered for the future were also sensible — that researchers should now begin to concentrate on finding out why people took drugs, and what effects the drugs had on the people who took them and on the community in general. But the Committee suffered from a limitation. Although it lacked the necessary evidence, there were some assumptions which, it felt, could safely be made. Most of them were little more than pious aspirations: 'the ordinary use of alcohol', its report advised, 'should not only be moderate, but should also be limited to the consumption of beverages of adequate dilution, taken at sufficient intervals of time to prevent a deleterious action on the tissues'. But one assertion, 'that alcohol is narcotic rather than stimulant in action', revealed that the Committee shared the orthodox view of the time that it was possible to categorise drugs as either narcotics or stimulants. And it based its classification not on everyday experience, but on research into the effects of alcohol on the body and the nervous system. Asked to examine alcohol's social effects, the Committee had castigated scientists for their reluctance to venture out of the laboratory. Yet its own diagnosis was derived from the lab, rather than the pub.

## Louis Lewin: Phantastica

The most influential pharmacologist of the time, Louis Lewin, suffered from the same limitation. He was anxious to show that drugs had been one of the most important of man's discoveries, and could be one of the most valuable of man's allies, and he did his best to popularise mescaline — without success, though experiments by Rouhier in France and Beringer in Germany bore out his claims. In his *Phantastica*, published in 1924, he set out his creed.

> If human consciousness is the most wonderful thing on earth, the attempt to fathom the depths of the psychological action of narcotic and stimulating drugs makes this wonder seem greater still, for with their help man is enabled to transfer the emotions of everyday life, as well as his will and intellect, to unknown regions; he is enabled to attain degrees of emotional intensity and duration which are otherwise unknown . . . By the exercise of their powers on the brain, they release marvellous stores of latent energy. They relieve the mentally tortured, massage the racking pains of the sick, inspire with hope those doomed to death, endow the overworked with new vitality and vigour such as no strength of will could attain, and replace for an hour the exhaustion and languor of the overworked by mental comfort and content.

Lewin was also well aware of the prevailing weakness of pharmacology; and he mocked those whose contribution had been simply to produce impressive-sounding terminology. 'Even today,' he wrote, 'we frequently meet with interpretations of the action of medicinal and poisonous substances which are merely pseudo-scientific descriptions of their effects.' They reminded him of the scene in Molière's *Malade Imaginaire* when the examination candidate, asked the reason for opium's soporific action, replies 'because it is endowed with narcotic and soporific properties' — which so delights his examiners that they immediately pass him. But Lewin then proceeded to follow the same course himself. He had not received the formal academic recognition which his abilities as a researcher and a teacher merited — perhaps because he was a Jew, and not given to disguising his contempt for those rash enough to disagree with him. The easiest way in which he could obtain it, in his own time, was to provide the classification of drugs according to their pharmacological properties which had eluded earlier researchers. He decided that there were five categories:

1 *Euphorica* — 'sedatives of mental activity, these substances diminish or even suspend the functions of emotion and perception'.
2 *Phantastica* — hallucinating substances.
3 *Inebriantia* — causing cerebral excitation followed by depression.
4 *Hypnotica* — sleep producing agents.
5 *Excitantia* — mental stimulants.

The trouble began when Lewin tried to squeeze all known drugs into the separate categories. His *Euphorica* were opium and its derivatives, and cocaine. Indian Hemp, however, was classified with the *Phantastica*, along with peyotl, the fly agaric, henbane, datura and caapi. In the *Inebriantia* section, alcohol was accompanied by chloroform, ether and benzine. The *Hypnotica* included chloral, veronal, paraldehyde, potassium bromide and — remarkably, in view of the results of his own research into it — kava. And the *Excitantia* had to provide room for all the rest — a weird miscellany; including camphor, betel, kat, coffee, tea, kola, maté, coca, tobacco, arsenic, and mercury.

Lewin was not unaware of the inconsistencies, which he did his best to iron out by tortuous rationalisations. Some *Hypnotica*, he admitted, were capable of being *Excitantia*; the reason was that 'like all toxins, they act on the brain', producing a euphoric state. The fact that the American Indians used tobacco not as *Excitantia*, but as *Phantastica*, to produce visions, proved more troublesome to explain. The best he could do was suggest that the hallucinatory effects must have been due to the carbon monoxide which they inhaled, together wth the tobacco fumes, whenever they lit their pipes.

The book had other limitations. Well-versed though he was in the pharmacological literature, Lewin's reading outside it was less than comprehensive; he quoted Surgeon Crombie's statistics about the insanity caused by hemp drugs, unaware that they had been demolished in the report of the Indian Hemp Drugs Commission. But this was of little importance compared with the decision to try to classify drugs according to their effects. Not that his categories were accepted; but they gave rise to further futile attempts along the same lines. The basic premise remained, that it *ought* to be possible to think in terms of the chemical action of a drug, rather than of the reaction of the people who take it; leading to such pontifications as the argument that the St. Bernard dogs who found lost travellers in the snow ought not to have carried brandy in their little barrels, because brandy is a depressant.

Largely as a result of this fixation, pharmacologists could not come to grips with the most serious problem which drugs presented: addiction. They could not even accept the traditional premise, that addiction represented a failure of will power, because will power was not quantifiable. A favourite proposition in the 1920s, as Evelyn Waugh recalled in *Brideshead Revisited*, was 'it's something chemical in him'; applied to alcoholics, it became 'the cant phrase of the time, derived from heaven knows what misapplication of popular science'. The available research funds were channelled into the search for metabolic disfunction, or defects in the endocrine system. And although by the 1930s there was more of a disposition to admit the explanation might be psychological, research in that area continued to be hampered by lack of resources, and by the divisions among the psychologists themselves. The Freudians looked for the causes of addiction in unconscious conflicts; the Pavlovians preferred to regard it as another conditioned reflex — similar to that which B. F. Skinner induced in rats, so that when they experienced the joy of a certain type of electric shock, they would return to it again and again, sacrificing food, fighting and sex for the chosen form of stimulation.

## Auto-suggestion

The break-through to a better understanding of the effect of drugs can be traced to an experiment undertaken in 1933 — though it was to be many years before its significance was appreciated. In the *Quarterly Journal of Medicine* in 1933 two London cardiologists, William Evans and C. Hoyle, described how they had given out pills which their patients, suffering from angina, assumed were pain-killing, but which were actually made from bicarbonate of soda. Over a third of the patients reported that their pain had been satisfactorily relieved.

It had long been known that people could be fooled by the fairground quack's coloured water, and come back for more. But it had been taken for granted they must be gullible souls, who only imagined they were better, or who perhaps had only imagined they were ill. This could hardly account for so high a proportion of angina patients reacting to a placebo, as if it had been the real thing. And by this time, there was a widely-publicised alternative explanation. From his experience as a chemist in Troyes, Emile Coué had become convinced that what cured many of his customers was not his medicines, but their belief in them; a conviction which he was able to test by giving them placeboes.

At the time, Evans and Hoyle's paper aroused only mild curiosity; and Coué's fame, though world-wide, turned out to be transitory. The imagination could be stimulated, he had suggested, with the aid of a simple formula; 'every day, in every way, I get better and better'. It was a reversion to ritual; and in a ritual-starved civilisation it caught on, throughout Europe and America, as well as in France, with people intoning it in the bath or on the bus. But his basic proposition, that the formula's function was simply to help bring the imagination into play — just as a drug might — was not grasped. It was assumed that he was calling for an exercise of the will. The ritual became a music-hall joke and, like many another craze of the twenties, Couéism soon became only a mildly absurd memory.

After the Second World War, however, research began at last to broaden its base. The psychologists did not compose their differences, but they managed to establish a measure of common ground, leading to acceptance of the proposition that there are addiction-prone individuals — or, rather, that some people are more addiction-prone than others, and are therefore more likely to become addicts if nudged in that direction by any of a variety of forces.

At first sight this was not far removed from the earlier idea that addicts lacked will power. But there was one essential difference. It had been believed that the addict could extricate himself if he really wanted to, by an effort of will. The new theory came closer to regarding addiction as a neurosis. There was no point in telling an addict to pull himself together, because the fact he had become an addict itself revealed that he was incapable of such self-discipline.

The reasons why one individual was more addiction-prone than his neighbour proved difficult to pin down. It was easy enough to show with the help of statistics that the Italians, in proportion to the amount of wine they drank, were far less likely to become alcoholics than the French; not so easy to determine why. Long-term monitoring projects began to turn up clues; they revealed, for example, that alcoholics were more likely to come from homes where there had been parental conflict. But there were scores of similar environmental possibilities to be considered, as well as interactions between them. All that could be claimed with assurance was that — as Howard Jones put it, in his study of alcoholism — addiction was not 'the invariable result of particular kinds of personality constellation', but 'the solution found when problems of adjustment arise because certain types of personality are confronted by certain types of environmental stress'.

This research therefore, though it contributed to a better understanding of the drug problem, did little to assist either prevention or cure. For a time it was hoped that new institutions, specialising in the treatment of drug addicts, would be the answer. Even hard-liners like Anslinger approved, because they wanted it to be demonstrated that addicts could learn, or be taught, self-control. The first such establishment was opened in Lexington, Kentucky, in 1935, subjecting heroin addicts to a rigorous course designed to dry them out and refit them for society; and by 1953, Anslinger was able to boast that of the 18,000 patients who had been through it, two-thirds had not returned. This should, he felt, give everyone confidence that the system worked. That confidence was soon shattered. Follow-up studies of those two-thirds, to find how they were faring, revealed that the great majority had relapsed. Lexington's success rate, it was estimated, was only around three per cent. Other institutions, more sympathetic in their approach, were to do a little better; but not much. As Brecher sadly noted in his *Licit and Illicit Drugs*, 'no effective cure for heroin addiction has been found'.

One reason for the failure of institutional treatment emerged when a few doctors began to study placebo effect in its own right. They found that the pharmacological content of a drug was not necessarily the determining factor in the patient's reaction to it. For example, when Dr Stewart Wolf — one of the pioneers of such studies in America — gave a woman an emetic, telling her it was a medicine designed to stop her feeling sick, not merely did she stop feeling sick, but her stomach juices, which were being monitored, reacted as if they were dealing with an anti-emetic — in other words, to her mental picture of what the drug's effects should be, rather than to the drug.

In his *Drugs and Human Relations*, published in 1970, Dr Gordon Claridge set out the evidence which had been accumulating to show the extent to which it is not the drug, but the expectation of the drug taker, which determines reactions. In a trial where one group took barbiturates, while a matched group were given placeboes, the barbiturates proved to be more effective sedatives only when the members of the group which was taking them were expecting sedation. Where they did not know what to expect from the pills, the reaction was the same whether they took the placebo or the drug. An experiment which Claridge himself undertook on behalf of the British army in 1961, to find out how the tranquilliser meprobamate affected soldiers' reactions, had a similar result. Although there was no significant difference between the reactions of those who took the drug, and those who took the placebo, both performed their set laboratory tasks less well than a third group who had not been given pills at all. The fact of taking pills, in other words, led to a deterioration in performance. 'Although none of the subjects was told what to expect', Claridge observed, 'most of them clearly associated drug taking with "being drugged", or being made less efficient in some way'.

It was not simply the lay public who could be deceived by placeboes. Doctors had been inclined to think they would not be good subjects in such tests, because they would know from training and experience how to recognise a drug's effects. But when in the late 1960s the members of the staff of the Department of Psychological Medicine in Glasgow University who had volunteered for tests were given pills which might be either amphetamines or placeboes, and were invited to guess which they had taken, their replies were scarcely more accurate than if they had decided by spinning a coin. One psychiatrist of several years' standing recognised his symptoms as coming from dexamphetamine. According to Claridge, 'during the next few hours he became more "high", and the following morning announced that participation in the experiment had considerably enhanced his enjoyment of a party the previous evening'. It had then to be broken to him that he had taken a placebo. Other members of the staff, equally convinced that they had taken placeboes, found that they had in fact taken amphetamines.

### In search of reality

At first sight, such evidence may seem hard to reconcile with the accounts of the effects of the vision-inducing drugs. It is conceivable that Huxley knew enough about mescaline, when he took it, for his imagination to take over; but not that Hofman could have known what was going to happen when he took LSD. Another experiment described by Claridge provides a clue. In it, one of the subjects who thought he had taken LSD described what he saw:

> . . . a lot of strange shapes and brilliant colour, after images, as if I looked through pebble finished glass, particularly this morning. Especially this morning colours were more brilliant than I have ever experienced. Voices were at times somewhat in the distance, along with a feeling of being in a real situation, a dream kind of state, time is distorted, goes rather slowly, and an hour is only 10 to 15 minutes when I look at my watch . . .

'A perfect description of the LSD state!', Claridge commented

— but the subject had in fact had a placebo. The mind, in other words, is capable of duplicating any drug experience; but this is not the same as saying that the drug is irrelevant. LSD is obviously a highly potent substance, capable of inducing striking changes in perception. What it cannot do is produce more than is already within the mind's own capability. The drug is essentially the trigger mechanism. That is why at different times, or in different cultures, reactions to the same drug have been so very different. Take, for instance the passage

> Shivering I rose from my seat, incapable of rest, when that heavenly and harp-like voice sang its own victorious welcome . . . a chorus of elaborate harmony displayed before me as in a piece of arras-work, the whole of my past life — not as if recalled by an act of memory but as if present and incarnated in the music; no longer painful to dwell upon, but the details of its incidents removed, or blended in some hazy abstraction, and its passion exalted, spiritualised, and sublimed

This, too, might have been written about an LSD 'trip'; it is, in fact, de Quincey's description of the effects of laudanum. Jean Cocteau reacted similarly to opium. All of us, he claimed, carry something folded up within us like those Japanese flowers made of wood which unfold in water

> opium plays the same role as the water. None of us carries the same kind of flower. It is possible that a person who does not smoke may never know the kind of flower that opium might have unfolded within him.

On other writers, however, the opiates have had the opposite effect. For William Burroughs, they diminished awareness so that they could only, he felt, be a hindrance to the artist; whereas cannabis gave him what he needed: 'unquestionably this drug is very useful to the artist, activating trains of association that would otherwise be inaccessible'. Others, again, have derived their inspiration from tobacco, about whose effects J. M. Barrie wrote in terms ordinarily applied only to a loved one.

An attempt to account for these variations was made by William James in his *Varieties of Religious Experience,* where he recalled the effect ether had had on him. He had found no reason, he wrote, to change the impression he had formed at the time.

> It is that our normal waking consciousness, rational consciousness as we call it, is but one special type of consciousness, whilst all about it, parted from it by the flimsiest of screens, there lie potential forms of consciousness entirely different. We may go through life without suspecting their existence; but apply the requisite stimulus, and at a touch they are there in all their completeness . . . How to regard them is the question — for they are so discontinuous with ordinary consciousness. Yet they may determine attitudes though they cannot furnish formulas, and open a region though they fail to give a map. At any rate, they forbid a premature closing of our accounts with reality

The function of the drug is to provide the stimulus: and any drug may serve, if it happens to suit the individual concerned. Ether had suited James; peyotl had made him sick — perhaps because he literally could not stomach it, perhaps because the circumstances in which he took it had been unfavourable.

But how does a drug, any drug, liberate the mind? Huxley believed the explanation must be sought in a theory advanced by Henri Bergson, and later elaborated by the Cambridge philosopher, Professor C. D. Broad. The original function of the brain, Broad thought, was basically not productive, but eliminative. It was designed 'to protect us from being overwhelmed and confused by the mass of largely useless and irrelevant knowledge, by shutting out most of what we should otherwise perceive or remember at any moment, and leaving only that very small and special selection which is likely to be practically useful'. This, Huxley decided, would explain what had happened to him, and to others who had had similar drug experiences. Ordinarily we get only a 'measly trickle' from the mind's vast resources. But a few individuals have a by-pass mechanism, enabling them to open the doors of perception; others construct one with the help of spiritual exercises; and others can utilise drugs.

On this hypothesis, the vision-inducing drug could be described as a password to open doors which, for most people, are ordinarily closed. There is no single password; each individual may have his own — or none. Only one drug in common use has rarely been employed for the purpose: alcohol. Alcohol and the hallucinogens, Humphrey Osmond has argued, are actually antithetical; alcohol

produces a downward transcendence, peyotl an upward one — the difference between levelling up and levelling down. Alcohol allows one to relate to others by being more sure of one's self. This, in small doses, is much better than not being able to relate at all, but it is a very precarious business, and selfishness may soon end in brawling and ill-temper. Peyotl acts not by emphasising one's own self but by expanding it into the selves of others, with a deepening empathy or in-feeling. The self is dissolved, and, in being dissolved, enriched . . .

Anthropological field workers, too, have reported that the shaman who takes a drink loses his powers of divination. It remains possible, therefore, that the pharmacological action of alcohol will eventually be shown to be qualitatively different from that of other drugs, so that the doors which it opens do not expand awareness but instead — as Malcolm Lowry suggested in *Under the Volcano* — facilitate the emergence of a second self, ordinarily kept hidden.

Even this, though, is uncertain. Alcohol may have the effects it does because in some as yet unexplained way our minds are programmed to react to it — as a shaman's is programmed to react to tobacco as a vision-inducer.

The most likely hypothesis is that although a measured quantity of a specific drug can, other things being equal, have statistically predictable effects within a culture, its effects can vary greatly with different cultures, as well as with different individuals, or with the same individual at different times — as Oliver Sacks' experiences treating patients with 'L Dopa', described in his *Awakenings*, so strikingly illustrated. The reactions to the drug, he found, appeared to be dictated not just by the personalities of the patients, but by fragmented elements of those personalities, too.

In ordinary circumstances, however, expectation is the most potent force in determining a drug's effects. When Dr Walter Pahnke tested a psylocybin mushroom derivative on theology students at Harvard, he found that the visions the students reported were indistinguishable from the visions they would have expected to get from a mystical experience. And from his study of the peyotl cult among the Huichol Indians of Mexico, Peter Furst concluded that beyond any sensations which could be attributed to the chemistry of the plant, 'there are powerful cultural factors at work that influence, if they do not actually determine, both content and interpretation of the drug experience'.

### Drugs and drink

Scientists, then, have at last begun to ask relevant questions about drugs, and are beginning to get some answers. But the answers have been largely ignored, or rejected, because they do not fit in with society's preconceptions about drugs. One of the commonest assumptions, for example, is that alcohol has in some measure been tamed, and consequently can safely be put in a different category from other drugs. But a research project undertaken by Dr Harris Isbell and his associates at Lexington has revealed that almost all the reactions of subjects who were given barbiturates in the experiment, from mild tipsiness to delirium tremens, duplicated those of alcohol — so closely, Brecher thought, that 'the barbiturates might be labelled a "solid alcohol" and alcohol classed as a "liquid barbiturate".' The differences between them were chiefly the consequence of the barbiturates being available in more concentrated form. Otherwise, the evidence suggested, there was no logical reason why the barbiturates and alcohol should not be placed on the same legal footing. Yet in practice, as Brecher put it,

> society takes a very different stance with respect to the twin drugs. Alcohol is treated as a non-drug; it is on sale in multi-dose bottles at 40,000 liquor stores and in countless other outlets as well; it is freely sold to those 'of age' in saloons, taverns, cocktail lounges, nightclubs, roadhouses, and even ordinary family restaurants; and more than $250 m a year is spent on advertising alcohol. The barbiturates, by contrast, are legally

saleable only on prescription in pharmacies; other sales are severely punishable criminal offences. It is a curious fact, indeed, that Americans today are bombarded with advertising urging them to buy a liquid that, if secured without a prescription in tablet or capsule form, could lead to imprisonment for both seller and buyer.

In clinical terms, Isbell's experiments have also showed that the effects of alcohol and the barbiturates on health are more serious than those of the opiates. If its social side effects are taken into consideration, alcoholism emerges as by far the most serious of the Western World's drug problems. According to an estimate published early in 1972 by the National Institute on Alcohol Abuse and Alcoholism in America, nearly ten per cent of the nation's drinkers at that time were alcoholics, doing incalculable damage to their health, wrecking their families' lives, costing $15 billion annually in damage to property, loss of working time, and welfare payments, and causing havoc on the roads. In the same year, Lord Rosenheim, Chairman of the Medical Council on Alcoholism in Britain, warned that the number of alcoholics was much higher than doctors realised — there were 350,000 in Britain, he estimated, but there might be as many as half a million — and that alcohol caused far more actual illness, as well as misery, than all the other drugs such as cannabis, heroin and LSD put together.

In both countries, too, the number of alcoholics has been rising — so rapidly, in Britain an international conference on the subject in London was told in 1973, that they would top the million mark by 1980. Many other countries in different parts of the world have reported the same trend. Zambia, Kenneth Kaunda complained that winter, was becoming a nation of drunkards; and he threatened to resign if they did not learn to control their excessive drinking habits. Yet the World Health Organisation, faced with such reports from all over the world, could do little more than file them. 'So far as I am concerned', Dr Dale Cameron, head of WHO's Drug Dependency Unit, said in 1971, 'alcohol is probably the king of the mountain,' but so far as the U.N. was concerned, the king could do no wrong, because by tacit consent alcohol had not been included in drug conventions. In logic, or sense, such an omission was impossible to justify — as the Shafer Committee recognised. American laws, its report noted, had made alcohol the preferred social drug, but 'that historical fact should not prevent further evaluation of this preference'. On the Committee's own evaluation, alcohol dependence was 'without question the most serious drug problem in this country today'.

This is not, of course, to suggest that a campaign to wean people away from alcohol could blithely stress the relative safety of, say, cannabis as an alternative. Indeed the latest reports on cannabis, published by the U.S. Senate Subcommittee on Internal Security, strongly suggest that the drug carries greater dangers, mental and physical, than has earlier been recognised. This discovery appears to be partly due to more, and more sophisticated, research projects; partly to the recent development of stronger, more dangerous forms of the drug; partly to some as yet unexplained psychological reaction among users (perhaps more people are taking it not for a 'lift', but as a narcotic).

The evidence provides a salutary reminder that any drug, and all drugs, can have adverse effects. To judge from the introduction to the published volume of evidence, by Senator James Eastland, though, the lesson that banning a drug is the certain way massively to increase the sales of it has not been learned. He is aware that ten times as much cannabis gets into the country as is seized ('a fairly conservative estimate'). He is also aware that in the past five years seizures of marihuana have increased tenfold, and of hashish, twenty-five-fold. But it still has not got through to him why. Dr Henry Smith Williams's 1938 prophecy has come true; prohibition of cannabis has brought a five billion dollar racket in its train.

# Postscript

ENDLESSLY, OVER THE PAST FEW YEARS, THE ISSUE HAS BEEN DEBATED; should cannabis, or mescaline, or LSD, be legalised? The record of history suggests that the question should be put the other way round: should such drugs be banned? For then, the answer can be given unequivocally: no. Prohibition has always failed in free enterprise societies — free, that is, to the extent that consumers who have the means can exercise freedom of choice. If they choose drugs, no law can stop them. Prohibition may restrict supplies, for a time, but that will only drive up prices, bringing in fresh supplies — or different drugs. And this flouting of the law breeds disrespect for it, alienates otherwise law-abiding citizens, and corrupts the law enforcers.

The question needs to be re-phrased: not, shall we legalise? but, how shall we legalise? And to this, unfortunately, history gives no satisfactory answer. It is easy to say, as drugs cannot be suppressed, they should be regulated; but at this point the same difficulty arises as with prostitution. The kind of man to whom drugs, or prostitutes, are anathema, whether he be an Anslinger or a Muggeridge, finds the prospect of regulating them distasteful. It implies recognition, and they do not want what they regard as a vice to be recognised. They consequently cling to the illusion that drugs can be suppressed, if only the law is enforced.

This leads to a further error of policy. Unwilling to accept the existence of a distinction between, say, cannabis and heroin, they justify banning both, by claiming 'soft drugs lead on to hard'. They sometimes do; but not nearly so inexorably as the *prohibition* of soft drugs leads on to hard. The reason is obvious; hard drugs are both easier and far more profitable to smuggle. The most striking example is what happened in Hong Kong when opium smoking, which had been tolerated for a century, and had never given the authorities any worry (the rate of addiction to opium among the Chinese, reports often pointed out, was far less serious than the rate of alcoholism among the Europeans on the island) was banned. After the ban, opium was squeezed out of the market by heroin; and by the 1970s, according to the Commissioner of Police, four-fifths of the men in the island's penal institutions had been involved in drug offences. Much the same happened in Vietnam, according to the investigator sent by the Pentagon to examine the drug situation there. The only beneficiaries from a campaign against marihuana, he reported, had been the heroin pushers.

But governments have ignored the evidence that prohibition cannot work. And this is not surprising, as they have a powerful financial interest in maintaining a situation in which certain suppliers are allowed to keep their hold over the legal drug market, in return for their massive contribution to the revenue. Legalising cannabis, admittedly, might have augmented the revenue; but there was always the risk that it would provide a diversion, reducing the quantity of liquor and tobacco sold. It is never wise to attribute calculation, in such matters, to ministers. Individually, perhaps, none of them may realise how the policies they have followed have come to be formulated. But revenue has tended to be the overriding consideration; and anything which has threatened it has been discouraged.

This has been illustrated recently in the elaborate efforts which governments have made to appear to be campaigning against cigarettes, as a danger to health, while in fact making very certain that their campaign will not, and cannot, succeed. Governments, in fact, are the real drug-pushers of our time. They seem to know — by the instinct of financial self-preservation — that the 'safe' drugs from their point of view are those on which users come to depend, socially as well as psychologically — drink and cigarettes; and they cling to the two of them, in spite of the ugly evidence that has been building up against them. Cannabis and LSD, which do not exert the same hold, would not serve the exchequer nearly as well.

State licensing, therefore, though less disastrous in its consequences than prohibition, is an unsatisfactory method. It controls
drugs, but to ensure their profitability rather than their safety. And
even where a measure of safety is sought by handing over responsibility to the medical profession, the results (though again,
better than prohibition) have been discouraging. There is little in
a medical student's training to qualify him to dispense drugs
wisely, and, as the medical journals frequently complain, the
lavish prescribing of drugs in recent years suggests that doctors are
often more concerned to save themselves time and trouble, than to
find the cause of the patient's disorder. Just as governments are
the pimps of the tobacco and liquor interests, so the medical
profession has allowed itself to become a licensed drug-peddler
for the pharmaceutical industry.

There is little to be hoped from State intervention, therefore,
until the electorate begins to grasp the lessons of the past. But as
Hegel once complained, what experience and history teach is that
'peoples and governments never have learnt anything from history,
or acted on principles derived from it'. And in the case of drugs,
there is an additional reason why the lessons have not been learned;
the existence of a deep irrational fear of them, which leaves
otherwise sensible and intelligent members of the community
unwilling to accept that there can be a case for legalisation, let
alone to listen to it — even when the objective is the reduction of
drug taking.

Such people will not accept the realities of the situation — for
example, that alcohol is a drug, and a much more dangerous one
than most of those which are banned. On the other hand, they
will swallow the corniest fantasies about other drugs. They believe
that heroin, say, has a built-in addictive attraction, so that anybody taking it once can be enslaved for life. Yet this was exploded
years ago by Louis Lasagna, researching into addiction in America:
most people given heroin for the first time, he found (other than
for the relief of pain), were either not interested, or actually
disliked the experience. As the Le Dain Committee put it, 'the
once popular notion that opiate narcotic experience is intrinsically pleasurable, or that physiological dependence develops so
rapidly that most who are subjected to it are promptly addicted,
is without support'.

Then, there is the persistent myth that drugs can turn the ordinary citizen into a maniac. It is as old as Marco Polo's tale of the Old Man of the Mountain; it has been told of almost every drug; and it still crops up. In 1940 the rumour spread — Evelyn Waugh recalled it in *Put Out More Flags* — that the German infantry then sweeping across France was composed of teenagers, drugged before battle to make them oblivious of danger, so that they advanced unhesitatingly even when being mown down by allied machine-gun fire. It later transpired that these drugs were amphetamines, issued in case the soldiers needed to stay awake. A quarter of a century later American troops in Vietnam brought back pills found on allegedly drug-crazed Vietcong, who had been wiped out in an insanely reckless attack. On analysis the pills turned out to be antibiotics, sent to Saigon at the expense of the American taxpayer, and then discreetly diverted by the minister who received them to the enemy, for the usual consideration.

This is not to dispute that a drug — any drug — may precipitate a character change; the gentle, quiet man who gets aggressive when drunk is all too familiar a figure to publicans. But the disorder lies in the individual, or in his life pattern; not in the drug. Most of the troubles which have arisen are due to society's failure to make this distinction. Yet a last line of argument in favour of the *status quo* remains. Drugs may not be the cause — any more than cars are the cause of road accidents; but in irresponsible hands drugs, like cars, can be lethal. Does this not require intervention, by the State or some duly authorised body, for society's protection?

Looked at from this point of view, drugs have three main dangers. Unquestionably the most serious is intoxication. In the long term, though man has an astonishing capacity to survive his chosen poisons, certain drugs can be shown to have deleterious consequences, on the evidence of mortality statistics; and in the short term, people under their influence — whether at the wheel of a car, or at the heel of a drunken argument — can be very destructive. But as the intoxicant which has the worst long-term health record is tobacco, and the one with the worst short-term accident record is alcohol, this represents an argument for stricter control of established drugs, rather than of those which are illegal.

The risk of addiction — the second reason commonly given when a repressive drug policy is being defended — has now been shown to be less a drug problem, in the strict sense, than a psychological disorder. Unless drugs of all kinds, including nutmeg and paint-remover, could be removed from the market, there is little point in hoping that it can be dealt with by legislation.

It is the third common consequence of drug-taking which presents the real challenge; the personality change which some people undergo as a result of introduction to cannabis or LSD. Their record in other respects is much better than alcohol and tobacco. They do not intoxicate, unless taken in improbably large doses; they are not addictive; and their adverse effects on health, so far as can be judged on the evidence available, are relatively insignificant. But they confront society with an issue that it has been unwilling to face. People may need these drugs; not in their own right, but as a preliminary to restoration of the link, largely lost, between man's consciousness, and all that lies beyond it. The personality change may be for their benefit.

The positive values people find in the drug experience — as the Le Dain Committee put it — 'bear a striking similarity to traditional religious values, including the concern with the soul, or inner self. The spirit of renunciation, the emphasis on openness and the closely-knit community, are part of it, but there is definitely a sense of identification with something larger, something to which one belongs as part of the human race.' This theme was taken up by Andrew Weil in his *The Natural Mind*. Weil argued that to think of drug-taking, or even of drug-addiction, as something to be prevented or cured is a mistake. The sensation, and the craving, are symptoms of a psychic need. He produced evidence which indicates that there is no great difficulty in getting people off even heroin, provided they have, as it were, something to look forward to — which suggests that withdrawal symptoms may represent not simply the body's resistance to being deprived of a drug, but the mind's resistance to being deprived of its effects.

To Weil, however, this does not entail believing that cannabis, say, should be legalised. On the contrary, in his testimony to the Shafer Commission he opposed it, on the ground that it would be used in ways as unintelligent as tobacco and alcohol ordinarily are. The drug scene cannot be changed by tinkering with the law, he argued, because it is 'a manifestation of useless ways of thinking at all levels of society — among users of drugs as well as of non-users'.

Drug use, and drug abuse, are a reflection of society, its tensions, its values, and its needs. To punish drug-takers is like a drunk striking the bleary face which he sees in the mirror. Drugs will not be brought under control until society itself changes, enabling men to use them with discrimination, and perhaps in time to dispense with them.

# Acknowledgements

ANYBODY KNOWN TO BE WRITING ABOUT DRUGS CAN COUNT UPON getting countless ideas and suggestions and occasionally a valuable lead towards books or authors he has never heard of. I have been very lucky, in this respect; finding myself more than once in possession of a scrap of paper with some reference on it, and remembering only that I had received it from some chance acquaintance at a party. To all those who have helped me in this way, my thanks; and especially to Frances Fitzgerald, Dr Griffith Edwards, Professor Max Gluckman, Professor Bernard Lewis, Dr Jonathan Miller, Dr Neal E. Miller, Professor Michael Shepherd, Dr Gerry Stimson, Frances Verrinder, R. G. Wasson, and Lyall Watson. Francis Huxley made some suggestions about the section on drugs in primitive societies which I was glad to incorporate; Raye Farr, and Bill Grundy read a preliminary draft (I hope I have profited from their astringent comments) and, along with Bernard Levin (I wish I could have included some of his asides) somehow also found the time to do the invaluable chore of proof-reading. I am also grateful to Jasper Woodcock and his team at the Institute for the Study of Drug Dependence; but my chief debt is to the London Library, for the help from its staff, and for the access to its shelves, where I could browse at random in the — to me — often unfamiliar territory into which the research so often lured me.

# Sources

IN HIS BOOK ON COCA, PUBLISHED IN 1901, W. G. MORTIMER WAS able to boast that he had collected 600 titles of articles and books on that drug alone. The bibliography compiled a few years ago by the U.N. Economic and Social Committee on Narcotic Drugs listed nearly 2,000 sources of material on cannabis. In its interim report on drugs in Canada, the Le Dain Committee stated that there were already some 3,000 reports on LSD in scientific journals. When Joseph Robert wrote his history of tobacco, in 1949, the standard research guide contained over 6,000 titles; when he came to revise the book in 1967, he found that the guide, which was also being revised, was expected to include a further 4,000 titles. Nobody, so far as I know, has tried to keep count of the works on opium and its derivatives, but they would certainly reach five figures. As for alcohol, the library at Rutgers University, which specialises in the subject, is reputed to contain 40,000 items.

The writer of any work purporting to be a history is ordinarily anxious that his bibliography should display the extent and depth of his research; in admitting that mine has been far from comprehensive, I can only plead these figures in mitigation. And there has been another difficulty. As my concern had been mainly with the social rather than the pharmacological effects of drugs, several academic disciplines have been involved. Information about attitudes to drugs can be found not only in many social histories, but in works on anthropology, ethnology, mythology, theology, phenomenology, ecology, etymology and archeology, as well as in the descriptions of travellers, explorers and botanists. It has consequently been an enormous advantage when some professional — or an inspired amateur, like R. G. Wasson — has already researched some part of the territory, and published his findings; but such ventures have been regrettably few.

There are also some gaps, which cannot be filled until more — or more reliable — information becomes available; drug use behind the Iron Curtain, for example. So the structure of the book, with each chapter devoted to a theme, is designed as far as possible to make use of the material which is available, to illustrate developments in attitudes, to, and legislation about, drugs, rather than to try to cover all the historical ground.

Where I have quoted from early sources, I have where necessary translated the text into modern English; standardised spelling (sometimes to personal preference: peyotl rather than the now more common peyote); and occasionally modified punctuation or grammar, for clarity.

## BIBLIOGRAPHY

For the sake of brevity, I have omitted standard histories, biographies, journals, etc.; nor have I listed the individual state papers which are the chief source of material for the later chapters.

The place and date of publication refer to the edition I have consulted, which is not necessarily the first edition.

Aaronson, Bernard, and Humphrey Osmond, *Psychedelics*, London, 1971

Abrams, Stephen, 'Cannabis Law Reform in Britain', (*Marijuana Papers*, 1972)

Adams, E. W., *Drug Addiction*, Oxford, 1937

Alexander, General R., *The Rise and Progress of British opium smuggling*, London, 1856

Alexander, H. G., *Narcotics in India and South Asia*, London, 1930

Allegro, John, *The Sacred Mushroom and the Cross*, London, 1971

Allen, Dr Nathan, *The Opium Trade*, Boston, 1850

Allsop, Kenneth, *The Bootleggers*, London, 1961

Anderson, J. W., *Fiji*, London, 1880

Andrews, George, and Simon Vinkenoog (editors), *The Book of Grass*, London, 1967

Anselmini, O., *ABC of Narcotic Drugs*, Geneva, 1931

Anslinger, Harry, and William Tompkins, *The Traffic in Narcotics*, New York, 1953

Anslinger, Harry, and Will Oursler, *The Murderers*, New York, 1961

Anslinger, Harry, and J. D. Gregory, *The Protectors*, New York, 1964

Anstie, Francis, *Stimulants and Narcotics*, London, 1864


Bailey, S. H., *The Anti-Drug Campaign*, London, 1936

Banks, Sir Joseph, *Journal 1768–71, London*, 1896

Baudelaire, Charles, *My Heart Laid Bare* (edited by Peter Quennell), London, 1950

Beaglehole, J. C., *The Journals of Captain Cook* (Hakluyt Society), Cambridge, 1961

Beattie, John, and John Middleton (editors), *Spirit Mediumship and Society in Africa*, London, 1969

Beecher, Henry K., 'The Powerful Placebo' (in *Journal of the American Medical Association*, December 24th, 1955)

Benzoni, Girolamo, *History of the New World* (tr. Admiral W. H. Smyth; Hakluyt Society), Cambridge, 1851

Bloomquist, E. R., *Marijuana*, Beverley Hills, 1968

Blue, Frederick, *When a State Goes Dry*, Ohio, 1961

Boyer, S. S., *Hemp*, New York, 1900

Brecher, Edward M., *Licit and Illicit Drugs*, Boston, 1972

Brereton, William H., *The Truth about Opium*, London, 1882

Brinton, Daniel G., *The Myths of the New World*, Philadelphia, 1896

Brooks, Jerome E. (editor), *Tobacco* (five volumes), New York, 1937

—— *The Mighty Leaf*, London, 1953

Brown, F. C., *Hallucinogenic Drugs*, Springfield, Ill., 1972

Burroughs, William, 'Points of distinction between sedatives and consciousness-expanding drugs' (*Marijuana Papers*, 1972)

Burton, Richard (translator), *The Book of the Thousand Nights and a Night*, Benares, 1885

Castaneda, Carlos, *The Teachings of Don Juan*, Los Angeles, 1971
—— *A Separate Reality*, London, 1971
Catlin, George, *Liquor Control*, London, 1931
Central Control Board (Liquor Traffic) Advisory Committee Report, *Alcohol: its action on the human organism*, London, 1918 (The D'Abernon Report)
Chang, Hsin-pao, *Commissioner Lin and the Opium War*, Harvard, 1964
Cherrington, Ernest, *History of the Anti-Saloon League*, Ohio, 1913
*Chinese Repository*, 1832 ff
Christlieb, Theodore, *The Indo-British opium trade and its effect* (translated by D. Croom), London, 1879
Claridge, Gordon, *Drugs and Human Behaviour*, London, 1970
Clark, Walter, *Chemical Ecstasy*, New York, 1969
Cocteau, Jean, *Opium: the diary of a cure* (translated by Margaret Crosland), London, 1957
Cohen, Sidney, *Drugs of Hallucination*, London, 1964
Collis, Maurice, *Foreign Mud*, London, 1946
Connell, K. H., *Irish Peasant Society*, Oxford, 1968
Cook, Captain, *Voyages of Discovery*, London, 1906
Costin, W. C., *Great Britain and China 1833–60*, Oxford, 1937
Cotlow, Lewis, *In Search of the Primitive*, London, 1967
Cust, Robert, *The Opium Question*, London, 1885
Czaplicka, M. A., *Aboriginal Siberia*, Oxford, 1914

D'Avenant, Charles, 'An Essay upon Ways and Means' (*Political and Commercial Works*, London, 1771)
Dennett, Tyler, *Americans in Eastern Asia*, New York, 1941
De Quincey, Thomas, *Confessions of an English Opium Eater*, London, 1967
D'Erlanger, Baron Henry, *The Last Plague of Egypt*, London, 1936
De Ropp, Robert S., *Drugs and the Mind*, London, 1958
De Vesme, Caesar, *Primitive Man*, London, 1931
Dowdeswell, G. F. 'The Coca Leaf' (*Lancet*, April 29th, May 6th 1876)
Drake, William Daniel Jr., *The Connoisseur's Handbook of Marijuana*, London, 1971
Dunn, Will, *The Opium Traffic in its International Aspects*, New York, 1920

Eatwell, W. C., *On the Poppy Cultivation*, Calcutta, 1851

Elaide, Mircea, *Myths, Dreams and Mysteries*, London, 1960

—— *Shamanism*, New York, 1964

Ellis, E. S., *Ancient Anodynes*, London, 1946

Ellis, Havelock, 'Mescal: a new artificial paradise' (*Contemporary Review*, January 1898)

Emboden, William, *Narcotic Plants*, London, 1972

Evans-Pritchard, Edward Evans, *Witchcraft among the Azande*, Oxford, 1937

—— *Nuer Religion*, Oxford, 1956


Fairbank, John, L., *Trade and Diplomacy on the China Coast 1841–54*, Cambridge, Mass., 1953

Fairholt, F. W., *Tobacco*, London, 1870

Fleming, Peter, *One's Company*, London, 1934

—— 'A Far Eastern Inquiry' (*Times*, March 8th, 1935)

Forsyth, Frederick, 'The Killer Poppy' (*Telegraph Magazine*, August 11th, 18th, 25th 1973)

Freeman-Mitford, A. B., *Attaché at Peking*, London, 1900

French, Richard, *Nineteen Centuries of Drink in England*, London, 1884

Fry, Edward, 'China, England and Opium' (*Contemporary Review*, February 1876)

Fry, William Storrs, *Facts and Evidence relating to the Opium Trade*, London, 1840

Fryer, John, *A New Account of East India and Persia* (Hakluyt Society), 1909

Fuller, Henry C., *The Story of Drugs*, London, 1922

Furst, Peter T., *Flesh of the Gods*, London, 1972


Garcilaso de las Vegas, *Royal Commentaries of the Incas* (translated by H. V. Livermore), Austin, 1966

Gautier, Théophile, *The Hashish Club* (translated by Ralph Gladstone; *Marijuana Papers*, 1972)

Gavit, John P., *Opium*, London, 1925

Gelfand, Michael, *Witch Doctor*, London, 1964

Geller, Allen, and Maxwell Boas, *The Drug Beat*, New York, 1969

Ginsberg, Allen, 'First manifesto' (*Marijuana Papers*, 1972)

Gluckman, Max, *Politics, Law and Ritual in Tribal Society*, Oxford, 1965

Goldenweiser, Alexander, *Early Civilisation*, London, 1923

Goode, Erich (editor), *Marijuana*, New York, 1969

—— *The Marijuana Smoker*, New York, 1970

Gorer, Geoffrey, *Africa Dances*, London, 1935

Green, Timothy, *The Smugglers*, London, 1969

Greenberg, Michael, *British Trade and the Opening of China, 1800–47*, Cambridge, 1951

Gustaitis, Rasa, *Turning On*, New York, 1969


Von Hagen, Victor, *Highway of the Sun*, London, 1856

Haggard, Howard W., *Devils, Drugs and Doctors*, New York, 1929

Von Hammer, *History of the Assassins*, (translated O. Wood), London, 1835

Hariot, Thomas, *The New Found Land of Virginia*, Ann Arbor, 1931

Harner, Michael J. (editor), *Hallucinogens and Shamanism*, Oxford, 1973

Harrison, Brian, *Drink and the Victorians*, London, 1971

Hassell, Arthur, 'Properties and Effects of Tobacco' (*Lancet*, February 21st, 1857)

Haynes, Roy, *Prohibition Inside Out*, London, 1924

Hayter, Alethea, *Opium and the Romantic Imagination*, London, 1968

Hemming, John, *The Conquest of the Incas*, London, 1970

Hesse, Erich, *Narcotics and Drug Addiction*, New York, 1941

Heward, Edward, *St. Nicotine*, New York, 1909

Hill, J. Spencer, *The Indo-Chinese Opium Trade*, London, 1884

Hillier, Sydney, *Popular Drugs*, London, 1910

Hollingworth, H. L., *The influence of caffeine on mental and motor efficiency*, New York, 1912

Holt, Edgar, *The Opium Wars in China*, London, 1964

Hosie, Sir Alexander, *On the Trail of the Opium Poppy* (two volumes), London, 1914

Hsü, Immanuel, *The Rise of Modern China*, New York, 1970

Huby, Pamela, and C. W. M. Wilson, 'The effect of centrally-acting drugs on ESP ability in normal subjects' (*Journal of the Society for Psychical Research*, June 1961)

Hunter, Monica, *Reaction to Conquest*, Oxford, 1936

Hunter, W. C., *The 'Fan-Kwae' at Canton*, Shanghai, 1911

Huxley, Aldous, *The Doors of Perception*, London, 1954

—— *Heaven and Hell*, New York, 1955

—— *Island*, London, 1962


Im Thurn, Everard, *Among the Indians of Guiana*, London, 1883


James I, King of England, *Counterblaste to Tobacco*, London, 1604

James, William, *The Varieties of Religious Experience*, New York, 1925

Johnson, Donald McI., *Indian Hemp; a Social Menace*, London, 1952

Johnston, James F. W., *The Chemistry of Common Life*, London, 1879

Jones, Howard, *Alcoholic Addiction*, London, 1963

Jones, John, *The Mysteries of Opium Revealed*, London, 1701


Kidd, Dudley, *The Essential Kafir*, London, 1904

Klüver, Heinrich, *Mescal*, London, 1928

Koskowski, W., *The Habit of Tobacco Smoking*, London, 1955

Kroeber, A. L., *Anthropology*, London, 1923

Kunnes, Richard, *The American Heroin Empire*, New York, 1973


La Barre, Weston, *The Peyote Cult*, New Haven, 1938

La Farge, Oliver, *A Pictorial History of the American Indians*, New York, 1956

La Guardia, Committee on Mar"uana, *Report*, New York, 1944

La Motte, Ellen N., *The Opium Monopoly*, New York, 1920

—— *The Ethics of Opium*, New York, 1924

—— *Opium at Geneva* (articles reprinted from the *Nation* magazine), London, 1930

Lane, E. W., *The Manners and Customs of the Modern Egyptians*, London, 1908

Lang, Andrew, *Myth, Ritual and Religion* (two volumes), London, 1887

Laurie, Peter, *Drugs*, London, 1967

Leary, Timothy, *The Politics of Ecstasy*, New York, 1965

Le Dain, Gerald, *et al.*, *The non-medical use of drugs* (interim report of the Canadian Government Inquiry, 1970), London, 1971

—— *Final Report*, Ottawa, 1973

Levy, Hermann, *Drink*, London, 1951

Lewin, Louis, *Phantastica*, London, 1931

Lewis, Bernard, *The Assassins*, London, 1967

Livingstone, David, *Missionary Travels*, London, 1857

Ludlow, FitzHugh, *The Hashish Eater*, New York, 1960


MacAndrew, Craig, and Robert Edgerton, *Drunken Comportment: a social explanation*, Chicago, 1969

McBain, Howard L., *Prohibition: legal and illegal*, New York, 1928

McCord, William, and Joan McCord, *Origins of Alcoholism*, London, 1960

Mackenzie, Compton, *Sublime Tobacco*, London, 1957

Malinowski, B., *Magic, Science and Religion and other essays*, Boston, 1948

Masters, Robert, and Jean Houston, *The Varieties of Psychedelic Experience*, London, 1967

Mattison, J. B., 'Cocaine drugs and cocaine addiction' (*Lancet*, May 21st, 1887)

Medhurst, W. H., *China*, London, 1840

Melland, Frank, *In Witch-bound Africa*, London, 1923

Michelet, Jules, *The Sorceress* (translated by A. R. Allison), London, 1905

Mill, J. S., *Essay on Liberty*, London, 1972

Mitchell, S. Weir, 'Remarks on the effects of the Anhalonium Lewinii (the Mescal Button)' (*British Medical Journal*, December 5th, 1896)

Monardes, Nicolas, *Joyful News out of the New Found World*, New York, 1925

Moore, James J., *et al.* (UN Social Defence Research Institute), *Psychoactive drug control: issues and recommendations*, Rome, 1973

Moorehead, Alan, *The Fatal Impact*, London, 1966

Morse, H. B., *International Relations of the Chinese Empire, 1834–60*, London, 1910

—— *The Chronicles of the East India Company trading to China, 1635–1834* (five volumes), Oxford, 1926

Mortimer, W. G., *Peru: History of Coca, the 'divine plant' of the Incas*, New York, 1901

Moser, Brian, and Donald Tayler, *The Cocaine Eaters*, London, 1965

Nadel, S. F., 'A Study of Shamanism in the Nube Mountains' (*Journal of the Royal Anthropological Society*, 1946 (1))

O'Shaughnessy, W. B., *On the Preparation of Indian Hemp*, Calcutta, 1842

Owen, David, *British Opium Policy in China and India*, New Haven, 1934

Payne, Ronald, *et al.*, 'Cannabis on Demand: Britain's drug dilemma' (*Sunday Telegraph*, November 19th, 26th, 1972)

'Philaretes', *Work for Chimney Sweepers*, London, 1602

Pliny, *Natural History* (four volumes), London, 1856

Puharich, Andrija, *The Sacred Mushroom*, New York, 1959

Raffles, Sir Thomas Stamford, *History of Java*, London, 1817

Rathbone, W., and L. Fanshawe, *Liquor Legislation in the United States and Canada*, London, 1895

Raymond, Irving, *The Teaching of the Early Church on the Use of Strong Drink*, New York, 1927

Reich, Charles, *The Greening of America*, New York, 1972

Robert, Joseph, *The Story of Tobacco in America*, University of N. Carolina, 1967

Rolleston, Humphrey, *Report of the Committee on morphine and heroin addiction*, London 1926

Rosenthal, Franz, *The Herb: Hashish in Medieval Muslim Society*, Leiden, 1971

Rouhier, Alexandre, *Le Petotl*, Paris, 1927

—— *Les Plantes Divinatoires*, Paris, 1927

Rowntree, Joseph, and Arthur Sherwell, *Public Control of the Liquor Traffic*, London, 1903

Rowntree, Joseph, *The Imperial Drug Trade*, London, 1906

Rush, Dr Benjamin, *An inquiry into the effects of ardent spirits upon the human body and mind*, Brookfield, 1814

Russell, Sir Thomas Wentworth, *Egyptian Service 1902–46*, London, 1949

Sacks, O., *Awakenings*, London, 1973

Schofield, Michael, *The Strange Case of Pot*, London, 1971

Schmidt, Jacob, *Narcotics*, Springfield, Ill., 1959

Schultes, Richard E, 'An overview of hallucinogens in the Western Hemisphere' (in Furst, 1972)

Shadwell, Arthur, *Drink, Temperance, and Legislation*, London, 1902

Shafer, Raymond, *et al.*, *Drug Use in America* (2nd Report of the National Commission on Marihuana and drug abuse) Washington, 1973

Shepherd, Michael, 'The classification of psychotropic drugs' (*Psychological Medicine*, May 1972)

Silvestre de Sacy, *Sure la dynastie des Assassins et sur l'origine de leur nom*, Paris, 1809

Sinclair, Andrew, *Prohibition*, London, 1962

Slotkin, J. S., *Menomini Peyotism*, Philadelphia, 1952

Smith, Sydney, 'The Licensing of Alehouses' (*Edinburgh Review*, September 1826)

Solomon, David (editor), *The Marijuana Papers*, London, 1972

Sonnini, C. S., *Travels in Egypt* (three volumes, translated by Henry Hunter), London, 1790

Stevenson, Robert Louis, *Works* (vol. XVIII), London, 1912


Talalay, Paul (editor), *Drugs in Our Society*, Baltimore, 1964

Taylor, Norman, *Narcotics; Nature's Dangerous Gifts*, London, 1963

—— *Plant Drugs that changed the world*, London, 1966

Terry, Charles, and Mildred Pellins, *The Opium Problem*, Montclair N.J., 1970

Thelwall, A. S., *The Iniquities of the Opium Trade with China*, London, 1839

Thomas, Keith, *Religion and the Decline of Magic*, London, 1971

Thomson, Basil, *The Fijians*, London, 1908

Tinling, J. F., *The Poppy Plague, and England's Crime*, London, 1876

Von Tschudi, J. J., *Travels in Peru*, London, 1847

Tuohy, Ferdinand, *Inside Dope*, London, 1834

Turner, F. S., *British Opium Policy*, London, 1876

Tylor, Edward B., *Primitive Culture* (two volumes), London, 1929

Underhill, Ruth M., *Papago Indian Religion*, New York, 1946

Wasson, E. A., *Religion and Drink*, New York, 1914

Wasson, R. G., and Valentina Wasson, *Mushrooms, Russia and History* (two volumes), New York, 1957

Wasson, R. G., *Soma; divine mushroom of immortality*, New York, 1968

Watson, Lyall, *Supernature*, London, 1973

Watt, George, *A Dictionary of the Economic Products of India*, London, 1892

Watts, Alan, *The Joyous Cosmology*, New York, 1971

Weddel, H. A., *Voyage dans le nord de la Bolivie*, Paris, 1853

Weil, Andrew, *The Natural Mind*, London, 1973

Whipple, Sidney B., *Noble Experiment*, London, 1964

Wighton, Charles, *Dope International*, London, 1960

Wilkinson, Paul, 'Cannabis Indica; a historical and pharmacological study of the drug' (*British Journal of Inebriety*, October 1929)

Williams, S. Wells, *The Middle Kingdom* (two volumes), New York, 1883

Willoughby, W. W., *Opium as an international problem*, Baltimore, 1925

Wilson, A. J. C., 'Ayahuasca, Peyotl, Yagé' (*Proceedings of the Society for Psychical Research*, 1949)

Wilson, George B., *Alcohol and the Nation*, London, 1940

Wolf, Stewart, 'Effects of suggestion . . . the pharmacology of placeboes' (*Journal of Clinical Investigation*, 1950)

Wolff, Pablo, *Marijuana in Latin America; the threat it constitutes*, Washington, 1949

Wootton Committee on drugs, *Report*, London, 1969

Zaehner, Robert, *Drugs, mysticism and make-believe*, London, 1972

# *Index*

Abbas, Shah, 44, 45
Acosta, Father Joseph de, 54
Aerosols, 220
Africa, and hemp, 108
African dances, 18–19
Agra, 104
Alabama, 188
Alcohol, 117, 120–1, 208; dangers of, 55–6, 58–9, 122–3, 226–7; as a drug, 10, 221; duties on, 67–8; research, 210 ff. *See also* Prohibition (U.S.A.)
*Alcohol: its Action on the Human Organism* (D'Abernon Report), 144–5
Aleppo, 48
Alexander, H. G., 164, 165
Alsace, 168
American Civil War, 134
*American Magazine*, 184
American Medical Association, 187
*American Medicine*, 178
Americas, drugs from, 11–12, 16, 47, 125
Amphetamines, 200–1, 221
Amurath, Sultan, 44
Anderson, J. W., 57, 58
Angoulême, 48
*Anhalonium lewinii*, 130
Anslinger, Harry, 183 ff., 187–9, 194, 196, 198, 216
Anstie, Dr Francis Edmund, 120–1, 129, 194
Anthropologists, 11, 15 ff., 206–7
Antibiotics, 228
Anti-Saloon League, 142–3

Antonio Julian, Don, 123
Aphrodisiacs, 10, 31
Arabs, and hemp, 98
'Arctic mania', 18
*Arrow* affair, 88–9
Aschenbrandt, Dr Theodor, 126
Assam, 106, 107; and opium, 94
Assassins, 98, 190
Associated Press, 163
Auto-suggestion, 215 ff.
Ayahuasca, 16
Azande, 19–20

Bailey, S. H., 176, 177
Balzac, Honoré de, 48
Bangor (Maine), 141
Banks, Sir Joseph, 55, 58
Barbiturates, 201, 222–3
Bargeton, Madame, 48
Baring, W. B., 96
Barrie, Sir James Matthew, 219
Bathurst, Allen (1st Earl), 67–8, 71, 81
Batten, G. H. M., 92
Baudelaire, Charles Pierre, 113–14
Bayon, Dr Rafael, 23
H.M.S. *Beagle*, 56
Beck, James, 147
Beer, 42, 54, 101, 118, 132, 136, 138, 142, 145
Belon, Pierre, 72
Benares, 164
Bengal: and hemp, 106; opium production, 73, 75, 77
Benzine, 202

Benzoni, Girolamo, 12
Bergman, Dr Robert L., 208
Bergson, Henri, 220
Beringer, 212
Berkeley, George (Bishop), 70
Berlin, botanical museum, 130
Bernays, Martha, 126
Berne, 45
Betel, 117
*Bhang*, 100–1
Bilharzia, 174
Birdwood, Sir George, 92
Black market, 179, 180, 199
Black Mass, 68
Blanco, A. E., 169–70; formula, 174, 175
Blum, Dr Richard, 204
Bolivia, 28
Bootlegging, 141, 149, 150–1, 179
Boston (Mass.), 141
Boyce, S. S., 182
Brandy, 58, 146
Bread, 117, 118
Brecher, Edward M., 179, 184, 188, 200–1, 205, 217, 222
Bretherton, William, 92
*Brideshead Revisited* (E. Waugh), 214
Britain, *see* England
British colonists, tobacco growing, 43–4, 46
British Columbia, 148
British Medical Association, 201
*British Medical Journal*, 130
British Raj, 99
British ships, in opium wars, 78, 83 ff.
Broad, C. D., 220
Bryan, William Jennings, 147
Burma, 107; and hemp, 103, 105; and opium, 94
Burroughs, William, 206, 219
Burton, Sir Richard, 99, 181

Caapi, 11, 16
Cacti, 24, 130. *See also* Peyotl
Caffeine, 116
Caine, W. S., 96
Cairo, 47
Cairo University, 170
California, 148, 154, 189, 208
California, University of, 21
Callaghan, James, 192
Cambridge (Mass.), 140
Cameron, Dr Dale, 223
Cameroons, and hemp, 108

Campbell, Dr Harry, 180
Canada: distillers, 148; drugs report, 231; liquor traffic, 150. *See also* Le Dain, Gerald
*Cangue*, 74
Cannabis, 132, 190–3, 200, 205, 224, 225, 231; Home Office report on, 192. *See also* Hemp, Indian; Marihuana
Canton, 73–5, 78; academy, 80; British and American merchants, 82–3, 85, 88; British leave, 83–4; Governors of, 79, 81; river, 76, 83, 84, 87
Capone, Al, 151
Carey, Dr James, 189
Caribbean islands, 11
Casas, Bartholomew de las, 37
Castaneda, Carlos, 23, 206
Catherine de Medici, 37
Cavazzoni, Signor, 165
Central Control Board (Liquor Traffic) Report, 144–5
Central Narcotics Board, 162–3
Chamberlain, Joseph, 143
Chang Hsiu-Pao, 82, 85
Channon, 'Chips', 200
*Charas* 101–1, 164
Charles II, King, 48
*Chemistry of Common Life, The* (J. F. W. Johnston), 116, 119
Chemists, 146
Chesterfield, Philip Dormer Stanhope (4th Earl of), 67, 68, 81
Chicago, 149
China: Communist, 209; Emperors, 83, 86–9; and England, opium agreement, 156; and international opium policy, 161–3; naval junks, 84; and opium, 73, 74, 87, 90–5; opium trade, 76 ff., 85, 89–90; smuggling laws, 75; Treaty Ports, 92, 157. *See also Arrow* affair; Opium Wars
*China* (W. H. Medhurst), 90
Chinese, in California, 154
Chinese historians, 79
*Chinese Repository*, 79
Chloroform, 120
Christianity, 20, 31; and peyotl, 206–8. *See also* Missionaries
Christison, Sir Robert, 124
Chrysostom, Saint, 31
Chu Tsun, 81–2
Chuckchi tribesmen, 14, 28
Church, Native American, 207

Church authority, 13, 29, 34, 35, 49, 50, 51, 53, 54
Church fathers, 31
Cider, 137
Clark, Dr H. Martyn, 93
Claridge, Dr Gordon, 217–18
Clement of Alexandria, 31
Clippers, opium, 76
Clive, Robert, 72, 73
*Club des Hachichins*, 113–15
Coca, 11, 15 ff., 28, 48–52, 94, 128–9, 231; international policies, 162; used by labourers, 50–2, 94, 108, 122–6, 128. *See also* Cocaine
'Coca Mama', 50
Cocaine, 167, 172, 201–2
Cocteau, Jean, 219
Coffee, 47–8, 117, 118, 123, 128, 174
Cohoba, 11
Coleridge, Samuel Taylor, 110, 111, 122
*Colliers*, 201
Collins, William Wilkie, 111
Collis, Maurice, 82
Colombia, 23
Colonialism, 56, 59
Columbus, Christopher, 11, 36
Commission on Indian Affairs, 206
*Commissioner Lin and the Opium War* (Chang Hsiu-Pau), 82
Comstock, Ada, 151
Conference of Commissioners on Uniform State Laws, 183
*Confessions of an English Opium Eater* (T. De Quincey), 77, 111
Connell, K. H., 112
Connolly, Cyril, 21 n.
*Conquest of the Incas, The* (J. Hemming), 51
Constantinople, 45
Consumers' Union, 190, 217
Cook, James, 55
Corn Mother, 50
Coué, Emile, 215
*Count of Monte Christo, The* (A. Dumas), 99
*Counterblast to Tobacco* (James I), 40–2
'Country ships', 73–4
Coventry, Henry, 48
Cowley, Abraham, 122–3
Coxe, William, 66
Crime (hemp drugs), 105–6
Crombie, Surgeon Lt. Col., 103–4, 106, 108, 214
*Curandero*, 23

Custer, George Armstrong, 59
Customs, 66, 172, 195, 197

D'Abernon, Sir Edgar Vincent (Viscount), Chairman of Central Control Board (Liquor Traffic), 144–5, 210–12
Dacca, 103, 104
Dangerous Drugs Act (1920), 179–80
Dangerous Drugs Act (1965), 192
Darwin, Charles Robert, 56
Datura, 11, 15
D'Avenant, Charles, 62
Davis, Sir John, 87
Davy, Sir Humphry, 111, 116
Deadly nightshade, 35, 117
Defence of the Realm Act, *see* 'DORA'
Defoe, Daniel, 63, 64
Democrats (U.S.A.), 140
'Denatured' alcohol, 146
De Quincey, Thomas, 77, 111, 112, 122, 219
D'Erlanger, Henry (Baron), 172–3
de Ropp, Robert S., 201
Derry Central Railway, 112
Diderot, Denis, 55–6
Diplomatic bags, 79, 193
Dissociation, 21, 26
Doctors, 128–9, 146, 178, 180, 193–4, 208, 227
*Does Prohibition Prohibit ?*, 141
Don Juan, 23
*Doors of Perception, The* (A. Huxley), 203
Dope peddling, 9, 190
'DORA', 144, 145
Dowdeswell, G. F., 125, 128
Draperstown (Ulster), 112
Driberg, Commissioner, 94
Drug classification (Lewin's), 213
Drugger, Abel, 43
Drugs: defined, 9–10; soft and hard, 225; synthetic, 176; vision-inducing, 10, 12–13, 59–60, 130–1, 202–5, 218–22; white and black, 171 ff.; addiction rate, 193–4; and crime, 105–6, 183–4, 188–9, 196 ff., 200–2, 226; and divination, 12–13, 17, 22–4; effects of, 119–21, 217, 227–30; international controls, 155 ff., 162 ff., failure, 173–7, 198–9; international scandals, 165 ff., legislation, 208–9, 225–9; medical tratement of, 181; pharmaceutical dangers of, 166,

Drugs—*contd.*
176; reasons for addiction, 174, 214 ff., 229–30; and youth, 188, 190–1, 205, 208. *See also* Pharmacology; Plant drugs; Prohibition
*Drugs and Human Relations* (G. Claridge), 217
*Drugs and the Mind* (R. S. de Ropp), 201
*Drunken Comportment* (C. MacAndrew and R. Edgerton), 58
'Dry' States, 141
'Dry' votes, 151–3
Dumas, Alexandre, 99, 113
du Pont, Dr Robert, 197
Duran, Diego, 13

East India Company, and opium trade to China, 73–7, 89
East Indies, and opium, 74, 161
Ecclesiastical Council (Lima, 1551), 50
Ecevit Government (Turkey), 199
Ecuador, 16
Edgerton, Robert, 58
*Edinburgh Review*, 136
Egypt: and hashish, 170 ff., 182; and heroin, 172; and international heroin policies, 173–4; and tea, 173–4
Egyptian Central Narcotics Bureau, 172
Elgin, James Bruce (8th Earl of), 89
Eleusinian cult, 34
Eliade, Mircea, 21, 54
Elizabeth I, Queen, 41
Elliot, Charles, 83–6
Ellis, Henry Havelock, 130, 204
Ellis, William (missionary), 56
Elwin, Rev. A. (missionary), 93
Embassies, 193
Endor, Witch of, 29
England: alcohol, illicit exports to U.S.A., 147; and cannabis, 190 ff.; and hashish, 99; heroin policy, 193–4; and international opium policies, 155 ff., 161; laboratories, 169; opium production, India, 72–7, 156–7, 159, 164, illicit exports to China, 78, 83, 85–6, 89–90, 95; temperance, 137, 141; Treasury, 41, 44, 67. *See also* Parliament; Prohibitions; Taxes
English Channel, 193
Epinay, Franz d', 99
Ergot, 203

Essay *On Liberty* (J. S. Mill), 137–8
*Essential Kafir, The* (D. Kidd), 23
Establishment, 17
Ether, 220
*Euphorica*, 213
Europe, 11–12, 35–6, 37, 45, 49; and coca, 122; and coffee, 47–8; and tobacco, 37 ff., 46; and tea, 47–8
Evangelical movement, 132
Evans, William, 215
Evans-Pritchard, Edward, 19–21
*Every Man out of his Humour* (B. Jonson), 38
Excise Reports, Indian hemp, 164
*Excitantia*, 213
Extra-sensory perception, 22
Ezekiel, 130

*Faery Queen, The* (E. Spenser), 38
Fanshawe, E. L., 139 ff.
Far East: and drugs, 96; opium enquiry into, 165–6; report of opium commission, 166–7
'Fast crabs', 76, 84, 148
Field, M. J., 20
Fielding, Henry, 68, 70
Fiji, 57, 59
*Fire in the Lake* (F. Fitzgerald), 195
First World War, 143–5, 179, 210
Fitzgerald, Frances, 195–6
Fleischl, Dr, 126, 127
Fleming, Peter, 176
*Flesh of the Gods* (ed. Peter T. Furst), 21, 23
Fly agaric, *see* Mushroom
*Foreign Mud* (M. Collis), 82
Formosa, opium, used by labourers, 94, 108
Forsyth, Frederick, 196
Fowler, Rev. Orin, 133
Fowler, Orson S., 134
France: alcohol, illicit exports to U.S.A., 148; and coca, 125; and hemp, 113; heroin production, 168, 198; and international opium policies, 161; laboratories, 166; in opium wars, 89; and tobacco, 37, 45; wines and brandies, 62, 71, 74
Frazer, Sir James, 17
French Indo-China, and opium, 161
Freud, Sigmund, 20, 122, 126–7
Freudians, 214
Fryer, John, 72
Fuller, Henry, 182
Furst, Peter T., 21, 222

G.I.s, 143, 149, 190, 195–6
Gandhi, 159
*Ganja*, 100 ff., 164
Gardner, Edmund, 39
Gauguin, Paul, 56
Gautier, Théophile, 113
Gavit, John P., 163, 166
Gelfand, Michael, 20
'Geneva' (gin), 62
Geneva Convention on drugs: (1925), 160 ff., 168, 176; (1931), 174–7, 178
*Gentleman's Magazine*, 67 n., 123
George, Dorothy, 79
George V, King, 144
Germany, laboratories, 166
Ghana, 20
Gin: dangers of, 62–4, 69–71; as a drug, 64; prohibition, 64–6; revenue from, 67–9
'Gin Lane' (W. Hogarth), 68
Ginsberg, Allen, 206
Glasgow University, Department of Psychological Medicine, 218
Gloucester, Bishop of, 70
Glue, 202
Gnostics, 31
*Golden Bough, The* (J. Frazer), 17
Goldenweiser, Alexander, 28
Goldsmith, Oliver, 14
Gothenburg experiment, 142–4
Grain alcohol, 146
Great Lakes, 149
Greece, Ancient, 30–1, 34
Green, Timothy, 193, 195, 201
*Guardian*, 199
Guiana, 17
Gulf of St. Lawrence, 58
Gutzlaff, Charles (missionary), 78, 80

Hague Convention on drugs (1911), 155, 157 ff., 162, 166, 169, 176, 179
Hair tonics, 147
Hallucinogens, *see* Drugs: vision-inducing
Hanway, Jonas, 48
Hariot, Thomas, 38
Harner, Michael, 35
Harrison Narcotics Act (1914), 178–9, 180, 184
Hashish, 31–4, 97, 112–15, 132, 170 ff., 190
Hastings, Warren, 73–4
Hayes, Herbert (missionary), 172

Haynes, Roy, 145 ff.
Health, Department of, 180, 194
Hegel, Georg Wilhelm Friedrich, 227
Hell Fire Club, 68
Hemming, John, 51
Hemp, Indian, 47, 112, 115, 117, 181; hemp drugs, 96 ff., 109; international policies, 162; opium compared, 96; peyotl compared, 208; used by labourers, 102, 108. *See also* Cannabis; Hashish; Indian Hemp Drugs Commission
*Hemp* (S. S. Boyce), 182
Henbane, 32, 35, 173
*Herb, The* (F. Rosenthal), 32
Herbert, Philip (Earl of Montgomery), 43–4
Herbert, Sir Thomas, 44
Hernandez, Francisco, 53
Herodotus, 32
Heroin, 95, 129, 178–9, 190, 200, 225 ff.; international controls, 167–8, 172–4. *See also* smuggling
Hervey, John (Baron Hervey of Ickworth), 67–8, 70, 81
Hillier, Sydney, 144
Hippies, 189, 208
Hispaniola, 12, 37
Hobson, Dr Benjamin, 91
Hofman, Dr Albert, 203, 218
Hogarth, William, 68
Holland: drug production, 158; and gin, 62, 70; and international opium policies, 161; laboratories, 166
Holstein, Duke of, 45
Homer, 34
Hong Kong, 84 ff.; and drugs, 226; Governor of, 91; and opium, 92, 94
Hong Kong *Daily News*, 154
Hood, Thomas, 135
Hoover, Herbert Clark, 151, 152
Hosie, Sir Alexander, 156
Hot gospelling, 185
House of Commons, *see* Parliament
House of Lords, *see* Parliament
Hoyle, C., 215
Hsien-feng, Emperor, 87
Hsü Nai-chi, memorandum on opium, 80–2
Huxley, Aldous, 203–4, 218, 220
Hypnosis, 17
*Hypnotica*, 213
Hysteria, 20

Illinois, 188
*Illinois Medical Journal*, 179
Im Thurn, Everard, 17
Inchcape Commission, 159
India: Aryanism, 27; banning of hemp drugs, 107; and opium, 73, 76, 77, 92–5; 161; and tobacco, 45
India, opium production, *see* England
Indian hemp, *see* Hemp, Indian
*Indian Hemp: a Social Menace* (D. M. Johnson), 190–1
Indian Hemp Drugs Commission, 96, 99 ff., 184, 186, 214; *Report*, 102, 105, 108
Indian High Commission, 193
*Indian Medical Gazette*, 103
Indian Native States, and opium, 75–6
Indiana trial (liquor selling), 149–5
Indians: Andean, 51, 122–3, 127–8; Apache, 208; Comanche, 206; of Hispaniola, 12; Huichol, 222; North American, 17, 38, 39, 57–8, 214; Navajo, 208; Papago, 60–1; Peruvian, 50–2; South American, 15, 122, 206 ff.
Industrial alcohol, 147
Industrial Revolution, 123
*Inebriantia*, 213
*Inquiry into the Effects of Ardent Spirits . . . , An* (B. Rush), 136
Inquisition, 13, 45, 53–4
Insanity (hemp drugs), 103–5
*Inside Dope* (F. Tuohy), 175
Institute for the Study of Drug Dependence, 232
International Conferences on drugs, *see* Geneva Convention; Hague Convention; Shanghai Conference
Intoxicants, 12–15, 30, 32–4, 129, 228
Iran, *see* Persia
Ireland: and spirits, 156; temperance, 137
*Irish Peasant Society* (K. H. Connell), 112
Iron Curtain countries, and drugs, 232
Isbell, Dr Harris, 222–3
Italy: heroin production, 198; and international opium policies, 165

James, William, 112, 130, 220
James I, King, 40–4, 48, 67
James II, King, 62

Japan: and morphine, 158; and opium (medical), 199; opium monopoly, 176
Jardine, William, 78, 82, 85
Jardine Matheson, 78, 91–2, 150
Java, and opium, 77
Jehangir Khan, Great Mogul, 45
Jekyll, Sir John, 64–5
Jenkins, Roy, 192
Jesus Christ, 31, 38, 206
Jimsonweed, 11
Jochelson, Vladimir, 18 n.
John the Baptist, Saint, 30, 38
Johnson, Dr Donald McIntosh, 190–1
Johnson, Dr Samuel, 48, 67 n., 122
Johnston, James F. W., 116 ff.
Jones, Howard, 216
Jones, Dr John, 110, 111
Jonson, Ben, 38, 43
Jordan, Sir John, 160
*Joyful News out of the New Found World* (N. Monardes), 13, 37
Jung, Carl Gustav, 20
Junks, 76

Kamchatkaland, 14–15
Kansas City, 141
Kaunda, Kenneth David, 223
Kava, 54–7, 129
Kidd, Dudley, 23
*Kif*, 98, 199
King, Charles W., 79
Kopek, Joseph, 22
Koran, 32–3
Koryak tribesmen, 14
Kraseninnikov, Stephan, 14
Kroeber, A. L., 26–7
*Kubla Khan* (S. T. Coleridge), 110
Kwantung, 80

LSD, 203 ff., 208, 218 ff., 225, 229, 231; ban on research, 205; dangers of, 204–5
La Barre, Weston, 49, 207
Lagae, Monsieur, 19
La Guardia, Fiorello, report on marihuana, 186–8
La Motte, Ellen N., 156–7, 160 ff.
*Lancet*, on coca, 125; on tobacco 134–5
Lane, Edward William, 135
Lasagna, Louis, 227
Laudanum, 110–11, 219
Laughing gas, 111, 112–15
Lavoisier, Antoine Laurent, 116

*Laws* of Plato, 30–1
L Dopa, 221
League of Nations, Opium Advisory Committee, 163, 165, 169, 170, 173, 174 ff., 178. *See also* Geneva Convention; Hague Convention
Leary, Dr Timothy, 206
Lebanon, 198
Lecky, W. E. H., 69
Le Clerq, Father Chrestien, 58
Le Dain, Gerald (report on drugs, Canada), 196, 197, 202, 227, 229, 231
Lehrer, Tom, 9
Leon, Cieza de, 50
Leslie, David, 23
*Letters from Turkey* (H. von Moltke), 135
Lettuce, 118
Lewin, Louis, 9, 129–30, 194, 204, 212–14
Lexington (Kentucky), 216–17
Liberal Governments: and hemp enquiry, 99–100; opium policy, 155
*Licit and Illicit Drugs* (E. M. Brecher), 179, 188, 217
Lima, 50, 52
Lin Tse-hsu, 82–5, 88, 173
Lintin island, 76
Liquor, *see* Alcohol
Livesey, Joseph, 138, 139
Livingstone, David, 108
Lloyd George, David, 143–4, 145, 210
London, and gin, 63–4; effect on population, 69–70
London Distillers' Guild, 62
*London Life in the Eighteenth Century* (D. George), 70
Lonsdale, Henry Lowther (3rd Viscount), 69
Lorchas, 88
Louisiana, 188
Lowry, Malcolm, 221
Ludlow, Fitzhugh, 114
Lyall, R. D., 106
Lysergic acid diethylamide, *see* LSD
Lytton, Edward George Bulwer (1st Baron), 135

MacAndrew, Craig, 58
Macao, 73, 78
McCullum, Major, 93
MacIntosh, H. J., 100
*Madame Bovary* (G. Flaubert), 48
Madras, 107

Madrid, 52
Mahomet, 31–2
Maine Law, 137 ff.
*Malade Imaginaire* (Molière), 213
Malay Straits Settlements, and opium, 93, 159
'Malwa', (opium), 75–6
Manchester, 136
Manchukuo opium monopoly, 176
Mandarins, 88
Manicheans, 31
*Manners and Customs of the Modern Egyptians, The* (E. W. Lane), 135
Mantegazza, Paolo, 124
Mao Tse-tung, 209
Marco Polo, 97–8, 228
Marihuana, 181 ff., 205. *See also* La Guardia, Fiorello
Marihuana Bill, 184
Mary II, Queen, 62
Massachusetts, 46–7, 143, 189
Mathew, Father Theobald, 137, 150
Mattison, Dr J. B., 127
Maugham, William Somerset, 200
Mecca, 47
Medhurst, Walter Henry (missionary), 90–1
Medical and Physical Society of Calcutta, *Transactions*, 97
Medical Council on Alcoholism in Britain, 223
*Medical Record*, 126
Medicine men, 12 ff.
Melland, Frank, 18–19
Mental hospitals (India), 103–4
Mescalero Reservations, 208
Mescaline, 129–30, 204, 205, 225
Mexico, 28, 53, 189, 206, 222
Michael, Tsar, 45
Michelet, Jules, 29
Michigan, 150
'Mickey Finn', 191
Middle East: and coffee, 47; and hemp, 98
Milan, 124
Mill, John Stuart, 137
Miller, Etta May, 150–1
Miquelon Island, 148
Missionaries, 11, 22; to American Indians, 58; China, 78–9, 90 ff.; Egypt, 172; India, 93–4, 100, 107; South Seas, 55–7, 59, 129
Missouri, 189
Mitchell, Silas Weir, 130
Mitford, Algernon Bertram Freeman (1st Baron Redesdale), 95

Moguls, 45, 73
Molière, 213
Moltke, Helmuth (Count von), 135
Monardes, Nicolas, 13, 37
Monet, Claude, 130
'Moonshine', 146, 147
Moreau, Dr Jacques, 112–13, 116
Morning glory, 11, 53, 206
Morocco, hemp production, 199
Morphine, 116, 122, 129, 164; international controls, 158–9. *See also* Smuggling
Morris, Corbyn, 69, 70
Mortimer, W. G., 127–9, 231
Moscow, 45
Moslems, 32; and hashish, 132; and tobacco, 119
'Mother Hubbards', 56
Muggeridge, Malcolm, 170–2
'Muggle', (marihuana), 185
Murphy, Patrick, 197
Murtagh, John M., 197
Mushroom, 11; amanita muscaria, 14; fly agaric, 14, 18, 27, 28, 54; psilocybe, 206, 222
Musicians, and cannabis, 190
Myers, Dr W., 94

'Naarden Case', 168–9
Nanking, Treaty of (1842), 87
Napier, William John (8th Baron), 78, 95
Napoleon Bonaparte, 112
Narcotics legislation, 178 ff.; and crime, 197. *See also* Drugs
*Nation*, 160
National Commission on Marihuana and Drug Abuse (Shafer Commission), 190, 224, 229
National Institute on Alcoholism, 223
National Prohibition Act (Volstead act), 139, 145 ff., 189; repeal, 151–3
*Natural Mind, The* (A. Weil), 230
Near East: drug traffic survey, 198; and hemp, 98
Nebraska, 140
Nepenthe, 34
New World, 11–12, 36, 46, 49
New York, and narcotics, 197
New York Academy of Medicine, 186
*New York Evening Post*, 162
New York Health Department, 197
*New York Magazine*, 201

Nicot, Jean, 37
Nicotine, *see* Tobacco
Nixon, Richard Milhous, 189, 190, 192
*Noble Experiment* (S. B. Whipple), 150
*Non-medical Use of Drugs, The* (G. Le Dain), 196, 202, 227, 229, 231
Norway, alcohol control, 142
Nutmeg, 229

*Obsevations upon the influence of . . . Tobacco* (B. Rush), 133
'Old Man of the Mountain', 97–8, 228
Old Testament, 29–30
Old World, 44, 47, 49
Ololiuqui, 11, 53
Opium, 99, 117, 121, 219, 231; benefits of, 90–5; Chinese, 89, 154 ff.; dens, 167, 176–7; Indian, 90, 154; international controls, 155 ff., 198–9; medicinal, 199; price fall, 175; and prohibition, 78–82; Royal Commission, 92, 94, 96; used by labourers, 94, 108. *See also* Heroin; Laudanum; League of Nations; Morphine
*Opium* (J. P. Gavit), 166
*Opium War Through Chinese Eyes, The* (A. Waley), 82
Opium Wars: First, 82–5; Second, 88–9; Prohibition compared, 147–9; treaty negotiations, 89–90
Oregon, 190
O'Shaughnessy, Sir William Brooke, 96–7, 116
Osmond, Humphrey, 10, 205–6, 221
Oviedo y Valdez, Gonzalvo Fernando d', 12
Oxford University, Chairs of Anthropology, 17, 19

Pahnke, Dr Alter, 222
Paint-remover, 229
'Palinurus', 21 n.
Palmerston, Henry John Temple (3rd Viscount), 78, 83, 84–6, 88, 91
Palomino, Eduardo Calderon, 23–4
Panama, report on marihuana, 186
*Papago Indian Religion* (R. M. Underhill), 60
Parliament: House of Commons, 43, 69, 96, 139; Committee (on East India Company), 77; House of Lords, 67; Members' distillery

Parliament—*contd.*
interests, 63, 70–1; opium debates, 86, 88, 91, 92, 155, 159; and prohibition, 63 ff., 143–5
'Parliament Brandy', 65
Pavlovians, 214
Pekin, 74–6, 79, 85, 89
Pennsylvania, 182, 183
Pentagon, 203, 226
'Pep pills', 200
Pepys, Samuel, 46; wife of, 47
*Perceptives* (O. Sacks), 221
Perfumes, 147
Perjury, 66–7
*Perla de America* (Don Antonio Julian), 123
Persia: and opium, 157; and tobacco, 44–5
Peru, and coca, 28, 49 ff., 94, 108, 124, 126
*Peru: History of Coca, the 'divine plant of the Incas'* (W. G. Mortimer), 239
Peyotl, 11, 23, 52–4, 130, 206–8, 232. *See also* Mescaline
*Phantastica*, 9, 213
*Phantastica* (L. Lewin), 212
Pharmacology, 116 ff., 212–14; chemical effects of drugs, 121–2, 125 ff., 130–1
*Pharmacopeia*, 125, 146
Philadelphia, 149
'Philaretes', 39–40
Philippines, and opium, 154–5
Pinchot, Giffard, 147
'Pipe of peace', 46
Pirates, and Prohibition, 148–9
Pizarro, Francisco, 15
Placeboes, 215–19
Plague, Great, 47, 70
Plant drugs, 11, 13, 21, 27–8, 116, 122
Plassey, 73
Plate, Thomas, 201–2
Plato, 30
Police, 173, 181, 195, 197
Pomare II, of Tahiti, 55–6
Pont St Esprit, 191
Pop: festivals, 189; Singers, 191
Poppies, 74, 77, 89, 156–7, 198–9, 209
*Popular Drugs* (S. Hillier), 144
Porter, Stephen, 160
Portugal, 37, 44; and opium trade, 73
Pottinger, Sir George, 86, 87
Prescriptions, 65, 146, 178, 180, 208, 227

Preston, 137
Priestley, Joseph, 116
Priests, and drugs, 24 ff. *See also* Religion
*Primitive Culture* (E. Tylor), 16
Princes, Indian, and opium, 75–6
Prohibition, 224, 225–6; alcohol, 143–5; gin, 64, 66–9; opium, 209; tobacco, 41 ff. *See also* Parliament
Prohibition (U.S.A.), 137, 139 ff., 145–53, 183, 189, 209, 225; Commission of Enquiry, 151; enforcement penalties, 141–2, 150. *See also* Bootlegging
*Prohibition inside out* (R. Haynes), 145
Prostitutes, 224. *See also* Drugs: and crime
Protection money, 150
Psychosis, 208
Pu Chi-t'ung, memorandum on opium, 83, 85
Pulteney, Sir William (Earl of Bath), 64–6
Punjab, and opium, 93
Puritanism, 38
*Put Out More Flags* (E. Waugh), 228

*Quarterly Journal of Medicine*, 215
Quinine, 116

Radicals, and opium debate, 88
Raffles, Sir Thomas Stamford, 77
Raleigh, Sir Walter, 38, 40
Rats, and electric stimulus, 214–15
*Reader's Guide to Periodical Literature, The*, 184
*Reasons for the Late Increase in Robbers* (H. Fielding), 68
Rechabites, 30
Reed, William B., 89
Reindeer, 14, 18 n.
Religion: Hinduism, 107, 164; Inca, 49–51; peyotism, 206–8; shamanism, 14, 16 ff., 25–9, 49, 52, 54, 59–60
Republicans (U.S.A.), 140, 142
*Review* (D. Defoe), 63
*Revue de deux mondes*, 113
Rhode Island, 189, 142
Rhodesia, 18, 20
Rich, Barnabe, 42
Richelieu, Cardinal, 45
Richet, Charles Robert, 114–15
*Rig Veda*, 27
Robert, Joseph, 47, 133, 231

Rolleston, Sir Humphrey, 180
Roosevelt, Franklin Delano, 153
Rosenheim, Lord, 223
Rosenthal, Franz, 32–4
Rouhier, André, 23, 212
Rowell, Earle Albert, 185–6
Rowntree, Joseph, 92
Royal Commission into opium, 92, 94, 96
Royal Society of Arts, 92
Rusby, Dr Henry, 127
Rush, Dr Benjamin, 133, 136
Russell, Thomas Wentworth ('Russell Pasha'), 171 ff.
Rutgers University, 231

Sacks, Oliver, 221
Sacy, Sylvestre de, 98
Saigon, 228
St Pierre and Miquelon, 148
Saloons, 142, 143, 149
Sandwich, John Montagu (4th Earl of), 68
Sandys, George, 44, 45
San Pedro Cactus, 24
Sarychev, Gavril, 14
Saul, King, 29
Savile, Henry, 48
Scotland, distillers, 148
'Scrambling dragons', 76
Scythians, 32
Searle, W. S., 128
Shafer Commission, see National Commission on Marihuana and Drug Abuse
Shaftesbury, Anthony Ashley Cooper (7th Earl of), 91
Shamanism, see Religion
Shamanism (M. Eliade), 21
Shanghai, 87, 89
Shanghai Conference on opium (1909), 155
Sharon, Douglas, 23–4
Shew, Dr Joel, 133
Shirley, Sir Anthony, 47–8
Siberia, 14, 22, 28, 54
Single Convention on Narcotic Drugs, 198
Sioux, 59
Sitting Bull, 59
Skinner, B. F., 214
Slavery, 181
Sljunin, Nikolai, 54
Slotkin, J. S., 207
Smith, Sydney, 136

'Smugglers' Reunion', 165
Smuggling: coca, 162; gin, 66, 70–1; hemp, 101, 162, 164, 168 ff., 195; heroin, 172–3, 193–5, 198–9; morphine, 168 ff.; opium, 73–7, 83–4, 87–8, 166, 175–7, 209; tobacco, 42 ff. See also Bootlegging; England; Prohibition (U.S.A.)
Smuggling craft, 148
Sniffing, 201
Society for the Study of Addiction, 191
Society for the Suppression of Opium Traffic, 164
Soft drinks, 149
Sogliardo, 38
Soldiers: and amphetamines, 228; and cocaine, 125–6; and meprobamate, 217; and opium, 79; and tobacco, 134
Solon, 34
Soma, 27–8
Soma (R. G. Wasson), 21, 27
Sonnini, C. S., 98
South Carolina, 182
South Sea Islands, 55–7
Spanish chroniclers, 11–13
Spanish colonists: and coca, 50–1, 122; and peyotl, 206; and tobacco, 37
Spenser, Edmund, 38
Spirits, see Alcohol
Spirits Licensing Act (1736), 64–8, 81
State authority, 10, 29, 30, 34, 49, 54
Stanford University, 204
Stanley, Edward George Geoffrey Smith (14th Earl of Derby), 137–8, 139
Stevenson, Robert Louis, 56, 58, 94
Stimulants, 120–1, 129
Stimulants and Narcotics (F. Anstie), 120
Story of Tobacco in America, The (J. C. Robert), 47, 231
Strahlenberg, Count Filip von, 14
Styx, 50
Suasionists, 137, 142
Sudan, 19
Sufis, 32
Summer Palace (Pekin), 89
Sun dance, 59
Sunday Telegraph, 192–3
Sunday Times, 147
Suppressionists, 137, 142, 143–4
Sweden, alcohol control, 142–3, 201

Switzerland, pharmaceutical industry, 158, 163, 166

Taft, William Howard, 143, 155
Tahiti, and alcohol, 54–6, 69
Taiping, The, 87–8
Tao-Kwang, Emperor, 79
Tavernier, Jean, 45
Taxes, 41–3, 45, 48, 50, 77
Taylor, Dr Norman, 198–9
Taylor, W. C., 106
Tea, 47–8, 74, 83, 85, 117, 118, 123, 128, 135, 173–4
'Tea', (marihuana), 187
Teare, James, 136
Temperance, 136
Ten Commandments, 45
Teng T'ing-chen (Governor of Canton), 81
Thomson, Basil, 59
*Thousand Nights and a Night, Book of the*, (R. Burton), 99
*Times, The*, 176; letters to (Sir G. Birdwood), 92, (Lord Stanley), 137–9
Tiverton, Lord Palmerston at, 88
Tobacco, 11, 22, 94, 116 ff., 127, 173, 185–6, 219, 231; attacks against, 132–6; dangers of, 37–40, 45 ff.; revenue from 41 ff.
Tobacco Court, 45
Toledo, Francisco de, 52
Tories, 136, 155; and *Arrow* affair, 88; China policy, 91; opium policy, 86
Toronto Lacrosse Club, and coca, 125
Trance state, 17–19, 21
*Travels in Peru* (J. J. von Tschudi), 15, 124
'Treating', 140, 145
*Trial of Tobacco* (E. Gardner), 39
Troyes, 215
Tschudi, Johann Jacob von, 15, 28, 123–4
Tuohy, Ferdinand, 175–6
Turkey: and international drug policies, 155, 168; and opium, 63, 72, 198; poppy cultivation, 199
Turnbull, John, 55, 56
Tylor, Edward, 16–17

Ulster, and ether, 111–12
*Under the Volcano* (M. Lowry), 221
Underhill, Ruth M., 60
Union, Jack, 87

United Kingdom Alliance, 137–9, 143
United Nations, 192, 197–9, 223
United Nations, Economic and Social Committee on Narcotic Drugs, 231
United States Congress, 181: Department of Agriculture, 182: Department of Health and Welfare, 194: Federal Bureau of Narcotics, 182 ff.: Federal Department of Labour, 143: Foreign Affairs Committee, 160: Treasury, 182, 184
United States of America: aid to Turkey, 199; alcohol legislation, 224; drug survey, 182; great crash, 153; and heroin, 179–80, 195 ff.; and international opium policy, 155 161; laboratories, 166; in opium wars, 89; and peyotl, 206–8. *See also* Prohibition (U.S.A.)
Universities (U.S.A.), 190
*Unquiet Grave, The* (C. Connolly), 21 n.

Valera, Blas, 51
*Varieties of Religious Experience, The* (W. James), 112, 220
Vietcong, antibiotics, 228
Vietnam: drug report, 226; and heroin, 190, 195–6
Villavicenzio, Manuel, 16
Virginia, 38, 43, 47, 182
Virginia Company, 44
Vollmer, August, 180–1
Volstead, Andrew J., *see* National Prohibition Act

Wade, Sir Thomas, 90
Waley, Arthur, 82
Wallace, Dr George B., 187
Walpole, Sir Robert, 63–4, 65–6, 71
Washington, George, 181
Washington, Narcotics Treatment Organisation, 197
Wasson, Rev. E. A., 146
Wasson, R. G., 21, 24, 27, 28, 232
Watt, George, 100, 107
Waugh, Evelyn, 214, 228
Webb-Kenyon Bill, 143
Weddell, H. A., 28
Weil, Andrew, 229
Wesley, John, 132, 136
West Indian immigrants, 190, 191

'Wet' States, 141
Whampoa (Canton), 76
Whipple, Sidney, 150
Whiskey, 64, 118, 140, 146
White House, 140
Wilberforce, William, 111
William III, King (Prince of Orange), 62
Willcocks, Major, 104
Williams, Dr Henry Smith, 186
Wine, 29–31, 136; communion, 146, 207
*Witch Doctor* (M. Gelfand), 20
Witch doctors, 16 ff.
Witches, 35–6
Wolf, Dr Stewart, 217
Wood alcohol, 146

Wootton of Abinger, Barbara (Baroness), 192, 193
World Health Organisation, Drug Dependency Unit, 223
*Work for Chimney Sweepers* ('Philaretes'), 39
Wounded Knee, 60


Yagé, 16
Yangona (kava), 57
Yeh Ming-Chen, 87–8
Yoga, 28, 230
Yonville, 48
Young, W. Mackworth, 100


Zambia, alcoholism, 223